Microsoft .NET for Programmers

D1359750

Microsoft .NET
for Programmers

FERGAL GRIMES

MANNING

Greenwich
(74° w. long.)

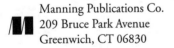

Manning Publications Co.   Copyeditor: Elizabeth Martin
209 Bruce Park Avenue   Typesetter: Dottie Marsico
Greenwich, CT 06830   Cover designer: Leslie Haimes

ISBN 1-930110-19-7

Printed in the United States of America
1 2 3 4 5 6 7 8 9 10 – VHG – 06 05 04 03 02

To Joe and Kate

contents

preface

As the title suggests, this book is written for programmers who want to learn about the Microsoft .NET platform. There is a lot to learn. .NET development embraces many areas including:

- Windows desktop development
- Web-based development
- Component development
- Development of remote objects and services
- Development of XML Web services

In addition, programmers need to become familiar with an extensive new class library and a new runtime environment. Even for seasoned Windows developers, this almost amounts to a fresh start.

About this book

The purpose of this book is to explore the many parts that make up .NET, to assemble them into a meaningful whole, and to do so within the confines of a compact and readable publication. Although many of the topics we'll explore, such as XML Web services, Windows Forms, or ADO.NET, are worthy of separate books in their own right, all are just pieces of the .NET jigsaw puzzle. I felt there was a need to examine each of the individual pieces, and to show how they relate to one another, and how they fit together. This book is the result.

The scope and size of .NET make it impossible to cover everything in a single book. So I've taken some shortcuts. In particular, I've tried to impart the essentials while avoiding unnecessary handholding, repetition, or padding. In general, the documentation, online help, and samples, which come with the .NET software development kit (SDK), are comprehensive and complete. So, armed with the knowledge gleaned from this book, you should be able to consult the documentation for supplementary information.

This book's audience

This book is written for intermediate and advanced programmers who plan to develop applications, components, or services for .NET. The typical reader will have some experience programming with Visual Basic, C++, or Java. This is not an absolute requirement, since I've included an appendix which provides an introduction to C#, the language used for the examples in the book.

To get the most out of chapter 4, "Working with ADO.NET and databases," you should have some knowledge of SQL database objects including databases, tables, and SQL queries. Likewise, chapter 8, "Creating the Web Forms user interface," assumes a basic understanding of the Web including HTML, HTTP, and forms processing.

Choosing a .NET programming language

.NET is a language-neutral platform, and comes with a huge set of class libraries that are accessible to all .NET-compliant languages. Therefore, you can code equally powerful programs using C#, Visual Basic .NET, JScript .NET, or a host of third-party languages. So which language should you choose?

The obvious candidates are C# and Visual Basic .NET since most Windows developers will be coming from a Visual C++ or Visual Basic background. At the outset, I considered including examples using both C# and Visual Basic .NET. However, it quickly became clear that the result would be a repetitious book, which might shortchange both groups of readers. I settled on C# since it was designed for use with .NET and carries no legacy baggage. Being designed with .NET in mind, it could also be argued that C# provides the most natural fit to .NET's object model.

It is worth noting that there is less difference between C# and Visual Basic .NET than you might think at first glance. Programmers from both camps will need to get comfortable with assemblies, namespaces, types, classes, structs, enums, interfaces, methods, properties, events, delegates, threads, and more. These are features of .NET, and not the preserve of a particular programming language. So the differences between C# and Visual Basic .NET are mostly syntax-related.

Ultimately, you'll choose the language(s) with which you are most comfortable. This book teaches .NET, not C#. I hope that, by placing the C# introduction in a separate appendix, it will help to distinguish the C# language from the (language-neutral) .NET platform.

Depending on the level of interest, I hope to be able to provide a Visual Basic .NET edition of this book in the future. Stay tuned.

Do I need Visual Studio .NET?

Visual Studio .NET is Microsoft's integrated development environment (IDE) for .NET programming. It provides an impressive array of features that automate many tedious development tasks, making your job easier. However, for the beginning .NET programmer, this automation hinders understanding. So we'll build our examples, and our case study, using the .NET SDK tools.

Although you don't need a copy of Visual Studio .NET to follow along, we won't completely ignore the IDE. In particular, we'll briefly explore the creation of Visual Studio .NET projects and the use of the drag-and-drop forms designer to create both Windows Forms and Web Forms.

Organization of this book

This book contains eight chapters and three appendixes:

Chapter 1 Introduction.   Chapter 1 provides an overview of the .NET architecture and introduces application development using the .NET Framework class library.

Chapter 2 Understanding types and assemblies.   In chapter 2, we look at fundamental .NET features including types, assemblies, and the Microsoft Intermediate Language, or IL. Also, to illustrate reflection, we develop a simple language compiler.

Chapter 3 Case study: a video poker machine.   The video poker case study is introduced and described in chapter 3. We develop simple COM-based and Internet Explorer-based versions of the game.

Chapter 4 Working with ADO.NET and databases.   Chapter 4 introduces ADO.NET and the new disconnected architecture for data access via the Internet. We also look at XML serialization, and we implement a data tier for the case study.

Chapter 5 Developing remote services.   In chapter 5, we explore the .NET remoting architecture and the activation models it offers. We also look at Windows Services and Microsoft Message Queuing, and we use what we learn to develop several new versions of the case study.

Chapter 6 Developing XML Web services.   Chapter 6 describes .NET's features for developing XML Web services. We look at SOAP, WSDL, and UDDI, and we present a Web service-based implementation of the case study.

Chapter 7 Creating the Windows Forms user interface.   We explore Windows Forms, the new class library for the creation of Windows GUI applications, in chapter 7. We examine the Windows Forms programming model, and we see how to design a GUI using the Visual Studio .NET forms designer. We also implement a Windows Forms-based version of the case study.

Chapter 8 Creating the Web Forms user interface.   Chapter 8 explores ASP.NET and the Web Forms classes for the creation of browser-based applications. We examine the new server controls and we learn how to create our own user controls. We also look at designing Web Forms inside Visual Studio .NET, and we develop a Web Forms-based version of the case study.

Appendix A Introduction to C#.   Appendix A provides an introduction to the C# programming language. For readers who have no exposure to C#, this material provides all you need to follow the book's examples.

Appendix B The poker engine listings.   Appendix B contains the C# code for the classes that make up the Poker.dll assembly.

Appendix C The WinPok.cs listing.   Appendix C presents the C# listing of the Windows Forms-based video poker machine.

Each chapter builds on previous material. So the chapters are best read in the order presented.

The programming samples

This book contains many short programs and code snippets designed to illustrate .NET programming. While writing the book I've had several discussions about so-called real-life examples and I've had reason to think about this. Witness the increasing number of programming books that use e-commerce as a vehicle for examples. I generally dislike this trend for the following reasons.

The obvious problem with real-life examples is that people's lives differ. The reader engaged in retail e-commerce may want to see an online shopping cart example. The banker might want to see a financial application. The list goes on.

The second problem is that real-life examples often deviate from established principles of good teaching. In general, an example should be just big enough to illustrate the point. Any bigger, and it can obscure it. This is particularly relevant for a new technology such as .NET. If you can demonstrate .NET remoting by invoking a method that says "Hello from Server X", then there is no need to distract the reader with details of an imaginary banking application.

However, there is no doubt that more substantial real-life examples can be useful, provided they are confined to a case study where they do not interfere with the presentation of basic concepts. Therefore, this book includes both short illustrative examples, and a complete case study. The case study provides a realistic example of a production .NET system consisting of several interrelated applications and components. For the most part, when introducing a concept for the first time, I use examples that are as short as possible. When we are acquainted with the concept, we apply what we've learned by integrating the feature into the case study.

The source code for all examples in this book is available for download from http://www.manning.com/grimes.

The case study

The case study is an implementation of a video poker gaming machine. I think it makes a good case study for the following reasons:

- Video poker is defined by a small set of simple rules that can be easily digested and remembered.
- It is most naturally implemented as a game engine and a set of interfaces. We'll reuse the same engine to implement different versions of the game based on COM, Internet Explorer, remoting, Windows services, message queuing, XML Web services, Windows Forms, Web Forms, and Mobile Forms. In doing so, we get a fairly complete tour of .NET development.
- The game looks nice on the screen.
- It will sharpen your poker skills!

Is this a real-life example? Yes. For a short period in the mid-1980s I made a meager living writing video poker machine software. For those of you who are interested, the game was coded in PL/M-80, an Intel language for its 8080 series processors. The software was compiled on an Intellec development system and transferred directly to EPROM for testing inside the machine. (We didn't have an in-circuit emulator.)

Any similarity between the game presented here and any commercial video poker machine, living or dead, is purely coincidental. In particular, the payout control strategy we explore is designed to illustrate ADO.NET database programming. It is not intended to be a serious payout management algorithm.

Organization of a typical chapter

Once we've established the basics and introduced the case study in the early chapters, the typical structure of the each chapter is:

- Briefly introduce the new topic; e.g., XML Web services or Windows Forms
- Present a simple example program to illustrate the topic
- Present and discuss incrementally more complex examples to reveal the topic in full
- Apply what we've learned to the case study

Therefore, the case study is a recurring theme throughout the book, and serves as a vehicle to implement what we've learned as we progress through the material.

Conventions used in this book

The following typographic conventions are used in this book:

- `Constant width` is used for all program code and listings, and for anything you would typically type verbatim.
- *Italic* font is used for file and directory names, and for occasional emphasis such as when a new term is being introduced.
- **NOTE** is used to indicate an important side comment to the main text.

acknowledgments

I would like to the thank the following people for their expertise, their support, and their hard work in getting this book to print.

A special thanks goes to Ruth Meade who helped conceive the original idea for the book, and reviewed and edited each draft of the manuscript. I am indebted to Ruth for her suggestions and advice which she always delivered with good humor.

There would be no book without the committed support and assistance of the team at Manning Publications. So I thank Marjan Bace, for publishing this book and for many hours of good conversation, and Ted Kennedy for coordinating the many reviews. To the production team, who worked extremely hard to get this book out on time, many thanks: Mary Piergies, Syd Brown, Dottie Marsico, and Elizabeth Martin. Thanks also to the rest of the Manning team, including Susan Capparelle, Leslie Haimes, and Helen Trimes.

There were many people who reviewed the manuscript at various stages of development. I am grateful to them all for their invaluable suggestions and comments: Daniel Anderson, Greg Bridle, Gary DeCell, Mitch Denny, Marc Hoeppner, Bob Knutson, Grace Meade, Darrel Miller, Devon O'Dell, and Mark Wilson. A special thanks to Eric Kinateder who reviewed the manuscript, the sample programs, and the case study for their technical accuracy.

Finally, I would like to thank my family for their encouragement and support. I'm especially grateful to my brother, Eoin, for pointing out, years ago, that Maslow's hierarchy is upside down.

author online

One of the advantages of buying a book published by Manning, is that you can participate in the Author Online forum. So, if you have a moment to spare, please visit us at http://www.manning.com/grimes. There you can download the book's source code, communicate with the author, vent your criticism, share your ideas, or just hang out.

Manning's commitment to its readers is to provide a venue where a meaningful dialog between individual readers and between readers and the author can take place. It is not a commitment to any specific amount of participation on the part of the author, whose contribution to the AO remains voluntary (and unpaid). We suggest you try asking the author some challenging questions lest his interest stray!

The Author Online forum and the archives of previous discussions will be accessible from the publisher's Web site as long as the book is in print.

about the cover illustration

The figure on the cover of *Microsoft .NET for Programmers* is a "Gran Visir," the Prime Minister to the Sultan in a medieval Arabic country. While the exact meaning of his position and his national origin are lost in historical fog, there is no doubt that we are facing a man of stature and authority. The illustration is taken from a Spanish compendium of regional dress customs first published in Madrid in 1799. The book's title page states:

> *Coleccion general de los Trages que usan actualmente todas las Nacionas del Mundo desubierto, dibujados y grabados con la mayor exactitud por R.M.V.A.R. Obra muy util y en special para los que tienen la del viajero universal*

Which we translate, as literally as possible, as:

> *General Collection of Costumes currently used in the Nations of the Known World, designed and printed with great exactitude by R.M.V.A.R. This work is very useful especially for those who hold themselves to be universal travelers.*

Although nothing is known of the designers, engravers, and workers who colored this illustration by hand, the "exactitude" of their execution is evident in this drawing. The "Gran Visir" is just one of many figures in this colorful collection which reminds us vividly of how culturally apart the world's towns and regions were just 200 years ago. Dress codes have changed since then and the diversity by region, so rich at the time, has faded away. It is now often hard to tell the inhabitant of one continent from another. Perhaps we have traded a cultural and visual diversity for a more varied personal life—certainly a more varied and interesting world of technology.

At a time when it can be hard to tell one computer book from another, Manning celebrates the inventiveness and initiative of the computer business with book covers based on the rich diversity of regional life of two centuries ago—brought back to life by the picture from this collection.

CHAPTER 1

Introduction

Since Microsoft unveiled .NET in the summer of 2000, many have had difficulty defining exactly what .NET is. According to Microsoft, ".NET is Microsoft's platform for XML Web Services." That's true, but it is not the whole story. Here are a few of the highlights:

- .NET is a new platform for the development and deployment of modern, object-oriented, "managed" applications.

- Fully functional .NET applications can be developed using any programming language that targets the .NET runtime.

- .NET provides a comprehensive framework of language-neutral class libraries.

- .NET supports the creation of self-describing software components.

- .NET supports multilanguage integration, cross-language component reuse, and cross-language inheritance.

- .NET introduces a new way to develop Windows desktop applications using the Windows Forms classes.

1

- .NET provides a new way to develop Web browser-based applications using the ASP.NET classes.

- .NET's ADO.NET classes provide a new disconnected architecture for data access via the Internet.

- .NET supports the creation of platform-independent XML Web services using standards such as SOAP (Simple Object Access Protocol) and WSDL (Web Service Description Language).

- .NET provides a new architecture for the development and deployment of remote objects.

- .NET makes many Windows technologies and techniques obsolete.

So .NET is big, and requires almost a fresh start for developers working with Microsoft platforms and tools. For Microsoft, the release of .NET is arguably the most important event since the introduction of Windows itself.

1.1 DEVELOPING FOR THE .NET PLATFORM

For Windows developers, .NET offers relief from the hegemony of Visual C++ and Visual Basic. .NET is independent of any programming language. There are .NET compilers available for several languages and more are planned. Available at the time of writing are C#, Visual Basic .NET, JScript .NET, COBOL, Perl, Python, Eiffel, APL, and others. You can also use the *managed extensions* for Visual C++ to write .NET applications. .NET supports these languages by supporting none directly. Instead, .NET understands only one language, Microsoft Intermediate Language (IL).

1.1.1 A language-independent platform

A language compiler targets the .NET platform by translating source code to IL, as we see in figure 1.1.

The output from compilation consists of IL and metadata. IL can be described as an assembly language for a stack-based, virtual, .NET "CPU." In this respect, it is similar to the p-code generated by early versions of Visual Basic, or to the bytecode emitted by a Java compiler. However, IL is fully compiled before it is executed. A further difference is that IL was not designed with a particular programming language in mind. Instead, IL statements manipulate common types shared by all .NET languages. This is known as the *Common Type System*, or CTS. A .NET type is more than just a data type; .NET types are typically defined by classes that include both code and data members.

At run time, the *Common Language Runtime* (CLR, in figure 1.1) is responsible for loading and executing a .NET application. To do this, it employs a technique known as *Just-In-Time* (JIT) compilation to translate the IL to native machine code. .NET code is always compiled, never interpreted. So .NET does not use a virtual machine to execute the program. Instead, the IL for each method is JIT-compiled when it is called for the first time. The next time the method is called, the JIT-compiled native code is

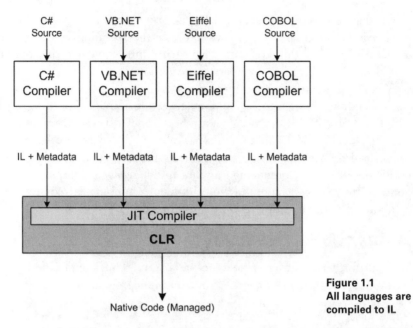

C#
Source

VB.NET
Source

Eiffel
Source

COBOL
Source

C#
Compiler

VB.NET
Compiler

Eiffel
Compiler

COBOL
Compiler

IL + Metadata   IL + Metadata   IL + Metadata   IL + Metadata

JIT Compiler

CLR

Native Code (Managed)

**Figure 1.1
All languages are
compiled to IL**

executed. (This is the general case, since .NET code can also be pre-JITted at installation time.)

The compilation process produces a Windows executable file in *portable executable* (PE) format. This has two important implications. First, the CLR neither knows, nor cares, what language was used to create the application or component. It just sees IL. Second, in theory, replacing the JIT compiler is all that's necessary to target a new platform. In practice, this will likely happen first for different versions of Windows including Windows CE and future 64-bit versions of Windows.

1.1.2   .NET and managed code

.NET applications, running under the scheme shown in figure 1.1, are referred to as *managed applications*. In contrast, non-.NET Windows applications are known as *unmanaged applications*. Microsoft recognizes that managed and unmanaged code will coexist for many years to come and provides a means to allow both types of code to interoperate. Most common will be the need for .NET applications to coexist alongside COM in the immediate future. Therefore, Microsoft has endowed .NET with the ability to work with unmanaged COM components. It is also possible to register a .NET component as a COM object. Similarly, for Win32 API access, .NET allows managed code to call unmanaged functions in a Windows dynamic-link library (DLL). We'll look at some examples of .NET/COM/Win32 interoperation in the following chapters.

In addition to JITting the code, the CLR manages applications by taking responsibility for loading and verifying code, garbage collection, protecting applications from each other, enforcing security, providing debugging and profiling services, and supporting versioning and deployment. Code management by the CLR provides an extra layer that decouples the application from the operating system. In the past, the services provided by this layer would have been implemented in the application itself, provided by the operating system, or done without.

You may be wondering about the metadata emitted along with IL by the language compilers shown in figure 1.1. This is a key feature of .NET. For those of you familiar with COM or CORBA, the metadata can best be described as a form of Interface Definition Language (IDL) that is automatically produced by the language compiler. Metadata describes types including their fields, properties, method signatures, and supported operations. By producing this data automatically at compile time, .NET components are self-describing and no additional plumbing is required to get .NET components, written in different programming languages, to interoperate seamlessly.

1.2 A FIRST .NET PROGRAM

Without further delay, let's take a look at a simple .NET application. The program shown in listing 1.1 is a simple C# command-line program which greets the user.

Listing 1.1   Hello from C#

```
// file    : hello.cs
// compile : csc hello.cs

using System;

class Hello {

  public static void Main() {
    Console.WriteLine("Hello from C#");
  }
}
```

Every C# program must contain at least one class. In this case, that class is `Hello` and its `Main` method is the program's entry point where execution begins. (A member function of a class is known as a *method*.) To display the greeting, the program calls:

```
Console.WriteLine("Hello from C#");
```

This calls the `WriteLine` method of the `Console` class, which is contained in the `System` namespace, to display the message. The `System` namespace is part of .NET's Framework class library. We could have coded this call, as follows:

```
System.Console.WriteLine("Hello from C#");
```

Instead we declared the `System` namespace at the start of our program:

```
using System;
```

This allows us to omit the namespace name and provides a shorthand for referring to `System` classes within our program.

This short example demonstrates the use of .NET's Framework class library, a huge repository of useful classes, which we can use in our .NET applications. These classes are grouped by function and logically arranged in namespaces. We'll look at some common namespaces in a moment.

1.2.1 Compiling the C# Hello program

To compile and test this example, you'll need a copy of the .NET SDK, or Visual Studio .NET. At the time of writing, the SDK could be downloaded from the Microsoft Developer Network site, http://www.msdn.com.

To compile and run this program, open a command window, and use the C# command-line compiler, as shown in figure 1.2.

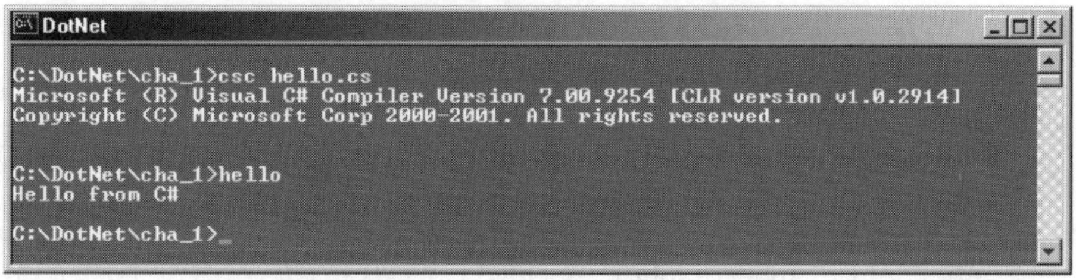

Figure 1.2   Compiling and running the C# Hello program

If *csc.exe* is not found, you'll have to add the directory where it resides to your path. This directory will depend on the version of .NET you are using and should look like *C:\WINNT\Microsoft.NET\Framework\<.NET Version>*.

We'll be using C# for the programming examples in this book. For readers unfamiliar with the language, a complete introduction is provided in appendix A. However, before we commit to C#, let's take a brief look at Visual Basic .NET.

1.2.2 A Visual Basic .NET Hello program

For comparison, listing 1.2 shows the same program coded in Visual Basic .NET.

Listing 1.2   Hello from VB.NET

```
' file    : hello.vb
' compile : vbc hello.vb

Imports System

module Hello

  sub main()
    Console.WriteLine("Hello from VB.NET")
  end sub

end module
```

You can see that the Visual Basic .NET version of the program is very similar. Specifically, the Visual Basic .NET program uses the same `Console` class from the `System` namespace. The Framework class library is part of the .NET platform and is not the preserve of a particular programming language.

In general, there is less difference between C# and Visual Basic .NET than you might expect, and those differences that exist are mostly syntax-based. C# and Visual Basic .NET programmers use the same framework classes and deal with the same .NET concepts, including namespaces, classes, the CLR, and so forth. Also, as we saw in figure 1.1, both C# and Visual Basic .NET programs are compiled to IL. If you were to examine the generated IL for the previous C# and Visual Basic .NET examples, you'd find the output almost identical.

1.3 THE PLATFORM VS. THE PROGRAMMING LANGUAGE

IL is not a typical assembly language in the tradition of machine assembly languages such as 8080 or 6809 assembler. Instead, it is comprised of an instruction set and an array of features that are designed to support the essential operations and characteristics of many modern, object-oriented languages. The focus of .NET is on a common object system instead of a particular programming language.

The CLR directly supports many features which might ordinarily be features of the programming language. This includes a language-neutral type system with support for classes, inheritance, polymorphism, dynamic binding, memory management, garbage collection, exception handling, and more. For example, the same garbage collector is responsible for deleting unused objects from the heap and reclaiming memory, no matter which programming language was used to code the application. So, inclusion of features such as these in the CLR provides a common bridge to facilitate language interoperation and component integration.

To facilitate cross-language interoperability, .NET includes a *Common Language Specification*, or CLS, that represents a common standard to which .NET types should adhere. This standard lays down rules relating to allowed primitive types, array bounds, reference types, members, exceptions, attributes, events, delegates, and so forth. Components and libraries which adhere to this standard are said to be CLS-compliant.

Cross-language inheritance presents no special challenge when CLS-compliant code is involved. You can create a base class using Visual Basic .NET, derive a C# class from it, and seamlessly step through both with a source-level debugger. This level of language interoperability is probably one of .NET's greatest strengths. Many powerful and elegant programming languages, commonly available on other platforms, have failed to become first-class citizens of the Windows world due to their limited integration with the platform. .NET promises to change this.

1.4 EXPLORING THE .NET FRAMEWORK CLASS LIBRARY

In the early days of Windows development, applications were typically coded in C and interaction with the operating system was through C-based API function calls into system DLLs. This was a natural consequence of the fact that much of Windows itself was written in C. Over the years, the emphasis has gradually shifted to more flexible COM-based interfaces that can be invoked by both traditional C-based applications and by scripting languages.

.NET supplants both these approaches with a new language-independent framework class library. Under the .NET Framework, everything is an object, from a humble C# or Visual Basic .NET array (`System.Array`), to a directory under the file system (`System.IO.Directory`), to the garbage collector itself (`System.GC`).

1.4.1 An overview of important namespaces

As we've already noted, the .NET Framework classes are grouped by function and logically organized into namespaces. There are almost 100 namespaces shipped with the .NET SDK, and some contain dozens of classes. Therefore we can't explore them all here. Even if we could, we'd soon forget most of them. So table 1.1 lists some of the more commonly used namespaces and provides a brief description of each.

Table 1.1   Common .NET namespaces

Namespace	Functional area of contained classes
Microsoft.CSharp	Compilation and code generation using the C# language
Microsoft.JScript	Compilation and code generation using the JScript .NET language
Microsoft.VisualBasic	Compilation and code generation using the Visual Basic .NET language
Microsoft.Win32	Windows registry access and Windows system events
System	Commonly used value and reference data types, events and event handlers, interfaces, attributes, exceptions, and more. This is the most important namespace
System.Collections	Collection types, such as lists, queues, arrays, hashtables, and dictionaries
System.ComponentModel	Run-time and design-time behavior of components
System.Configuration	Access to .NET Framework configuration settings
System.Data	ADO.NET types
System.Data.SqlClient	SQL Server .NET Data Provider types
System.Data.SqlTypes	Native SQL Server data types
System.Diagnostics	Application debugging and tracing. Also Windows Event Log class.

continued on next page

Table 1.1   Common .NET namespaces *(continued)*

Namespace	Functional area of contained classes
System.DirectoryServices	Active Directory access using service providers such as LDAP and NDS
System.Drawing	Windows GDI+ graphics types
System.Globalization	Culture-related types embracing language, string sort order, country/region, calendar, date, currency and number formats
System.IO	Reading and writing of streams and files
System.Messaging	Sending, receiving, and managing queued messages (MSMQ)
System.Net	Simple API for network protocols such as DNS and HTTP
System.Net.Sockets	API for TCP/UDP sockets
System.Reflection	Access to loaded types and their members
System.Reflection.Emit	Metadata/IL emission and PE file generation
System.Resources	Creation and management of culture-specific application resources
System.Runtime.InteropServices	Accessing COM objects and native APIs
System.Runtime.Remoting	Creation and configuration of distributed objects
System.Runtime.Remoting.Channels	Managing remoting channels and channel sinks
System.Runtime.Remoting.Channels.Http	HTTP (SOAP) channel management
System.Runtime.Remoting.Channels.Tcp	TCP (binary) channel management
System.Runtime.Remoting.Lifetime	Managing the lifetime of remote objects
System.Security	Accessing the underlying CLR security system
System.Security.Permissions	Controlling access to operations and resources based on policy
System.Security.Policy	Code groups, membership conditions, and evidence, which define the rules applied by the CLR security policy system
System.Security.Principal	Identity/Principal classes, interfaces, and enumerations used in role-based security
System.ServiceProcess	Windows service installation and execution
System.Text	Text encoding and conversion for ASCII, Unicode, UTF-7, and UTF-8
System.Text.RegularExpressions	Access to the built-in regular expression engine
System.Threading	Classes and interfaces for multithreaded programming
System.Timers	Timer component for raising events at specified intervals
System.Web	Browser/server communication including commonly used ASP.NET classes such as HttpApplication, HttpRequest, and HttpResponse
System.Web.Configuration	ASP.NET configuration classes and enumerations

continued on next page

Table 1.1   Common .NET namespaces *(continued)*

Namespace	Functional area of contained classes
System.Web.Services	Building and using Web services
System.Web.Services.Description	Describing a Web service using WSDL
System.Web.Services.Discovery	Discovering Web services via DISCO
System.Web.SessionState	Access to ASP.NET session state
System.Web.UI	Creation of ASP.NET Web pages and controls
System.Web.UI.Design	Extending design time support for Web Forms
System.Web.UI.Design.WebControls	Extending design time support for Web controls
System.Web.UI.HtmlControls	Creating HTML server controls
System.Web.UI.WebControls	Creating Web server controls
System.Windows.Forms	Creating Windows Forms-based user interfaces and controls
System.Windows.Forms.Design	Extending design-time support for Windows Forms
System.Xml	Standards-based XML support
System.Xml.Schema	Standards-based support for XML schemas
System.Xml.Serialization	Serializing objects into XML documents or streams
System.Xml.XPath	The XPath parser and evaluation engine
System.Xml.Xsl	Support for XSL transformations

The list of namespaces in table 1.1 includes only the more commonly used namespaces, most of which are used in examples in the chapters that follow.

1.4.2   Programming with the .NET Framework classes

Namespaces provide a convenient way to logically group related classes together. They also prevent name clashes where two or more classes have the same name, but reside in different namespaces. The classes themselves physically reside in DLL files that are shipped with the .NET Framework. Depending on the version of .NET you are using, these DLLs can be found in the *C:\WINNT\Microsoft.NET\Framework\<.NET Version>* directory.

The most common classes reside in the core library file, *mscorlib.dll*. When you use classes that reside in other DLLs, you must refer to the DLL when you compile your program. For example, the `SecurityIdentity` class from the `System.EnterpriseServices` namespace resides in the *System.Enterpriseservices.dll*. To compile a C# program that uses this class, you need to use the C# compiler's `/reference` option and provide the DLL name:

```
csc /reference:System.Enterpriseservices.dll MyProg.cs
```

Or, for short:

```
csc /r:System.Enterpriseservices.dll MyProg.cs
```

Note that there isn't a one-to-one correspondence between namespaces and DLLs. A DLL may contain classes from several different namespaces, while classes from the same namespace may be physically distributed among several DLLs.

NOTE   For each class in the Framework, the .NET reference documentation gives both the containing namespace name, and the name of the physical file where the class resides.

Figure 1.3 illustrates how the Framework fits into the .NET development model.

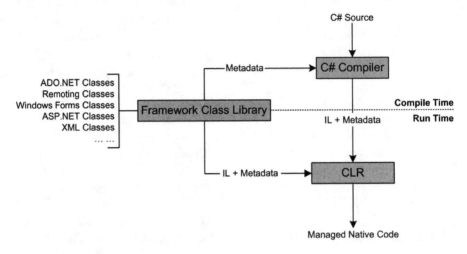

Figure 1.3   Architecture of .NET

Metadata flows from the Framework class library to the C# compiler. The compiler uses the metadata to resolve references to types at compile time. Unlike C and C++, C# does not use header files, nor is there an explicit linkage stage in the build process.

In figure 1.3, we also see the CLR pulling in the IL and metadata for both the application and the Framework classes it uses. This process is analogous to dynamic linking under Windows, but with the extra .NET bells and whistles described earlier, such as verifying type-safety and enforcing version policy.

1.4.3   What happened to ASP and ADO?

You may be familiar with Active Server Pages (ASP) and ActiveX Data Objects (ADO), and you may wonder how they fit into the .NET puzzle. In fact, they are implemented as part of the class library. For example, the `System.Data`, `System.Data.Sql-Client`, and `System.Data.SqlTypes` namespaces, shown in table 1.1, make up part of the new ADO.NET subsystem. Likewise, the `System.Web`, `System.Web.UI`, and several other namespaces listed in table 1.1, make up part of the new ASP.NET subsystem. In the same way, the Framework also embraces Windows GUI development with the Windows Forms classes in `System.Windows.Forms`.

This is consistent with the .NET approach in which previously disparate and often-unrelated areas of Windows and Web-based development are combined in a single new framework. The historical division of skills between Visual C++ component developers, Visual Basic graphical user interface (GUI) developers, and VBScript/HTML Web developers, is a thing of the past.

Under .NET, coding Web-based applications is no longer a separate discipline and the artificial divide between component development and scripting no longer exists. For example, you can include C# code in an ASP.NET page. The first time the page is requested, the C# compiler compiles the code and caches it for later use. This means that the same set of programming skills can be employed to develop both Windows and Web-based applications. Likewise, Visual Basic developers have the full power of Visual Basic .NET with which to develop ASP applications, while VBScript has been retired.

1.5   PUTTING .NET TO WORK

The breadth of coverage of .NET, and the way it unifies previously separate programming disciplines makes it possible to develop and deploy complex distributed applications like never before. Let's consider an example. Figure 1.4 depicts a loan department in a bank together with the applications, and users, involved with the system.

Let's see how we use .NET to develop the applications and components required to build and deploy a loan system like this:

1 *Loan database*—The database contains the data for individual loan accounts. It also contains views of the bank's customer database. The loan database might be stored in SQL Server, Oracle, Informix, DB2, or some similar database management system.

2 *Data tier*—This is the data tier in an N-tier, client/server arrangement. The data tier uses ADO.NET to talk to the database system and it presents an object-oriented view of the data to the logic tier. In other words, it maps database records and fields to objects that represent customers, loans, payments, and so forth. We could use C#, or Visual Basic .NET, or some other .NET-compliant language to implement the data tier.

3 *Logic tier*—The logic tier contains the business rules. We can look upon this layer as the engine at the heart of the system. Once again, we can use C# or Visual Basic .NET, or some other .NET language here. Our choice of programming language is not affected by the language used to develop the data tier. Cross-language compatibility, including cross-language inheritance, means that we can pick the best language for the task at hand. The CLR and the CLS combine to ensure that we can freely mix and match languages, as required.

4 *Internal loan department applications*—We would probably choose to develop internal-use applications as traditional Windows GUI applications. Using typical client/server techniques, these internal applications would talk directly to

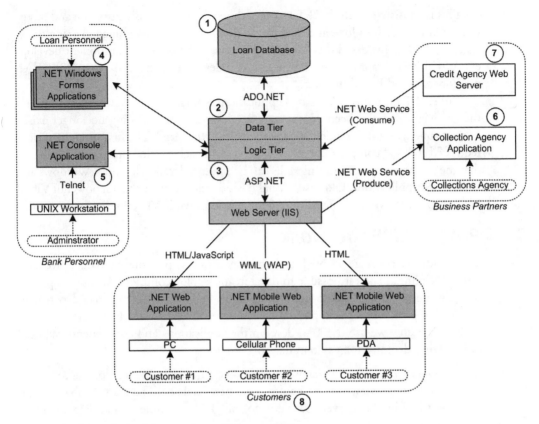

Figure 1.4 A sample bank loan system which uses .NET

the logic layer across the bank's local area network. The traditional Windows GUI model is known in .NET as Windows Forms. It is similar to the tried-and-tested Visual Basic forms model. Using Visual Studio .NET, forms can be designed using a drag-and-drop approach. Windows Forms can contain all the familiar Windows controls, such as the buttons, check boxes, labels, and list boxes. It also contains a new version of the Windows Graphical Device Interface (GDI), a new printing framework, a new architecture for controls and containers, and a simple programming model similar to Visual Basic 6.0 and earlier versions of Visual Basic.

5 *Administrator console applications*—Perhaps the bank uses Informix on UNIX as the database management system. If so, we may have administrators who wish to run .NET applications from their UNIX workstations. .NET's humble `System.Console` class can be used to create command line applications that operate over a telnet connection. For example, using Visual Basic .NET or C#, we might write a console application to allow an administrator on another

platform to archive expired loans. Console I/O and a modern GUI cannot be compared for usability, but it is useful and appropriate in a case such as this.

6 *Business partner Web service (produce)*—Here we have a business partner, a collection agency, hired by the bank to pursue payment of delinquent loans. In the past, we might have designed a batch application to extract delinquent accounts every day and export them to a flat file for transmission to the collection agency. With .NET, we can implement this function as a Web service that exposes delinquent accounts to remote clients. This means that the collection agency can hook its own applications into the bank's loan system and extract delinquent accounts as required. While human surfers consume Web sites, Web services are consumed by other applications. They promise a future, federal model where independent Web services will be produced, consumed, reused, and combined in the creation of powerful, interconnected applications. The simplicity of the Web service model will likely give rise to a rapid increase in automated, business-to-business, e-commerce applications.

7 *Business partner Web service (consume)*—The loan system might also be a consumer of Web services produced by other business partners. Here, we see a credit agency that produces a Web service to enable commercial customers to perform credit checks on loan applicants. .NET provides the tools to build a client to consume this service and integrate it into our loan system.

8 *Customer Web-based applications*—Using ASP.NET, we can quickly deploy a Web-based loan application system which gives the customer immediate access to the loan system. Also, .NET's Mobile Internet Toolkit means that we can deploy and integrate an interface that allows customers with handheld devices, such as Web-enabled phones and personal digital assistants (PDAs), to access the loan system for balance enquiries and transfers.

Perhaps it's more instructive to consider what's missing from figure 1.4. For example, there are no CORBA or DCOM components. Instead, we leverage the Web server using ASP.NET's XML Web services infrastructure to expose system functions to remote callers.

Neither do we employ any additional servers or filters to support multiple mobile devices such as Web-enabled phones and hand-held PCs. We use the controls from the Mobile Internet Toolkit to take care of detecting and supporting multiple devices.

Although not evident in figure 1.4, no special steps are taken to support multiple browsers. Instead, we use ASP.NET controls that automatically take care of browser compatibility issues. This means that our ASP.NET applications can take advantage of the extended features of higher-level browsers, while automatically producing plain old HTML for older browsers.

This example depicts a moderately complex system involving multiple interfaces and different user types, including bank staff, customers, and business partners, who are distributed in different locations working on multiple platforms. .NET provides us with everything we need to build and deploy a system such as this.

Starting in chapter 3, we begin a case study containing all the essential features of the system depicted in figure 1.4. We develop a video poker machine and deploy it as a console application, a Windows application, a Web-based application, a remote object, a mobile application, an XML Web service, a Windows service, and a message-based service. We implement a 3-tier client/server architecture, and our poker machine will exhibit all the essential features of a modern, multi-interface, distributed application.

1.6   *SUMMARY*

We have taken a first look at the features of the .NET platform. We learned about the CLR and that .NET is fundamentally agnostic about the choice of programming language. We explored the Framework class library and we noted that subsystems such as ADO.NET and ASP.NET are integral pieces of the Framework. We also considered the case of a distributed bank loan system and how we might use .NET to build it.

In the next chapter, we explore .NET types and assemblies, the fundamental building blocks of .NET applications.

CHAPTER 2

Understanding types and assemblies

Creating a .NET application involves coding types, and packaging them into assemblies. .NET types are similar to data types in non-object-oriented languages except that they contain both data, in the form of fields, and behavior in the form of methods. .NET types are also language-neutral. An assembly containing types coded in one language can be used by an application coded in a different language. So types and assemblies are the basic building blocks and they are important concepts for .NET developers.

In this chapter, we explore .NET types and assemblies. .NET provides both value and reference types and uses an elegant mechanism called boxing to convert between the two. Value types provide a lightweight, stack-based means of creating runtime objects, thus avoiding the overhead of garbage collection. As we'll see, most of the primitive .NET types are value types.

We examine both private and shared assemblies. Private assemblies enable developers to ship DLLs while avoiding the potential problems associated with their public accessibility and versioning. A shared assembly, on the other hand, is shared by multiple applications. We also develop a small sample program that downloads and installs an assembly on demand.

The .NET Framework provides reflection classes to enable applications to inspect assemblies and to discover and instantiate types at run time using late binding. The `System.Reflection.Emit` namespace provides classes that can be used to dynamically generate new types and assemblies at run time. We use these classes for our final example in this chapter when we develop a complete compiler for a simple programming language.

If you are new to C#, now would be a good time to refer to appendix A. There, you'll find an introduction to the language that should equip you with the skills to work through the examples in this chapter, and in the remainder of the book.

2.1 INTRODUCING TYPES

Every object in a .NET program is an instance of a type that describes the structure of the object and the operations it supports. Table 2.1 lists the built-in types available in C#, Visual Basic .NET, and IL, and their relationship to the underlying .NET types.

Table 2.1   .NET built-in types

NET	C#	VB.NET	IL	Value or Reference
System.Boolean	bool	Boolean	bool	Value
System.Byte	byte	Byte	unsigned int8	Value
System.Char	char	Char	char	Value
System.DateTime	-	Date	-	Value
System.Decimal	decimal	Decimal	-	Value
System.Double	double	Double	float64	Value
System.Int16	short	Short	int16	Value
System.Int32	int	Integer	int32	Value
System.Int64	long	Long	int64	Value
System.Object	object	Object	object	Reference
System.SByte	sbyte	-	int8	Value
System.Single	float	Single	float32	Value
System.String	string	String	string	Reference
System.UInt16	ushort	-	unsigned int16	Value
System.UInt32	uint	-	unsigned int32	Value
System.UInt64	ulong	-	unsigned int64	Value

From the table, we can see that the built-in language types are just aliases for underlying .NET types. For example, .NET's `System.Single`, which represents a 32-bit floating-point number, is known as `float` in C#, `Single` in Visual Basic .NET, and `float32` in IL. This cross-language type system is known as Common Type System (CTS), and it extends beyond the primitive types. The CTS defines how types are declared, used, and managed in the runtime, and it establishes the basis for cross-language integration. In fact, it provides an object-oriented model that supports the implementation of many modern programming languages, and it defines rules to ensure that objects written in different languages can interoperate.

As we see in table 2.1, not all primitive types are directly supported in every language. Visual Basic .NET provides a built-in `Date` type that is not provided by C#. Likewise, C#'s unsigned integer types are not supported by Visual Basic .NET, and IL does not have a `decimal` type. In such cases, you can always use the underlying .NET type directly:

```
// C# date...
System.DateTime d = System.DateTime.Now;

' VB unsigned integer...
Dim u As System.UInt32

// IL decimal...
.locals (valuetype [mscorlib]System.Decimal d)
```

The CTS forms the foundation for .NET's cross-language abilities. Since new types are defined in terms of the built-in .NET types, mixed language application development presents no special difficulty for .NET developers. However, since not all types will be available in all languages, the Common Language Specification (CLS) specifies a subset which should be used when developing libraries for cross-language use. Such libraries are termed CLS-compliant.

For example, `System.SByte`, `System.UInt16`, `System.UInt32`, and `System.UInt64`, are not CLS-compliant nor are they available as primitive types in Visual Basic .NET. Generally, non-CLS-compliant types may not be directly supported by some languages and should not be exposed as public members of programmer-defined types in libraries designed for cross-language use. If you annotate your code with the `CLSCompliant` attribute, the C# compiler will warn you about noncompliance. (See appendix A for a discussion of attributes.)

Table 2.1 also includes the IL names of the .NET types. You can program directly in IL and, later in this chapter, we'll develop a skeleton program that can be used as a starter template for your own IL programs. The low-level nature of IL makes it an unsuitable choice for general-purpose application development. However, if you intend to use the `System.Reflection.Emit` classes to generate your own assemblies, an understanding of IL will be essential.

We can explicitly create a new type by defining a class, as in listing 2.1.

Listing 2.1   A Person class in C#

```
// file : person.cs

public class Person {

  public Person(string firstName, string lastName, int age) {
```

```
    FirstName = firstName;
    LastName = lastName;
    Age = age;
  }

  public readonly string FirstName;
  public readonly string LastName;
  public readonly int Age;
}
```

New types are defined in terms of their constituent types. In this example, the FirstName, LastName, and Age field members are instances of the types System.String, System.String, and System.Int32, respectively. Members can be fields, methods, properties, or events.

Using the new operator, we can create instances of the Person type, as follows:

```
Person p = new Person("Joe", "Bloggs", 40);
System.Console.WriteLine(
  "{0} {1} is {2} years old.",
  p.FirstName,
  p.LastName,
  p.Age
); // displays "Joe Bloggs is 40 years old."
```

2.2   *VALUE VS. REFERENCE TYPES*

.NET types can be divided into value types and reference types. In table 2.1, we see that the built-in types, with the exception of string and object, are value types. Typically, value types are the simple types such as int, long, and char, which are common to most programming languages. Objects, strings, and arrays are examples of reference types:

```
object o = new System.Object();
string s = "Mary had a little lamb";
int[] a = {1, 2, 3};
```

In this example, o is an object reference, s is a string reference, and a is a reference to an array of integers. All, therefore, are reference types. A reference is a bit like a pointer in C or C++. It is not in itself an object, rather, it refers to an object. In .NET, all reference types implicitly derive from System.Object.

Space for value types is allocated on the stack. When a method returns, its local value types go out of scope and the space allocated to them is automatically reclaimed. The compiler creates the necessary code to do this automatically, so there is no need for the program to take explicit steps to delete value types from memory. In contrast, reference types are created on the managed heap. Figure 2.1 illustrates the distinction.

Both i and j in figure 2.1 are local integer value types. When their definitions are encountered, two distinct data values are created on the stack. When their containing method ends, they go out of scope.

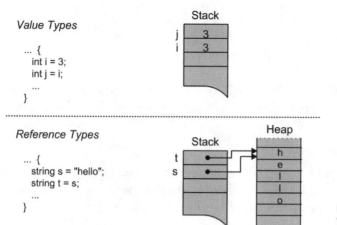

Figure 2.1
Value vs. reference types

Both s and t are reference types. The assignment, string s = "hello", causes the string "hello" to be stored on the managed heap and a reference to the string, s, to be created on the stack. So a reference type embodies a combination of both location and data. Copying one reference type to another does not copy the data and so the assignment, string t = s; creates a second reference, t, to the same object. When their containing method ends, both references go out of scope, and are destroyed. However, the string, "hello", although inaccessible, remains on the heap until its space is recovered by the runtime. The recovery process is known as garbage collection. Since it is an automatic process, the programmer generally does not have to worry about it. Garbage collection means that there is no equivalent of the C++ delete operator in C#.

A reference type can be null, while a value type cannot:

```
string s = null; // ok
int i = null;    // error - value type
```

Here, s is declared as a string reference, but no string space is allocated. All references are type-safe meaning that they can only refer to objects of the correct type. This means that s, in this example, can refer to null, or to a string, or to its base class, System.Object. We could not, for example, store a reference to a Person type in s.

2.2.1   The C# struct

Typically, when we create our own types, we create reference types by defining a class type, such as the Person class in listing 2.1. However, we can create value types too. In C#, we use a struct to create a new value type. The following example defines a struct to represent the x and y coordinates of a point:

```
public struct Point {
  public Point(int x, int y) {
    this.x = x;
```

```
    this.y = y;
  }
  private int x;
  private int y;
}
```

A struct is typically used for a lightweight class and often contains data members, but no methods, as in this example. We use the same new operator to create an instance of a struct:

```
Point p = new Point(10, 20);
```

Small structs can be more efficient than classes because they avoid the extra level of indirection associated with a reference, and they don't have to be garbage collected. However, when you pass a struct to a method, a copy of the struct is passed. In contrast, when you pass a class instance, a reference is passed. Therefore, passing large structs as parameters can negatively impact performance.

A struct cannot inherit from another struct or class, nor can it serve as a base for inheritance. However, a struct can implement interfaces.

2.2.2   Boxing and unboxing

To preserve the "everything is an object" philosophy, .NET provides a corresponding reference type for every value type. This is known as the value type's boxed type. For example, if you store a value type in a reference type, the value type is automatically boxed:

```
int i = 123;
object o = i;
```

In this example, we define i as an integer with the value 123. Then, we create an object reference, o, and assign i to it. This causes an implicit boxing operation.

Boxing causes the runtime to create a new object, containing a copy of i's value, on the heap. A reference to this object is stored in o. The original value type, i, is unaffected by the operation.

In contrast, unboxing must be explicitly requested with a cast:

```
int i = (int)o; // unbox o to i
```

In this case, we're unboxing o into an integer i. For this to succeed, o must contain a reference to an integer type and we must make our intentions clear by casting o to an integer. Any attempt to unbox to an incompatible type, such as from a string to an integer, will generate an InvalidCastException error at run time.

Boxing and unboxing provide an elegant way to allow programs to use small, efficient value types without the overhead of full-blown heap-allocated objects, while, at the same time, allowing such values to take on the form of an object reference whenever necessary.

Note that automatic boxing means that you can use an array of objects as a generic collection:

```
object[] arr = {"cat", 1, 2.3, 'C'};
```

This example creates an array containing string, integer, double, and character elements. However, you'll need to cast the individual array elements to the correct type when unboxing.

2.3   EXPLORING SYSTEM.OBJECT

System.Object is the ultimate superclass from which all .NET reference types implicitly derive. It provides several useful members that you should become familiar with:

- Equals—An overloaded method that comes in both static and virtual instance versions, and tests whether two object instances are equal. The default implementation tests for reference equality, not value equality. Therefore Equals returns true if the object passed as an argument is the same instance as the current object. It may make sense to override this method. For example, the built-in string type overrides Equals to return true if the two strings contain the same characters.

- Finalize—A protected virtual instance method that is automatically executed when an object is destroyed. You can override this method in derived classes to free resources and perform cleanup before the object is garbage collected. In C#, this method is not directly overridden. Instead C++-style destructor syntax is used, as we'll see in a moment.

- GetHashCode—A public virtual instance method that produces a hash code for the object. GetHashCode returns an integer value that can be used as a hash code to store the object in a hash table. If you override Equals, then you should also override GetHashCode, since two objects, which are equal, should return the same hash code.

- GetType—A public instance method that returns the type of the object, thereby facilitating access to the type's metadata. Under .NET, applications and components are self-describing and that description is stored with the component in the form of metadata. This contrasts with alternative schemes in which such data was typically stored as IDL, or in TypeLibs, or in the registry. GetType returns a Type object that programs can use to retrieve details of the type's members and even create an instance of the type and invoke those members. This process of type inspection and dynamic invocation is known as *reflection*, and we examine it in more detail later in this chapter. GetType is not virtual because its implementation is the same for all types.

- MemberwiseClone—A protected instance method that returns a shallow copy of the object.

- ReferenceEquals—A public static method that tests whether two object instances are the same instance. If you've overridden the Equals method to test for value equality, then you can use ReferenceEquals instead to test for reference equality.

- ToString—A public virtual instance method that returns a string representation of the object. By default, ToString returns the fully qualified name of the object's type. In practice, ToString is typically overridden to provide a more meaningful string representation of the object's data members.

2.3.1 Overriding System.Object methods

Let's see how we might leverage System.Object in a class of our own. Suppose we had a class representing a pixel in a 256 x 256 pixel graphics coordinate system. Listing 2.2 illustrates how we might implement this class while overriding Equals, GetHashCode, and ToString, to our advantage.

Listing 2.2   Overriding System.Object methods

```
public class Pixel {

  public Pixel(byte x, byte y) {
    this.x = x;
    this.y = y;
  }

  private byte x;
  private byte y;

  public override string ToString() {
    // return "(x,y)"...
    return "(" + x + "," + y + ")";
  }

  public override bool Equals(object o) {
    try {
      Pixel p = (Pixel)o;
      return p.x == x && p.y == y;
    } catch (Exception) {
      return false;
    }
  }

  public override int GetHashCode() {
    // shift x one byte to the left...
    // and add y...
    return (x<<8) + y;
  }
}
```

The implementation of `ToString` simply returns the x and y coordinates in parentheses, separated by a comma. Methods such as `Console.WriteLine` automatically call the `ToString` method on their arguments. Therefore, in this example, we can create and display a pixel, p, as follows:

```
Pixel p = new Pixel(200, 150);
Console.WriteLine(p); // displays "(200,150)"
```

`Equals` returns `true` if the argument is a pixel with identical coordinates, while `GetHashCode` combines the coordinates into a single integer value suitable for use as a unique key. This ensures that pixels, which are in fact equal, will hash to the same value.

2.4   *UNDERSTANDING FINALIZATION*

As we saw above, reference types are created on the managed heap. Management of the heap is performed automatically by the runtime and involves garbage-collecting unused objects when necessary to reclaim heap space. `System.Object` includes a protected, virtual, instance method called `Finalize` that can be "overridden" by all classes in order to free resources before an object is reclaimed by the garbage collector. In C#, you do not directly override `Finalize` as you would other `System.Object` methods such as `Equals` or `ToString`. Instead C# uses the familiar C++ destructor notation, `~ClassName()`, to identify the finalization method.

2.4.1   Coding a finalizer

Listing 2.3 provides a simple example of a base class and a derived class, each containing a finalizer that displays a message when the object is finalized.

Listing 2.3   Finalization of a derived class

```
// file    : finalize.cs
// compile : csc finalize.cs

using System;

public class BaseClass {
  public BaseClass() {
    Console.WriteLine("creating BaseClass");
  }

  ~BaseClass() {
    Console.WriteLine("finalizing BaseClass");
  }
}

public class DerivedClass : BaseClass {
  public DerivedClass() {
    Console.WriteLine("creating DerivedClass");
  }

  ~DerivedClass() {
```

```
      Console.WriteLine("finalizing DerivedClass");
    }
  }

public class Go {
  public static void Main() {
    DerivedClass dc = new DerivedClass();
  }
}
```

The `Go.Main()` method simply creates an instance of `DerivedClass` and exits. The output generated, when you compile and run this program, is shown in figure 2.2.

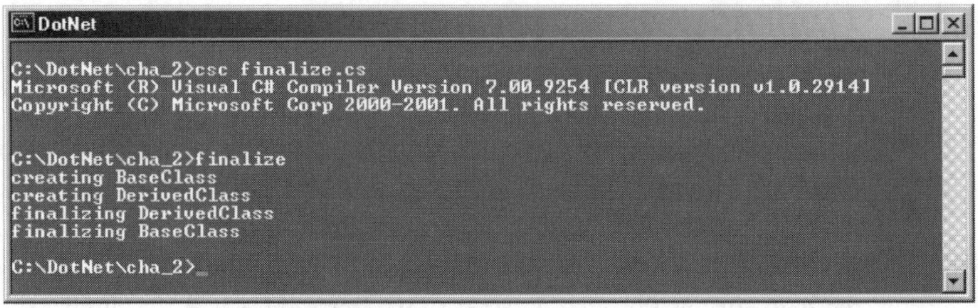

Figure 2.2   Finalization of a derived class

Note that the base class constructor is automatically called before that of the derived class. The finalizers are called in reverse order when the derived object is garbage collected. This ensures that the base class object is not destroyed while a derived object still exists, and thus ensures that the finalization chain is correctly followed.

Typically, since finalization takes time, you should avoid coding a finalizer unless your program absolutely requires it, such as when it needs to close files, or network connections.

2.4.2   Finalization and the Dispose method

If it is necessary to explicitly free resources when an object is destroyed, the .NET documentation recommends writing a `Dispose` method and calling it explicitly, as we do in listing 2.4. The `System.IDisposable` interface is provided for this purpose.

Listing 2.4   Implementing the IDisposable interface

```
// file    : dispose.cs
// compile : csc dispose.cs

using System;

public class MyClass : IDisposable {

  public MyClass(string name) {
    Console.WriteLine("creating " + name);
```

```
      this.name = name;
    }

  ~MyClass() {
    Console.WriteLine("finalizing " + name);
    Dispose();
  }

  public void Dispose() {
    Console.WriteLine("disposing " + name);
    // free resources here, and...
    // suppress further finalization...
    GC.SuppressFinalize(this);
  }

  private string name;
}
public class Go {

  public static void Main() {

    MyClass obj1 = new MyClass("obj1");

    object obj2 = new MyClass("obj2");
    if (obj2 is IDisposable)
      ((IDisposable)obj2).Dispose(); // explicitly dispose of obj2

    // garbage collection (finalization) will dispose of obj1
  }
}
```

In this example, we implement the System.IDisposable interface and provide a Dispose method to free resources. Dispose also suppresses any further finalization by calling the static GC.SuppressFinalize(this). We include a finalizer method that simply calls Dispose. This arrangement allows for explicit freeing of resources by calling Dispose or implicit disposal by allowing finalization to do its work. Figure 2.3 shows the output generated when we compile and run this example.

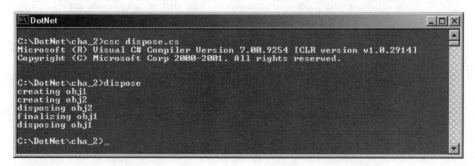

Figure 2.3 Finalizing and disposing objects

The Framework classes include many examples of `Dispose`. A related method, `Close`, is sometimes used instead of `Dispose` if the object can be reopened or reused after it has been closed. A good example would be a class that represents a file or stream that can be closed and reopened without creating a new object instance. On the other hand, if clean-up means that the object is no longer usable, `Dispose` is preferred. Remember that finalization costs time and should only be implemented if an object needs to explicitly release resources.

2.5 INTRODUCING ASSEMBLIES

A .NET application is packaged into an *assembly*, which is a set of one or more files containing types, metadata, and executable code. The .NET documentation describes the assembly as the smallest versionable, installable unit in .NET. It is the functional unit for code sharing and reuse. It is also at the center of .NET's code security and permissions model. All executable code must be part of an assembly.

When we compile a simple program, the compiler creates an assembly consisting of a single executable file. However, assemblies can contain multiple files including code module files and files containing resources such as GIF images. Therefore, an assembly can be viewed as a "logical" DLL.

The assembly contains a manifest that stores metadata describing the types contained in the assembly, and how they relate to one another. The runtime reads this manifest to retrieve the identity of the assembly, its component files and exported types, and information relating to other assemblies on which the assembly depends. When an assembly consists of multiple files, one file will contain the manifest.

2.5.1 Creating a multifile assembly

In listing 2.1, we defined a `Person` class using C#. Let's save this to a file called *person.cs*, and compile it to a module, as follows:

```
csc /target:module /out:person.mod person.cs
```

The `/target:module` option tells C# to create a module target. Both C# and Visual Basic .NET compilers support four different types of target output:

- *exe*—A console application
- *winexe*—A Windows GUI executable
- *library*—A nonexecutable assembly with its own manifest; typically one or more components packaged as a DLL
- *module*—A file, without a manifest, suitable for adding to an assembly

Listing 2.5 shows how to create a separate program which creates `Person` objects.

Listing 2.5   A C# program to create Person objects

```
// file    : people.cs
// compile : csc /addmodule:person.mod people.cs

using System;

public class People {
  public static void Main() {

    Person p  = new Person("Joe", "Bloggs", 40);
    Console.WriteLine(
      "{0} {1} is {2} years old.",
      p.FirstName,
      p.LastName,
      p.Age
    );
  }
}
```

You can compile and execute this program, as shown in figure 2.4.

```
C:\DotNet\cha_2>csc /addmodule:person.mod people.cs
Microsoft (R) Visual C# Compiler Version 7.00.9254 [CLR version v1.0.2914]
Copyright (C) Microsoft Corp 2000-2001. All rights reserved.


C:\DotNet\cha_2>people
Joe Bloggs is 40 years old.

C:\DotNet\cha_2>_
```

Figure 2.4   Building a multifile assembly

The /addmodule compiler option is used to link the *person.mod* module into the *People* assembly. This gives us a multifile assembly consisting of two module files, *people.exe* and *person.mod*. The assembly's manifest is contained in *people.exe*. The organization of the assembly is illustrated in figure 2.5.

A multifile assembly is always installed in its own directory tree. At run time, all modules added with /addmodule must be in the same directory as the file containing the manifest.

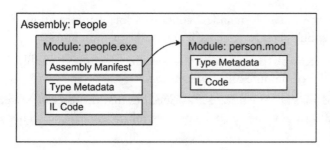

**Figure 2.5
The People assembly**

2.5.2 Disassembling with ILDASM

The .NET SDK provides a utility, *ildasm.exe*, which we can use to inspect .NET modules, libraries, and executables. To launch *ildasm.exe* and explore the *people.exe* file, issue the following command:

```
ildasm people.exe
```

If *ildasm.exe* is not found, you'll have to add the directory where it resides to your path. Depending on your installation, the directory will look something like *C:\Program Files\Microsoft.NET\FrameworkSDK\Bin*.

By default, *ildasm.exe* presents a tree-like view of the assembly containing both the assembly manifest and the disassembled code. Double-click the manifest and you should see the window shown in figure 2.6.

```
MANIFEST
.module extern person.mod
.assembly extern mscorlib
{
  .publickeytoken = (B7 7A 5C 56 19 34 E0 89
  .hash = (09 BB BC 09 EF 6D 9B F4 F2 CC 1B 5
             22 88 EF 77 )
  .ver 1:0:2411:0
}
.assembly people
{
  // --- The following custom attribute is ad
  //   .custom instance void [mscorlib]System.
  //
  .hash algorithm 0x00008004
  .ver 0:0:0:0
}
.file person.mod
    .hash = (FC 7B 55 3F B7 33 BA 09 16 0D E5
               96 28 3D 7E )
.class extern public Person
{
  .file person.mod
  .class 0x02000002
}
.module people.exe
// MVID: {B0270105-88B3-42D2-850A-1472302C3A5
.imagebase 0x00400000
.subsystem 0x00000003
.file alignment 512
.corflags 0x00000001
// Image base: 0x034a0000
```

Figure 2.6
Viewing the assembly manifest

As you can see, the assembly manifest contains a lot of information. We won't go through it line by line here. Instead, we'll note some relevant entries:

- .module extern person.mod—Specifies that the assembly includes an externally linked module called *person.mod*.

- .assembly extern mscorlib—Specifies that the assembly references version 1.0.2411.0 of the shared core assembly, *mscorlib.dll*. This entry also includes the public key of the originator of the referenced assembly and a cryptographic hash to verify its integrity. At run time, .NET uses this information, together with the versioning policy set by an administrator, to locate, verify, and load the correct version of an external assembly. We'll look at shared assemblies in a moment.

- `.assembly people`—Specifies the name of this assembly and its version, 0.0.0.0.
- `.file person.mod`—Specifies a hash value for the linked *person.mod* file.
- `.class extern public Person`—Specifies that the `Person` class resides in the linked *person.mod* module.
- `.module people.exe`—Defines various flags relating to the *people.exe* module.

The manifest enables an assembly, which may contain several physical files and references to other assemblies on which it depends, to be managed as a single logical unit. Depending on the needs of an application, installing an assembly on a target machine can be a simple matter of copying the assembly directory to that machine. (Uninstalling would simply involve deleting the directory.) This is known as an *XCOPY* installation, named after the MS-DOS `XCOPY` command which copies files and directory trees. We look at alternative deployment strategies in this and following chapters.

2.6   *PRIVATE VS. SHARED ASSEMBLIES*

The assembly we created in the previous example is a private assembly, that is, one that is used by a single application. .NET also supports shared assemblies. Installing a shared assembly is analogous to placing a legacy Windows DLL file into the *Windows\System* directory. The problem with such DLLs was that installing a new version often broke something in one or more applications that used the DLL. Furthermore, there was nothing to prevent a DLL being installed over an unrelated DLL of the same name. .NET solves these problems using shared assemblies with so-called strong names, while also allowing multiple versions of a shared assembly to coexist side-by-side.

2.6.1   Shared assemblies and versioning

Under .NET, the format of an assembly's version number is <major number>.<minor number>.<build number>.<revision number>, as we see in table 2.2.

Table 2.2   Assembly version numbering

Major	Minor	Build	Revision	Description
1	0	0	0	Original version
1	0	0	1	A revision (maybe a bug fix)

continued on next page

Table 2.2 Assembly version numbering *(continued)*

Major	Minor	Build	Revision	Description
1	0	1	0	A new build
1	1	0	0	A new minor version
2	0	0	0	A new major version

In general, a new version of an assembly, which is incompatible with the previous version, should be given a new major or minor version number. Compatible new versions should be given a new build or revision number. Note that the run time performs version checking on shared assemblies only.

2.6.2 Generating a strong name for a shared assembly

Let's explore assembly versioning by creating a shared *person.dll* assembly with multiple versions. In other words, this time we deploy the Person class in its own assembly. We'll need to generate a strong name for the assembly. Since strong names are based on public key encryption, we first need to use the strong name utility, *sn.exe*, to generate a public-private key pair, as shown in figure 2.7.

Figure 2.7   Generating a cryptographic key pair

We save the key pair to *key.snk*. At compile time, we can use the private key to sign the assembly, thus identifying its originator. The runtime uses a combination of the assembly name, version number, and the originator's public key to uniquely identify the assembly and to support the side-by-side existence of multiple versions of the same assembly.

> **NOTE** In practice, an organization might safeguard its private key so that it is not available to the development team. In such cases, using only the public key at compile time, you can use delayed signing to reserve space in the assembly for the strong name signature, while deferring the actual signing until just before the assembly is shipped. For details refer to the *-Vr* and *-R* options of the *sn.exe* utility.

The next step is to compile the *person.cs* file into a single file assembly and sign it with the key. We're going to create two side-by-side versions of this assembly, each with the same file name. So we create two subdirectories called *person1000* and *person2000*. Create the new *person.cs* file, shown in listing 2.6, and place it in the *person1000* subdirectory.

Listing 2.6 Declaring assembly version and key file attributes

```
// file    : person.cs
// version : 1.0.0.0
// compile : csc /target:library
//                 /out:person1000\person.dll
//                 person1000\person.cs
// note    : compile from parent directory

using System;
using System.Reflection;

[assembly:AssemblyKeyFile(@"..\key.snk")]
[assembly:AssemblyVersion("1.0.0.0")]

public class Person {

  public Person(string firstName, string lastName, int age) {

    AssemblyName aName = GetType().Assembly.GetName();
    Console.WriteLine("--------------------");
    Console.WriteLine("name     : {0}", aName.Name);
    Console.WriteLine("version : {0}", aName.Version);
    Console.WriteLine("--------------------");

    FirstName = firstName;
    LastName = lastName;
    Age = age;
  }

  public readonly string FirstName;
  public readonly string LastName;
  public readonly int Age;
}
```

The new file contains some changes from the example we saw earlier. First, we declare a key file attribute to enable the assembly to be signed at compile time using the *key.snk* file generated in figure 2.7. We also insert an assembly version attribute to declare that this is version 1.0.0.0. (The use of attributes is discussed in appendix A.) Finally, we insert code into the Person constructor to display the name and version of the assembly in which the class resides.

Copy *person1000\person.cs* to the new *person2000* subdirectory. Then edit it to change the version declaration from:

```
[assembly:AssemblyVersion("1.0.0.0")]
```

to:

```
[assembly:AssemblyVersion("2.0.0.0")]
```

Now we have two different versions of an otherwise identical assembly. Each will announce its version number when a new `Person` object is instantiated. Compile both versions, as shown in figure 2.8.

Figure 2.8   Compiling the shared person assemblies

Next, we're going to install both assembly versions side-by-side.

2.6.3   Installing shared assemblies into the global assembly cache

We explicitly share the two assemblies by installing them into the global assembly cache. We use the *gacutil.exe* utility to do this, as shown in figure 2.9.

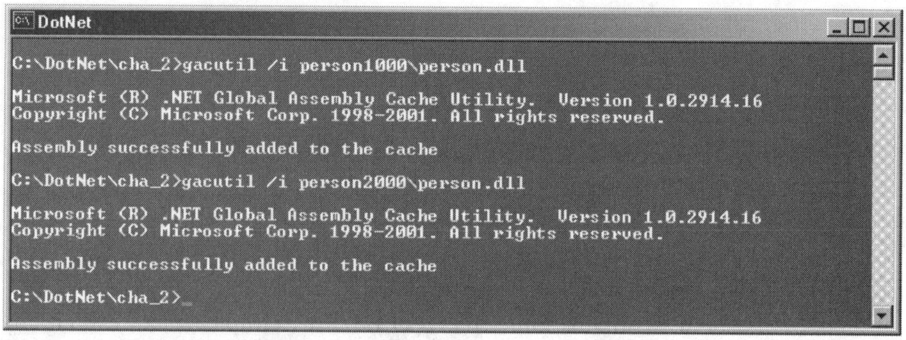

Figure 2.9   Installing the shared person assemblies

To check our work, we can launch Windows Explorer and browse the global cache at *C:\WINNT\Assembly*. (See figure 2.10.)

The global cache shows both versions of the assembly installed side-by-side. Note the public key token that identifies the originator of the assembly. To test our work, recompile the *people.cs* program, referencing version 1.0.0.0 of the *Person* assembly, and execute it, as shown in figure 2.11.

The program should execute as expected, announce that it is using version 1.0.0.0 of the *Person* assembly, and create an instance of the `Person` class. Without modifying or rebuilding the application, we can make it use version 2.0.0.0 of the referenced assembly. To do so, we must create an application configuration file. The ability to

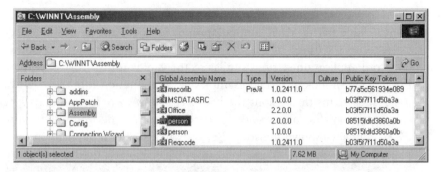

Figure 2.10   Exploring the global assembly cache

```
C:\DotNet\cha_2>csc /r:person1000\person.dll people.cs
Microsoft (R) Visual C# Compiler Version 7.00.9254 [CLR version v1.0.2914]
Copyright (C) Microsoft Corp 2000-2001. All rights reserved.


C:\DotNet\cha_2>people

name      : person
version  : 1.0.0.0
----------------------
Joe Bloggs is 40 years old.

C:\DotNet\cha_2>_
```

Figure 2.11   Using version 1.0.0.0 of the Person assembly

configure compiled applications to use different versions of shared DLLs goes a long
way toward solving the DLL compatibility problems of the past.

2.6.4   Creating an application configuration file

.NET applications can be configured using an application configuration file. By
default, this file resides in the same directory as the application and has the same
name as the application with *.config* appended on the end. For example, we would
create the file *MyApp.exe.config* to configure *MyApp.exe*. The configuration file is an
XML file with the layout shown in listing 2.7.

Listing 2.7   Configuration file layout

```
<configuration>

  <startup>
    ...
  </startup>

  <runtime>
    ...
  </runtime>

  ...

</configuration>
```

The file is divided into sections nested inside <configuration> tags. These sections include startup data, configuration data for the run time and for remoting services, security settings, and more. You can also use the application configuration file to record application settings similar to the way you might have used an INI file in the past. We'll look at several examples of configuration files as we explore different .NET subsystems throughout the book. For now, we're interested in specifying versioning policy for our *people.exe* application. We do this by creating the *people.exe.config* file shown in listing 2.8, and saving it to the application directory.

Listing 2.8   Configuring the People.Exe application

```
<configuration>
  <startup>
    <requiredRuntime safeMode="true"/>
  </startup>
  <runtime>
    <assemblyBinding xmlns="urn:schemas-microsoft-com:asm.v1">
      <dependentAssembly>
        <assemblyIdentity name="person"
                          publicKeyToken="08515fdfd3860a0b"
                          culture=""/>
        <bindingRedirect oldVersion="1.0.0.0"
                         newVersion="2.0.0.0"/>
      </dependentAssembly>
    </assemblyBinding>
  </runtime>
</configuration>
```

In the <startup> section, the <requiredRuntime safeMode="true"> causes the runtime startup code to search the registry to determine the runtime version. This is not necessary here and is included to illustrate that the CLR itself is versioned. Where multiple versions of the CLR are installed, you can specify the version used to run the application, as follows:

```
<requiredRuntime version="v1.0.2901"/>
```

The value specified should be identical to the name of the subdirectory where the corresponding version of the run time is installed. (In this case, version 1.0.2901.0 can be found at *C:\WINNT\Microsoft.NET\Framework\v1.0.2901*.)

In the <runtime> section, we can specify assembly binding information. In this example, we specify that the application is dependent on the *Person* assembly and we use the <assemblyIdentity> tag to provide the name and public key token of the assembly. (The latter can be found by browsing the assembly cache, seen in figure 2.10.) We could specify culture information here if we had different assemblies for different cultures. For our purposes, the most important item is the binding redirect information:

```
<bindingRedirect oldVersion="1.0.0.0"
                 newVersion="2.0.0.0"/>
```

This tells the runtime to redirect references to version 1.0.0.0 of the *Person* assembly to the newer 2.0.0.0 version. Saving the configuration file and executing the *people.exe* application causes the application to run with the newer version, as shown in figure 2.12.

Figure 2.12   Using version 2.0.0.0 of the Person assembly

.NET's facility to allow multiple versions of shared assemblies to coexist is a major feature of the platform and goes a long way toward solving the "dll hell" of the past. Using appropriate configuration file entries, an application, which has been broken by the installation of a new version of a shared dependent assembly, can be restored to health. However, remember that private assemblies are the default under .NET. They are not installed in the global assembly cache and are not subject to versioning by the runtime. Instead, it is the responsibility of the application to deploy the correct versions of assemblies to its own private directory tree. Installing a shared versioned assembly is recommended only if the assembly is to be shared across multiple applications.

2.7   *DOWNLOADING ASSEMBLIES*

The potential to deliver software as a service, instead of shipping it in a shrink-wrapped box, has become a reality with the widespread adoption of the Internet and, in particular, the Web. There are several different potential models. For example, there are the browser-hosted applications including popular, Web-based email and shopping services. These applications are server-based and simply transport the user interface to the user in the form of a Web page. We explore the development of such applications in chapter 8 when we look at ASP.NET and the Web Forms programming model.

Alternative models include using .NET's remoting or XML Web services classes, which facilitate the development of applications that can call, or expose, remote objects across the network or across the Web. This approach enables applications to aggregate remote services into a meaningful whole, effectively leveraging the Internet as a huge runtime library. We look at remoting in chapter 5 and XML Web services in chapter 6.

.NET also supports the downloading of assemblies at run time enabling an application to incrementally install features as required. This approach could be used to support a pay-as-you-go model where users pay for only those features they use. For example, a Word processor might only download the spell-checking assembly, if the user requested the feature and was willing to pay for it.

2.7.1 Downloading the Person assembly from the Web

Let's take our *person.dll* assembly and deploy it to the Web server. First, we need to delete both shared versions of this assembly from the global cache. You can delete them from Windows Explorer, or use *gacutil.exe* with the -u option.

Now, create a new virtual directory on your Web server. Call this virtual directory *deploy* and map it to the *person1000* subdirectory, thus making the assembly available at http://localhost/deploy/person.dll, as seen in figure 2.13.

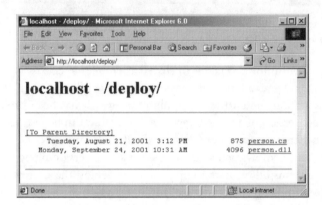

Figure 2.13
Deploying the Person assembly on the Web

Next, edit the application configuration file, *people.exe.config* as shown in listing 2.9.

Listing 2.9 Configuring an assembly download

```
<configuration>
  <startup>
    <requiredRuntime safeMode="true"/>
  </startup>
  <runtime>
    <assemblyBinding xmlns="urn:schemas-microsoft-com:asm.v1">
      <dependentAssembly>
        <assemblyIdentity name="person"
                          publicKeyToken="08515fdfd3860a0b"
                          culture=""/>
        <codeBase version="1.0.0.0"
                  href="http://localhost/deploy/person.dll"/>
      </dependentAssembly>
    </assemblyBinding>
  </runtime>
</configuration>
```

This time we use the `<codeBase/>` tag to specify that version 1.0.0.0 of the *Person* assembly can be downloaded at http://localhost/deploy/person.dll, if it is not already on the machine. The program should run with the new configuration file as normal. To satisfy yourself that the assembly has been downloaded, take a look at the assembly download cache, as shown in figure 2.14. Depending on your installation, you'll find it at *C:\WINNT\Assembly\Download*. Alternatively use *gacutil.exe* with the `/ldl` option to list the contents of the download cache.

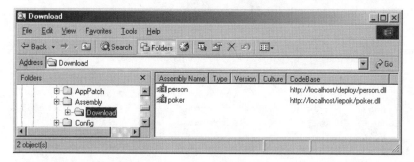

Figure 2.14   Exploring the assembly download cache

The .NET SDK also includes a utility called the Assembly Binding Log Viewer, which you can use to diagnose failed attempts to bind to a referenced assembly. To launch it, execute *fuslogvw.exe* from the command line.

To clear the contents of the download cache, use *gacutil.exe* with the `/cdl` option.

2.8   PROGRAMMING IN IL

.NET's native tongue is IL, the Microsoft Intermediate Language. IL is a stack-based assembly language that is fully compiled at load time. Its instruction set includes instructions for common operations such as loading and storing values, arithmetic and logical operations, and branching. It also includes specialized instructions for object-oriented programming. While a detailed knowledge of IL is not a prerequisite for day-to-day application programming, you will require an understanding of IL if you plan to take advantage of many of the advanced classes in the `System.Reflection.Emit` namespace. These can be used to generate executable code and dynamically build assemblies at run time. Later in this chapter, we'll use the classes in the `System.Reflection.Emit` namespace to build a simple compiler.

2.8.1   Inspecting generated IL

The best way to learn about IL is to create short C# programs, compile them, and inspect the generated IL using *ildasm.exe*. The following short C# program adds two integers and displays the result:

```
public class Test {
  public static void Main() {
```

```
    int i = 10;
    int j = 13;
    i += j;

    // display the result
    System.Console.WriteLine(i);
  }
}
```

If you launch ILDASM and inspect the code generated for the Main method, you should see something like the following:

```
...
.locals (int32 V_0, int32 V_1) // integers i and j in C# program

IL_0000:  ldc.i4.s   10 // load constant 10 as 4-byte signed int
IL_0002:  stloc.0       // store at location V_0
IL_0003:  ldc.i4.s   13 // load constant 13 as 4-byte signed int
IL_0005:  stloc.1       // store at location V_1
IL_0006:  ldloc.0       // load V_0
IL_0007:  ldloc.1       // load V_1
IL_0008:  add           // add them
IL_0009:  stloc.0       // store result
IL_000a:  ldloc.0       // load result

// display the result
IL_000b:  call void [mscorlib]System.Console::WriteLine(int32)

...
```

I've added comments to the IL to clarify the generated code. (The identifiers of the form IL_NNNN are just statement labels and can be ignored.) The stack-based nature of IL means that instructions typically operate on one or more operands on the top of the stack. (FORTH programmers will likely be comfortable with this programming idiom, although that's where the similarity ends.) In this example, the generated IL loads the 4-byte signed integer constants, 10 and 13, onto the stack, adds them, and calls System.Console::WriteLine(int32) to display the result on the console. The C# local variables, i and j, become V_0 and V_1 respectively, in the generated IL version of the program. Note the use of :: as in Class::Method. Also, the call is preceded by the name of the library where the Console class resides, mscorlib.dll. Later in this chapter, we'll create a skeleton IL program that we can use as a template for our own IL programs.

2.8.2   Boxing and unboxing in IL

Using *ildasm.exe*, we can see what boxing and unboxing look like underneath the covers. To find out, create the short C# file, *box.cs*, shown in listing 2.10.

| Listing 2.10   Boxing and unboxing in C# |

```
class Box {
  public static void Main() {
```

```
        int i = 123;
        object o = i;
        int j = (int)o;
    }
}
```

When we compile and disassemble this file, we get the IL shown in listing 2.11.

```
...

.locals (int32 V_0, object V_1, int32 V_2)  // i, o, and j
IL_0000:  ldc.i4.s 123                      // load 123
IL_0002:  stloc.0                           // store in i
IL_0003:  ldloc.0                           // load i
IL_0004:  box [mscorlib]System.Int32        // box i
IL_0009:  stloc.1                           // store ref in o
IL_000a:  ldloc.1                           // load o
IL_000b:  unbox [mscorlib]System.Int32      // unbox ref
IL_0010:  ldind.i4                          // load value via ref
IL_0011:  stloc.2                           // store in j

...
```

The first thing we notice is that the box and unbox operations are IL primitives. Boxing and unboxing are features of the platform, not the preserve of C#. The box operation takes a value type from the top of the stack, stores it in a new reference type which it creates on the managed heap, and places a reference to the newly created type on top of the stack. In this example, that reference is then stored in V_1, or o in C#. Unboxing involves the reverse operation and leaves the unboxed value type on top of the stack. In this case, the result is stored in V_2, or j in our C# program.

2.8.3   Coding IL programs

You can write your own IL programs and assemble them using .NET's *ilasm.exe* assembler. Depending on your installation, you should find *ilasm.exe* at *C:\WINNT\Microsoft.NET\Framework\<.NET Version>*. Listing 2.12 presents a skeleton program that you can use as a template for your own IL programs.

```
// file       : skel.il
// assemble   : ilasm skel.il

.assembly extern mscorlib {}    // reference the core assembly
.assembly 'skel' {}             // this assembly name
.module 'skel.exe'              // this module

.class Skel extends ['mscorlib']System.Object {
```

```
.method public static void
  Main(class System.String[] args) cil managed {

  .entrypoint            // program starts here
  .maxstack 8            // maximum number of stack slots

  .locals (

    // local variables here ////////////

  )

  // main code goes here ///////////////
  ldstr "IL Skeleton Program!"
  call void ['mscorlib']System.Console::WriteLine(string)

  ret // exit
}

// methods go here /////////////////////

// constructor follows...
.method public hidebysig specialname rtspecialname
  instance void .ctor() cil managed {
  .maxstack 8
  ldarg.0
  call instance void ['mscorlib']System.Object::.ctor()
  ret
}
}
```

The program begins by accessing the .NET core assembly, *mscorlib.dll*, in which many of the classes in fundamental namespaces, such as System, reside. To use the skeleton for your own IL programs replace the comments to insert required local variables, the main line code, and any methods your program may require. Figure 2.15 illustrates how to assemble and execute the result.

Figure 2.15   Assembling and executing the skeleton IL program

2.8.4 Generating native images

To speed program loading, assemblies can be pre-JITted to create a native image which can then be installed in the assembly cache. To pre-JIT an assembly use the *ngen.exe* utility. In figure 2.16, we pre-JIT the *skel.exe* assembly to create a native image and install it into the assembly cache.

Figure 2.16   Pre-JITting and assembly

Figure 2.17 shows the pre-JITted assembly in the cache.

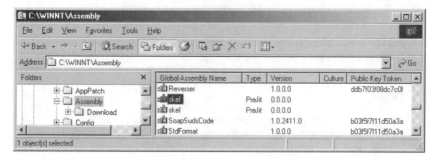

Figure 2.17   The pre-JITted skel assembly

To delete the native image from the cache, use `ngen` with the `/delete` option.

2.9   *TYPES, ASSEMBLIES, AND REFLECTION*

Reflection is a mechanism that allows programs to inspect assemblies and types at run time. This capability is provided by the classes in the `System.Reflection` namespace. Using these classes we can compile a list of types in an assembly, and a list of methods, fields, properties, events, and attributes for each type. We can use this information to create instances of these classes using late binding and invoke their methods on the fly.

2.9.1   An example of reflection

Listing 2.13 explores reflection with a new version of the `Person` class we created earlier.

Listing 2.13 Using reflection

```csharp
// file    : reflect.cs
// compile : csc reflect.cs

using System;
using System.Reflection;
using System.Text.RegularExpressions;

public class Person {

  public Person(string firstName, string lastName) {
    FirstName = firstName;
    LastName = lastName;
  }

  public void DisplayFirstName() {
    Console.WriteLine("First Name={0}", FirstName);
  }

  public void DisplayLastName() {
    Console.WriteLine("Last Name={0}", LastName);
  }

  public void ShowAll() {
    Console.WriteLine("Person...");
    Console.WriteLine("First Name={0}", FirstName);
    Console.WriteLine("Last Name={0}", LastName);
  }

  public readonly string FirstName;
  public readonly string LastName;
}

public class Reflect {
  public static void Main() {

    // get the Person type...
    Type typ = Type.GetType("Person");

    // create array of constructor arguments...
    object[] args = {"Joe", "Bloggs"};

    // create an instance of the Person type...
    Object obj = Activator.CreateInstance(typ, args);

    // get a list of Person methods...
    MethodInfo[] met = typ.GetMethods();

    // find and invoke all display methods...
    Regex r = new Regex("^display", RegexOptions.IgnoreCase);
    foreach (MethodInfo m in met)
      if (r.IsMatch(m.Name))
        m.Invoke(obj, null); // invoke display method
  }
}
```

This version of the `Person` class has two display methods, `DisplayFirstName` and `DisplayLastName`. It also has a method called `ShowAll` that displays both the first and last names. The `Reflect.Main` method retrieves the type of the `Person` class and uses `Activator.CreateInstance(typ, args)` to invoke its constructor and pass the required arguments. The arguments are passed as an array of objects. The program then loops through the type's methods using a regular expression to identify and call all methods whose names begin with the string `"Display"`. The regular expression is created by:

```
Regex r = new Regex("^display", RegexOptions.IgnoreCase);
```

This expression will match any method names beginning with the string `"Display"` while ignoring case.

Note that nowhere in our `Main` method do we declare a `Person` object. Instead we dynamically retrieve the `Person` type. Then we use reflection to discover its methods, and we use late binding to create a run time instance of the type and call its methods. When we save the file as *reflect.cs*, compile it, and run it, we get the result shown in figure 2.18.

Figure 2.18 Dynamically creating a Person object using reflection

We use the static `Type.GetType` method to retrieve the `Person` type. We can also search external assemblies by file name. For example, we could have used the following code:

```
Assembly asm = Assembly.Load("reflect");
Type typ = asm.GetType("Person");
```

2.9.2 The System.Reflection.Emit namespace

`System.Reflection.Emit` is another important namespace in the reflection class library. The classes in this namespace enable IL to be generated and emitted on the fly thereby creating a dynamic assembly at run time. Such features are typically used by compilers, interpreters, script engines, and servers. For example the ASP.NET engine uses this facility to compile and execute code in a Web page when a client requests the page. In the next section, we use the `Reflection.Emit` classes to build a compiler for a simple programming language.

2.10   BUILDING A SIMPLE COMPILER

So far, our assemblies have been created for us by the C# compiler. Our final example in this chapter is a little more ambitious. We will use our knowledge of assemblies, types, and IL to create a compiler for a simple arithmetic language, we'll call AL, which adds, subtracts, and displays integers. We use the classes in the `System.Reflection.Emit` namespace to generate the executable code. These classes provide a fully object-oriented framework for code generation.

The ability to generate IL can be useful in the development of certain types of applications such as simple search languages, or rule-based systems, or in the implementation of our own .NET scripting language.

We can create a compiler for our simple language in fewer than 200 lines of code. Doing so clarifies the relationship between the language compiler, JIT compiler, and CLR. In particular, we'll see that we don't have to concern ourselves with native code generation, since .NET automatically takes care of that difficult task.

2.10.1   The AL language

Listing 2.14 presents a sample AL program.

```
        Listing 2.14   A Sample AL Program

- file        : example1.al
- description : a sample al program
- compile     : alc example1.al

add 3
add 47
add 390
print       - displays 440
add 12
print       - displays 452
reset
print       - displays 0
sub 7
add -4
print       - displays -11
add 11
print       - displays 0
```

Like IL, AL is a simple stack-based language. It consists of just four statements as illustrated in table 2.3.

AL allows just one statement per line and the program executes from top to bottom with no variation in control flow. In spite of its simplicity, however, it provides a good vehicle for experimenting with code generation and the `System.Reflection.Emit` classes.

Table 2.3 The AL programming language

Statement	Description
add i	Adds integer i to value on top of stack, and leaves the result on the stack in its place
sub i	Subtracts integer i from value on top of stack, and leaves the result on the stack in its place
reset	Sets value on top of stack to zero
print	Writes value on top of stack to the console

In listing 2.14, we use the hyphen (-) to delimit comments. In fact, our compiler will simply ignore lines that don't start with one of the four statements in the language. Also, it will ignore any text after a statement and its argument, if present. So we can insert comments directly after statements on the same line without using the comment delimiter, if we like.

The output from the compiler, *alc.exe*, will be a PE format Windows executable. If the input file is called *progname.al*, the output will be written to *progname.exe*.

2.10.2 Translating AL to IL

Let's explore how we translate AL to IL. The IL program will need somewhere to store the result of AL's arithmetic operations so we'll use a single local integer variable that we'll initialize to zero at start up. Therefore, we need to emit the following IL to start:

```
.locals (int32 V_0)
ldc.i4.0
stloc.0
```

This creates the local integer variable, V_0, then loads zero, and stores it in V_0 to initialize it. From then on, each AL instruction will generate code to update V_0 with the result of each arithmetic operation. With this scheme in mind, we can translate AL's add statement, with just a few lines of IL. For example, add 123 would be translated, as follows:

```
// example AL statement...
// add 123
// compiles to...

ldloc.0      // load V_0
ldc.i4 123   // load constant 123
add          // add
stloc.0      // store result back in V_0
```

We load the local V_0, add the integer constant 123 to it, and store the result back in V_0. The sub statement is almost identical:

```
// example AL statement...
// sub 123
// compiles to...
```

```
ldloc.0      // load V_0
ldc.i4 123   // load constant 123
sub          // subtract
stloc.0      // store result back in V_0
```

The reset statement simply sets V_0 to zero:

```
// example AL statement...
// reset
// compiles to...

ldc.i4.0     // load constant zero
stloc.0      // store in V_0
```

To implement AL's print statement, we'll use System.Console.WriteLine to display V_0 on the console:

```
// example AL statement...
// print
// compiles to...

ldloc.0      // load V_0
call void [mscorlib]System.Console::WriteLine(int32) // display V_0
```

2.10.3   Dynamically generating an assembly

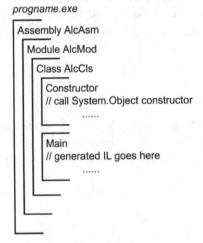

Figure 2.19 The assembly generated dynamically by the AL compiler

We know that we're going to need some sort of assembly to contain the executable code. Since AL does not support objects or methods, we'll use a simple translation scheme. To create the executable program, we'll generate an assembly with a Main method into which we'll place all the generated IL. Figure 2.19 illustrates the structure of the executable produced by the compiler.

The compiler takes *progname.al*, compiles it, and generates an executable called *progname.exe*. The latter represents a single-file assembly, AlcAsm, which in turn contains a single module, AlcMod, containing a single class AlcCls. The compilation process automatically generates a default constructor for AlcCls which simply calls the base class, System.Object, constructor. AlcCls.Main is where we place the IL generated by the compilation process.

2.10.4   Coding the AL compiler

We'll use the Framework's System.Reflection.Emit classes to create each of these building blocks, and we'll discuss them in turn. The full compiler program is presented in listing 2.15. It is presented here in outline form.

The AL compiler is implemented as a class called `ArithLang.ALC`:

```
namespace ArithLang {

    using System;
    using System.IO;
    using System.Threading;
    using System.Reflection;
    using System.Reflection.Emit;

    class ALC {

        public static void Main(string[] args) {
            Console.WriteLine("Arithmetic Language Compiler...");
            if (args.Length != 1) {
                Console.WriteLine("usage: alc progname.al");
                return;
            }
            new ALC(args[0]); // launch AL compiler
        }

        public ALC(string filePath) {

            ...

            init();

            ...

        }

        ...

        private string inFile;
        private string outFile;

        private AssemblyBuilder alcAsm;
        private ModuleBuilder alcMod;
        private TypeBuilder alcCls;
        private ILGenerator alcILG;

        private MethodInfo writeIntMethod;

    }
}
```

The program starts by declaring the reflection namespaces that we'll use to manage types and build the assembly. When the compiler starts, it checks for a command line argument containing the name of the AL source file. If this is absent, the compiler aborts with a message. The private string fields, `inFile` and `outFile`, contain the paths of the input source file and target executable file. We also declare references to an `AssemblyBuilder`, a `ModuleBuilder`, a `TypeBuilder`, and an `ILGenerator`, which we use to build the target assembly, its types, and the generated IL. The `writeIntMethod` will be used to reference the `System.Console.WriteLine` method call that we'll insert into the IL to display the value on top of the stack.

The `init()` method creates the assembly in which the executable will be stored:

```
// create dynamic assembly...
AssemblyName asmName = new AssemblyName();
asmName.Name = "AlcAsm";
alcAsm = Thread.GetDomain().DefineDynamicAssembly(
  asmName,
  AssemblyBuilderAccess.Save
);
```

The `AssemblyName` class is used to uniquely identify an assembly by its name, culture, originator, and version number. In this case, we're only interested in the name of the assembly, and we call it `AlcAsm`. Next, we define a new dynamic assembly in the current application domain. .NET uses application domains to separate executing applications. We'll look at application domains in more detail when we explore remoting in chapter 5. In this case, we're just going to save the assembly to disk. We specify this using the `AssemblyBuilderAccess.Save` option.

Next, we create a module in the assembly:

```
// create module...
alcMod = alcAsm.DefineDynamicModule(
  "AlcMod",
  outFile
);
```

We call the module `AlcMod` and we specify the path, `outFile` of the executable file produced.

Now, it's time to create the `AlcCls` class:

```
// define AlcCls class.
alcCls = alcMod.DefineType(
  "AlcCls",
  TypeAttributes.Public
);
```

This creates the `AlcCls` class and specifies that it is public. Next, the constructor:

```
// create AlcCls class constructor...
ConstructorBuilder alcCon = alcCls.DefineConstructor(
  MethodAttributes.Public | MethodAttributes.HideBySig,
  CallingConventions.Standard,
  new Type[0]
);
```

We specify that the constructor is public and that it is hidden by its method signature, and not by its name alone. We also specify `CallingConventions.Standard` for the constructor. Alternatives include the ability to call with variable arguments, or with a `this` reference included in the argument list.

Now that we have a constructor, we need to generate some IL. For our default constructor, we just call the base constructor in `System.Object`:

```
// generate constructor IL...
ILGenerator conILG = alcCon.GetILGenerator();
ConstructorInfo conObj =
  typeof(object).GetConstructor(new Type[0]);
conILG.Emit(OpCodes.Ldarg_0);
conILG.Emit(OpCodes.Call, conObj);
conILG.Emit(OpCodes.Ret);
```

We create an `ILGenerator` instance and create a reference, `conObj` to `System.Object`'s constructor. We use `ILGenerator.Emit` to write IL into the constructor. The `OpCodes` enumeration contains enumerated names for all the instructions in IL.

The real work happens in the `Main` method:

```
// create AlcCls.Main() method...
MethodBuilder mainMethod = alcCls.DefineMethod(
  "Main",
  MethodAttributes.Public |
  MethodAttributes.Static |
  MethodAttributes.HideBySig,
  Type.GetType("void"),
  null);
```

This code generates IL similar to that which would result from compiling the C# signature for `Main()`:

```
public static void Main() {
  ...
}
```

We need to set `Main()` as the program's entry point. We also need to create the local integer variable that AL programs will use to store the result of arithmetic operations:

```
// set Main as program entrypoint...
alcAsm.SetEntryPoint((MethodInfo)mainMethod);

// generate IL for Main.
alcILG = mainMethod.GetILGenerator();

// create local integer variable...
LocalBuilder v_0 = alcILG.DeclareLocal(
  Type.GetType("System.Int32"));

// set IL local V_0 to 0...
alcILG.Emit(OpCodes.Ldc_I4_0);
alcILG.Emit(OpCodes.Stloc_0 );
```

We use a `LocalBuilder` reference to insert the local integer variable declaration into the emitted IL and we emit the opcodes necessary to initialize the variable to zero.

That completes the creation and setup of the building blocks that our assembly requires. We'll be inserting calls to `System.Console.WriteLine` into the IL. So the final initialization step is to obtain, and store, a reference to the version of this method which takes an integer as an argument:

```
// get method for displaying integers...
Type[] argTypes = {typeof(int)};
writeIntMethod = typeof(Console).GetMethod(
  "WriteLine",
  argTypes
);
}
```

With these building blocks in place, we simply loop through the source file, scanning for AL statements and emitting the appropriate IL. For example, for AL's add statement we call the doAddStatement method:

```
private void doAddStatement(string arg) {
  alcILG.Emit(OpCodes.Ldloc_0);
  alcILG.Emit(OpCodes.Ldc_I4, Int32.Parse(arg));
  alcILG.Emit(OpCodes.Add);
  alcILG.Emit(OpCodes.Stloc_0 );
}
```

This attempts to parse the integer operand from the arg string passed in. If it fails, the compiler will report an error and the offending line number, as shown in figure 2.20.

Figure 2.20 Reporting compiler errors

The remaining statements are implemented using similar methods. The complete program is presented in listing 2.15.

Listing 2.15 The AL compiler

```
// file    : alc.cs
// compile : csc alc.cs

namespace ArithLang {

  using System;
  using System.IO;
  using System.Threading;
  using System.Reflection;
  using System.Reflection.Emit;

  class ALC {

    public static void Main(string[] args) {
      Console.WriteLine("Arithmetic Language Compiler...");
```

CHAPTER 2 UNDERSTANDING TYPES AND ASSEMBLIES

```
    if (args.Length != 1) {
      Console.WriteLine("usage: alc progname.al");
      return;
    }
  new ALC(args[0]); // launch AL compiler
}

public ALC(string filePath) {

  inFile = filePath;
  outFile = Path.ChangeExtension(inFile, "exe");

  int lineNum = 0;
  string line = "";
  StreamReader sr = null;

  try {
    sr = File.OpenText(inFile);  // open source file
    init(); // create new assembly

    char[] separator = {' '};
    while ((line = sr.ReadLine()) != null) {

      lineNum++;
      string[] tokens = line.Trim().ToLower().Split(separator);

      if (tokens[0].Equals("add")) {
        doAddStatement(tokens[1]);
        continue;
      }

      if (tokens[0].Equals("sub")) {
        doSubStatement(tokens[1]);
        continue;
      }

      if (tokens[0].Equals("print")) {
        doPrintStatement();
        continue;
      }

      if (tokens[0].Equals("reset")) {
        doResetStatement();
        continue;
      }
    }
  } catch (Exception e) {
    Console.WriteLine("ERROR LINE({0}): {1}", lineNum, line);
    Console.WriteLine(e.Message);
    return;
  } finally {
    if (sr != null) sr.Close();
  }
  save();
  Console.WriteLine("Done!");
}
```

```
private void init() {
  // create dynamic assembly...
  AssemblyName asmName = new AssemblyName();
  asmName.Name = "AlcAsm";
  alcAsm = Thread.GetDomain().DefineDynamicAssembly(
    asmName,
    AssemblyBuilderAccess.Save
  );

  // create module in this assembly...
  alcMod = alcAsm.DefineDynamicModule(
    "AlcMod",
    outFile
  );

  // create class in this module...
  alcCls = alcMod.DefineType(
    "AlcCls",
    TypeAttributes.Public
  );

  // create AlcCls class constructor...
  ConstructorBuilder alcCon = alcCls.DefineConstructor(
    MethodAttributes.Public | MethodAttributes.HideBySig,
    CallingConventions.Standard,
    new Type[0]
  );

  // generate constructor IL...
  ILGenerator conILG = alcCon.GetILGenerator();
  ConstructorInfo conObj =
    typeof(object).GetConstructor(new Type[0]);
  conILG.Emit(OpCodes.Ldarg_0);
  conILG.Emit(OpCodes.Call, conObj);
  conILG.Emit(OpCodes.Ret);

  // create AlcCls.Main() method...
  MethodBuilder mainMethod = alcCls.DefineMethod(
    "Main",
    MethodAttributes.Public |
    MethodAttributes.Static |
    MethodAttributes.HideBySig,
    Type.GetType("void"),
    null);

  // set Main as program entrypoint...
  alcAsm.SetEntryPoint((MethodInfo)mainMethod);

  // generate IL for Main.
  alcILG = mainMethod.GetILGenerator();

  // create local integer variable...
  LocalBuilder v_0 = alcILG.DeclareLocal(
    Type.GetType("System.Int32"));
  ,
```

```csharp
      // set IL local V_0 to 0...
      alcILG.Emit(OpCodes.Ldc_I4_0);
      alcILG.Emit(OpCodes.Stloc_0 );

      // get method for displaying integers...
      Type[] argTypes = {typeof(int)};
      writeIntMethod = typeof(Console).GetMethod(
        "WriteLine",
        argTypes
      );
    }

    private void doAddStatement(string arg) {
      alcILG.Emit(OpCodes.Ldloc_0);
      alcILG.Emit(OpCodes.Ldc_I4, Int32.Parse(arg));
      alcILG.Emit(OpCodes.Add);
      alcILG.Emit(OpCodes.Stloc_0 );
    }

    private void doSubStatement(string arg) {
      alcILG.Emit(OpCodes.Ldloc_0);
      alcILG.Emit(OpCodes.Ldc_I4, Int32.Parse(arg));
      alcILG.Emit(OpCodes.Sub);
      alcILG.Emit(OpCodes.Stloc_0 );
    }

    private void doPrintStatement() {
      alcILG.Emit(OpCodes.Ldloc_0 );
      alcILG.Emit(OpCodes.Call, writeIntMethod);
    }

    private void doResetStatement() {
      alcILG.Emit(OpCodes.Ldc_I4_0 );
      alcILG.Emit(OpCodes.Stloc_0 );
    }

    private void save() {
      alcILG.Emit(OpCodes.Ret); // emit return statement
      alcCls.CreateType(); // create our new type
      Console.WriteLine("Writing " + outFile);
      alcAsm.Save(outFile); // save the assembly
    }

    private string inFile;
    private string outFile;

    private AssemblyBuilder alcAsm;
    private ModuleBuilder alcMod;
    private TypeBuilder alcCls;
    private ILGenerator alcILG;

    private MethodInfo writeIntMethod;
  }
}
```

2.10.5 Building and testing the AL compiler

The first step is to compile the AL compiler. Then, we use the compiler to compile the AL program in listing 2.14. Finally, we execute the resulting AL program. These steps are shown in figure 2.21.

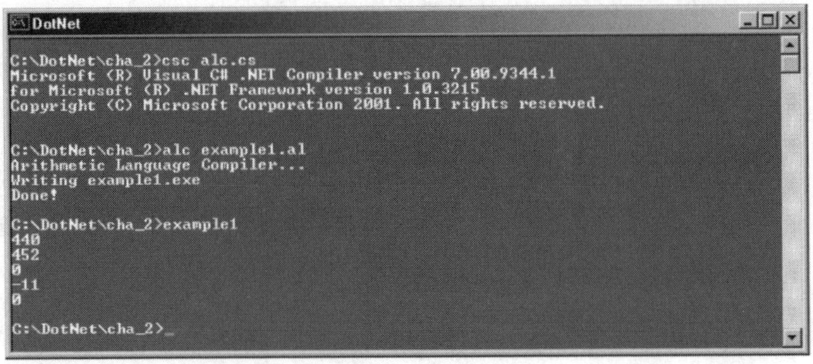

Figure 2.21 Compiling and running the AL compiler

How about that? We've just created our own language compiler with less than 200 lines of code, although it is hardly likely to shake up the computer science community. Note that we don't care about back-end generation of native code. The CLR's JIT compiler looks after that difficult problem for us at program load time. Alternatively, we can use *ngen.exe* to generate a native image and install it in the assembly cache.

2.11 SUMMARY

In this chapter we looked at types and assemblies. We saw how both are independent of the programming language used to develop the application or component. A type implemented in one .NET language can be used by an application coded in a different language and this language interoperability even extends to cross-language inheritance. We also explored the difference between value and reference types and how the runtime uses boxing and unboxing to convert between the two.

We explored `System.Object`, the ultimate superclass from which all types derive, and we learned about finalization under .NET. We looked at assemblies, the smallest versionable, installable unit in .NET and we saw how to install a shared assembly and how to download an assembly from the Web on demand.

Finally, we looked at IL and we used the reflection classes to discover the methods exposed by a type. We also used the classes in `System.Reflection.Emit` to dynamically generate our own assembly and to build a compiler for a simple programming language.

In the next chapter, we begin our case study, a video poker machine. We'll develop multiple versions of the poker machine in following chapters. In doing so, we'll explore important elements of .NET including ADO.NET, ASP.NET, Windows Forms, remoting, and XML Web services.

C H A P T E R   3

Case study: a video poker machine

In chapter 1, we considered the architecture of a loan management system for a bank. In doing so, we saw how .NET gives us the building blocks we need to create multi-tier applications with shared back-end systems and multiple interfaces to customers, business partners, and other bank departments. In this chapter, we begin a case study in which we employ these building blocks to implement a 3-tier, multiuser, distributed video poker machine.

I've chosen video poker for several reasons:

- Unlike examples from mainstream business or commerce, the rules of poker can be fully explained in a few paragraphs, leaving us free to concentrate on .NET development.

- A video poker machine can have all the important ingredients of a distributed, client/server, multi-interface application. It can be naturally implemented as a game engine and a set of interfaces. We'll reuse the engine to implement different game applications based on COM, Internet Explorer, remoting, Windows services, message queuing, XML Web services, Windows Forms, Web Forms, and Mobile Forms. We'll also use SQL Server and ADO.NET to store play history and provide data to drive the payout management algorithm.

- Video poker is a real-world application which generates millions of dollars in profits each year in places like Las Vegas and Atlantic City.

- Best of all, we'll need to play lots of poker to test our work.

We'll develop the poker engine, a DLL assembly, in this and the next chapter. In later chapters, we'll develop different interfaces to the engine using most of the important features of .NET. In doing so, we'll get a reasonably complete tour of .NET application development. In the meantime, we take a short break from .NET and play a little poker.

3.1 PLAYING VIDEO POKER

Video poker took the casino industry by storm in the early 1980s. In Las Vegas casinos, and elsewhere, it now accounts for a greater share of income than traditional slot machines. The game is simple. You play against a machine which acts as dealer and you insert money to receive credits. Then you make a bet and hit the Deal button. The machine displays five cards from the deck. The idea is to make the best possible poker hand out of these five cards by holding onto the best cards and drawing replacements for those you wish to discard. You do this by selecting the cards you want to hold and clicking Draw. The cards you hold are retained while the others are replaced. At this point the hand is scored and you either win or lose. Typically to win you need a pair of jacks or better. If you win, your winnings are calculated by multiplying the score for the hand by the amount of your bet. The total is added to your existing credits.

Figure 3.1 shows the Windows Forms version of the game. The screenshot shows the state of the game after we have placed our bet and received five cards. At this stage the bet text box in the top right of the screen is disabled to prevent us from changing our bet mid-game. In the top left we can see that we have 98 credits remaining. Underneath the two jacks we have checked the checkboxes to indicate that we want to hold onto these two cards when we draw. By doing so, we are guaranteed to win since the minimum scoring hand is a pair of jacks or better.

At this point we would click DRAW and the three remaining cards would be replaced. Drawing a third jack would result in a scoring hand known as *three of a kind*.

Figure 3.1
The Windows Forms version of video poker

3.1.1 Winning poker hands

Table 3.1 lists the winning poker hands, their scores, and some examples. We use a two-character identifier for a card's name. For example, the ace of diamonds has the name "AD", and so forth. This gives us a user-friendly shorthand for displaying cards on the console.

Table 3.1 Winning video poker hands

Hand	Example	Score	Description
Royal Flush	TD JD QD KD AD	10	A straight to the ace in the same suit
Straight Flush	3H 4H 5H 6H 7H	9	A straight in the same suit
Four of a Kind	5C 5D 5H 5S QH	8	Four cards of the same number
Full House	KC KH KD 8C 8S	7	Three of a kind with any pair
Flush	9S 3S QS TS AS	6	5 cards of the same suit
Straight	8C 9S TC JC QH	5	5 cards with consecutive numbers
Three of a Kind	TD 4C 4S 3S 4D	4	Three cards of the same number
Two Pair	AD QH QD 7C 7D	3	Any pair with any pair
Jacks or Better	KD 8C 7D KS 5C	2	A pair of jacks, queens, kings, or aces

If a player bets 5 and scores three of a kind, the player's credits increase by 20 (5 times 4). Note that a card's number is the number on the card. The non-numbered cards, jack, queen, king, and ace are given the numbers, 11, 12, 13, and 14 respectively. (An ace can also double as the bottom card in a straight to the 5; e.g., AC 2D 3D 4C 5H.)

3.1.2 A profitable video poker machine

In the bottom right of the screenshot in figure 3.1, we can see statistics for the machine. These statistics are based on data collected at the end of each game and stored in SQL Server. The figures include the total amounts taken in and paid out by the machine. The differences between these two figures is the profit. The house margin is the percentage profit, while the target margin represents the machine's target profit. These figures reflect data for all games played by all players and provide an overview of profitability from the machine's perspective and not from the current player's point of view.

You may be wondering about target profit. How can we set a target profit for a machine which is governed by chance? We do it by implementing a payout control algorithm which continually adjusts the odds in an effort to keep the machine on target. In figure 3.1, the machine has a 25% profit goal.

The delta figure is the difference between the target margin and the house margin. If delta is positive, then bias is zero. In other words, if the machine is meeting or exceeding its profit target, then no machine bias is necessary. Otherwise bias is calculated by taking the absolute value of delta and rounding it to an integer. The effect of this is that bias increases as the machine increasingly falls short of its profit goal. The bias value is used to tilt the odds back in favor of the machine, thus restoring profitability and reducing bias toward zero once again. In figure 3.1, the actual percentage profit is 17.54%, and the machine is falling 7.46% short of its 25% profit target. Therefore, bias is 7 and the machine will be harder to beat. The payout control algorithm is presented in detail in the following chapter.

3.2 THE POKER.CARD CLASS

We'll start with a simple version of the game consisting initially of just a couple of classes to represent playing cards and hands. Later in this chapter, we'll explore the design of the distributed, 3-tier version of video poker.

3.2.1 Designing the Card class

It's pretty obvious that we're going to need a class to represent a playing card, and a class to represent a hand. In fact, that's all we need to get a simple game engine up and running. Figure 3.2 depicts some sample card objects.

The card class will have three public properties, Number, Suit, and Name. A card's number can range from 2 to 14 and its suit will be an integer ranging from 1 to 4 representing clubs, diamonds, hearts, and spades in alphabetical order. We'll use

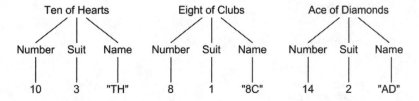

Figure 3.2   Example Card objects

the two-character identifier for the card's name. This simple scheme supports the efficient generation of random cards with a user-friendly way to display them as text.

3.2.2   Coding the Card class

Before we code the `Card` class, we observe that card objects are immutable. As in a real game, once a card is drawn from the deck, its number, suit, or name cannot be altered. Therefore, we can gain a little in both efficiency and simplicity by implementing a card's properties as public, read-only fields.

We'll need the ability to construct random playing cards to simulate dealing and drawing cards from the deck. We'll also need the ability to construct specific playing cards on demand. The code for the `Card` class is presented in listing 3.1.

Listing 3.1   The Poker.Card class

```
using System.Reflection;
[assembly:AssemblyVersion("1.0.0.0")]

namespace Poker {

  using System;

  internal class Card {

    public Card() : this(new Random()) {}

    public Card(Random r) {
      Number = r.Next(2, 15);
      Suit = r.Next(1, 5);
      Name = numberArray[Number - 2] + suitArray[Suit - 1];
    }

    public Card(string name) {
      string n = name.Substring(0, 1);
      string s = name.Substring(1, 1);
      Number = numberString.IndexOf(n) + 2;
      Suit = suitString.IndexOf(s) + 1;
      Name = name;
    }

    public readonly int Number;
    public readonly int Suit;
    public readonly string Name;

    public override string ToString() {
```

```
        return Name;
    }

    public override bool Equals(object o) {
        try {
            Card c = (Card)o;
            return c.Number == Number && c.Suit == Suit;
        } catch (Exception) {
            return false;
        }
    }

    public override int GetHashCode() {
        return (Suit<<4) + Number;
    }

    // private fields...
    private static string[] numberArray
        = {"2","3","4","5","6","7","8","9","T","J","Q","K","A"};
    private static string[] suitArray = {"C","D","H","S"};
    private static string numberString = "23456789TJQKA";
    private static string suitString = "CDHS";
    }
}
```

The Card class begins by specifying the version number of the *Poker* assembly where the Card class will reside. We could specify this in any of the source files which make up the assembly and choose to do so here only for convenience.

We place the code for the Card, and all other poker classes, inside a new namespace called Poker. We also specify internal access to the Card class, as it should be accessible only to a Hand object within the same assembly.

The Card class contains three constructors. The default constructor simply creates a new random number generator and calls the second constructor. To facilitate the generation of a valid pseudorandom sequence when dealing cards, we'll typically use the second constructor and pass a random number generator from the calling application. This constructor uses the private numberArray and suitArray as look up tables to create the Name. The third constructor accepts a card name as an argument and builds the corresponding Card object. This allows us to create specific cards to order when necessary.

The rest of the Card class should look familiar. We override Equals to return true if the two cards have the same number and suit. Therefore, we should override GetHashCode to ensure that cards, which are equal, hash to the same code. In this case, we combine number and suit into a single unique integer hash code. We also override ToString to display the card's name.

That completes the Card class. It provides us with a means of creating cards, displaying them on the console, comparing them for equality, and storing them in a hash table.

3.3 THE POKER.HAND CLASS

In video poker, cards are always assembled into a hand consisting of 5 cards. The machine starts by dealing 5 cards at random. The user can discard none, some, or all of these cards in an attempt to improve the hand's score. Therefore, a hand is an obvious choice for an application class.

3.3.1 Designing the Hand class

The Hand class represents a poker hand consisting of 5 cards. Figure 3.3 depicts a Hand object for a royal flush in spades.

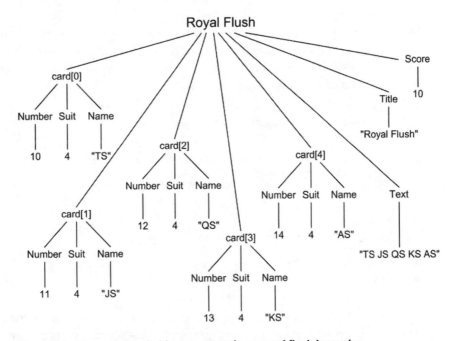

Figure 3.3 Example Hand object representing a royal flush in spades

The Hand class contains a private array of 5 card objects. It also contains public Score, Title, and Text properties. As shown in figure 3.3, for a royal flush in spades, Score is 10, Text is "TS JS QS KS KS", and Title is "Royal Flush".

3.3.2 Coding the Hand class

We know that the Hand class will require one or more constructors, together with properties representing the hand's score, text, and title. The score will need to be calculated according to the scheme shown in table 3.1.

Although the Hand class is simple, calculating the hand's score takes quite a few lines of code. The full source code for the Hand class is presented in listing 3.2. In the meantime, we'll go through the code in outline here.

We begin the Hand class with the default constructor which simply creates a hand of 5 cards taking care to avoid duplicates:

```
public Hand() {
  Random r = new Random();
  for (int i = 0; i < 5; i++) {
    while (true) {
      cards[i] = new Card(r);
      if (containsCard(cards[i], cards, i)) continue;
      break;
    }
  }
}
```

When a player selects cards to hold, and then draws, we'll need to create a new hand from the old. To do this, we'll need a constructor that takes an existing hand, and a list of cards to hold, and creates a new hand. In fact we'll provide three different constructors to do this, as follows:

```
public Hand(string handText) {
  cardsFromString(handText);
}

public Hand(string handText, string holdString) {
  cardsFromString(handText);
  holdCards(holdString);
  draw();
}

public Hand(Hand hand, string holdString) {
  this.cards = hand.cards;
  holdCards(holdString);
  draw();
}
```

In each case the handText argument is a string representation of an existing hand which we get from the hand's Text property. These constructors support the creation of new hands from existing hands, as follows:

```
Hand newHand = Hand(oldHand.Text)
...
Hand newHand = Hand(oldHand.Text, "13") // hold 1st and 3rd cards
...
Hand newHand = Hand(oldHand, "52") // hold 5th and 2nd cards
```

Although not obvious at this point, these constructors will provide a convenient means of drawing cards in both the text-based, Windows GUI, and Web versions of the poker game.

We could implement a scheme that uses just a single hand object for each game played, as follows:

```
Hand h = new Hand();
...
h.Hold(1); // hold 1st card
h.Hold(4); // hold 4th card
...
h.Draw(); // replace 2nd, 3rd, and 5th cards
```

While this scheme would work fine, it requires maintaining the state of a single hand for the duration of a game. In contrast, we'll find that using an immutable hand object, which is discarded and replaced by a new hand when cards are drawn, provides a better model for loosely coupled, remote and Web-based versions of the game.

The rest of the Hand class is straightforward. Note that we only compute the Score property on demand:

```
public int Score { get {
  if (score < 0) calcScore();
  return score;
} }
```

We're not interested in the score until cards have been drawn and the game is over. The calcScore, while a little long, is simple. It simply checks for a scoring hand starting with a royal flush and ending with jacks or better.

The full Hand class is presented in listing 3.2.

Listing 3.2   The Poker.Hand class

```
namespace Poker {

  using System;

  public class Hand {

    public Hand() {
      Random r = new Random();
      for (int i = 0; i < 5; i++) {
        while (true) {
          cards[i] = new Card(r);
          if (containsCard(cards[i], cards, i)) continue;
          break;
        }
      }
    }

    public Hand(string handText) {
      cardsFromString(handText);
    }

    public Hand(string handText, string holdString) {
      cardsFromString(handText);
      holdCards(holdString);
      draw();
    }

    public Hand(Hand hand, string holdString) {
```

```
    this.cards = hand.cards;
    holdCards(holdString);
    draw();
  }

  public int Score { get {
    if (score < 0) calcScore();
    return score;
  } }

  public string Title { get {
    return titles[Score];
  } }

  public string CardName(int cardNum) {
    return cards[cardNum - 1].Name;
  }

  public string Text { get {
    return  CardName(1) + " " +
            CardName(2) + " " +
            CardName(3) + " " +
            CardName(4) + " " +
            CardName(5);
  } }

  public override string ToString() {
    return Text;
  }

  private void cardsFromString(string handText) {
    char[] delims = {' '};
    string[] cardStrings = handText.Split(delims);
    for (int i = 0; i < cardStrings.Length; i++)
      cards[i] = new Card(cardStrings[i]);
  }

  private void holdCards(string holdString) {
    for (int i = 0; i < 6; i++) {
      int cardNum = i + 1;
      if (holdString.IndexOf(cardNum.ToString()) >= 0)
        isHold[cardNum - 1] = true;
    }
  }

  private void draw() {

    // remember which cards player has seen...
    Card[] seen = new Card[10];
    for (int i = 0; i < 5; i++) {
      seen[i] = cards[i];
    }

    int numSeen = 5;
    Random r = new Random();
    for (int i = 0; i < 5; i++) {
```

```
      if (!isHold[i]) {
        while (true) {
          cards[i] = new Card(r);
          if (containsCard(cards[i], seen, numSeen)) continue;
          break;
        }
        seen[numSeen++] = cards[i];
      }
    }
  }

  private bool containsCard(Card c, Card[] cs, int count) {
    for (int i = 0; i < count; i++)
      if (c.Equals(cs[i]))
        return true;
    return false;
  }

  private void calcScore() {
    // are cards all of the same suit?
    bool isFlush = true;
    int s = cards[0].Suit;
    for (int i = 1; i < 5; i++) {
      if (s != cards[i].Suit) {
        isFlush = false;
        break;
      }
    }

    // sort card values...
    int[] sortedValues = new int[5];
    for (int i = 0; i < 5; i++)
      sortedValues[i] = cards[i].Number;
    Array.Sort(sortedValues);

    // do we have a straight?
    bool isStraight = true;
    for (int i = 0; i < 4; i++) {
      if (sortedValues[i] + 1 != sortedValues[i+1]) {
        isStraight = false;
        break;
      }
    }
    // is it a straight to the ace?
    bool isTopStraight = (isStraight && sortedValues[4] == 14);

    // maybe it is a straight from the ace (i.e. A, 2, 3, 4, 5)
    if (! isStraight)
      if (sortedValues[0] == 2 &&
          sortedValues[1] == 3 &&
          sortedValues[2] == 4 &&
          sortedValues[3] == 5 &&
          sortedValues[4] == 14) // ace on top
```

```
    isStraight = true;

// now calculate score...

// royal flush...
if (isTopStraight && isFlush) {
  score = 10;
  return;
}

// straight flush...
if (isStraight && isFlush) {
  score = 9;
  return;
}

// four of a kind...
if (sortedValues[0] == sortedValues[1] &&
    sortedValues[1] == sortedValues[2] &&
    sortedValues[2] == sortedValues[3]) {
  score = 8;
  return;
}
if (sortedValues[1] == sortedValues[2] &&
    sortedValues[2] == sortedValues[3] &&
    sortedValues[3] == sortedValues[4]) {
  score = 8;
  return;
}

// full house...
if (sortedValues[0] == sortedValues[1] &&
    sortedValues[1] == sortedValues[2] &&
    sortedValues[3] == sortedValues[4]) {
  score = 7;
  return;
}
if (sortedValues[0] == sortedValues[1] &&
    sortedValues[2] == sortedValues[3] &&
    sortedValues[3] == sortedValues[4]) {
  score = 7;
  return;
}

// flush...
if (isFlush) {
  score = 6;
  return;
}

// straight...
if (isStraight) {
  score = 5;
  return;
```

```
        }
        // three of a kind...
        if (sortedValues[0] == sortedValues[1] &&
            sortedValues[1] == sortedValues[2]) {
          score = 4;
          return;
        }
        if (sortedValues[1] == sortedValues[2] &&
            sortedValues[2] == sortedValues[3]) {
          score = 4;
          return;
        }
        if (sortedValues[2] == sortedValues[3] &&
            sortedValues[3] == sortedValues[4]) {
          score = 4;
          return;
        }

        // two pair...
        if (sortedValues[0] == sortedValues[1] &&
            sortedValues[2] == sortedValues[3]) {
          score = 3;
          return;
        }
        if (sortedValues[0] == sortedValues[1] &&
            sortedValues[3] == sortedValues[4]) {
          score = 3;
          return;
        }
        if (sortedValues[1] == sortedValues[2] &&
            sortedValues[3] == sortedValues[4]) {
          score = 3;
          return;
        }

        // jacks or better...
        if (sortedValues[0] > 10 &&
          sortedValues[0] == sortedValues[1]) {
          score = 2;
          return;
        }
        if (sortedValues[1] > 10 &&
          sortedValues[1] == sortedValues[2]) {
          score = 2;
          return;
        }
        if (sortedValues[2] > 10 &&
          sortedValues[2] == sortedValues[3]) {
          score = 2;
          return;
        }
        if (sortedValues[3] > 10 &&
```

```
                 sortedValues[3] == sortedValues[4]) {
                 score = 2;
                 return;
               }
               score = 0;
               return;
             }
             private Card[] cards = new Card[5];
             private bool[] isHold = {false, false, false, false, false};

             private static string[] titles = {
               "No Score",
               "",
               "Jacks or Better",
               "Two Pair",
               "Three of a Kind",
               "Straight",
               "Flush",
               "Full House",
               "Four of a Kind",
               "Straight Flush",
               "Royal Flush",
             };

             private int score = -1;
           }
         }
```

3.4 SimPok: A SIMPLE POKER GAME

Now it is time to build our first version of video poker. This version will provide a simple poker machine class which can deal and draw cards, but which ignores game histories and omits profit calculations for now. We also implement a simple console interface to this machine.

3.4.1 The Poker.SimpleMachine class

Listing 3.3 presents a class called SimpleMachine which represents a simple poker machine with the ability to deal and draw hands.

Listing 3.3   The Poker.SimpleMachine class

```
namespace Poker {
  public class SimpleMachine {
    public Hand Deal() {
      return new Hand();
    }
    public Hand Draw(Hand oldHand, string holdCards) {
      return new Hand(oldHand, holdCards);
    }
```

```
      public Hand Draw(string oldHand, string holdCards) {
        return new Hand(oldHand, holdCards);
      }
   }
}
```

■

`SimpleMachine` is really just a wrapper class for constructing `Hand` objects. We'll build a more powerful machine with database support, and payout control, in the following chapter.

Appendix B contains the code for all the classes, which make up the poker engine, together with a makefile to build the DLL. These files can also be downloaded from http://www.manning.com/grimes. If, however, you wish to build the DLL with the classes presented so far, you can issue the following compiler command:

```
csc /t:library /out:poker.dll card.cs hand.cs simplemachine.cs
```

3.4.2   The SimPok console interface

Let's create a short console program to deal and draw cards. Listing 3.4 illustrates.

Listing 3.4   The SimPok program

```
// file    : simpok.cs
// compile : csc /r:poker.dll simpok.cs

using System;
using Poker;

class SimPok {

  public static void Main() {
    new SimPok(); // start game
  }

  public SimPok() {
    Console.WriteLine("A simple poker game...");
    Console.WriteLine("Hit Ctrl-c at any time to abort.\n");
    machine = new SimpleMachine(); // create poker machine
    while (true) nextGame(); // play
  }

  private void nextGame() {

    Hand dealHand = machine.Deal(); // deal hand
    Console.WriteLine("{0}", dealHand.Text); // display it

    // invite player to hold cards...
    Console.Write("Enter card numbers (1 to 5) to hold: ");
    string holdCards = Console.ReadLine();

    // draw replacement cards...
    Hand drawHand = machine.Draw(dealHand, holdCards);
    Console.WriteLine(drawHand.Text);
    Console.WriteLine(drawHand.Title);
```

```
        Console.WriteLine("Score = {0}\n", drawHand.Score);
    }

    private SimpleMachine machine;
}
```

The program starts by greeting the user and creating a new instance of `SimpleMachine`. Then it repeatedly calls `nextGame` until the user presses CTRL+C to abort. The `nextGame` method deals a hand, displays it to the user, and asks the user which cards to hold. (Cards are identified by their positions, 1 to 5.) The user's reply is captured in `holdCards` and cards are drawn by constructing a new hand from the old, as follows:

```
    Hand drawHand = machine.Draw(dealHand, holdCards);
```

Compile and execute this program, as shown in figure 3.4.

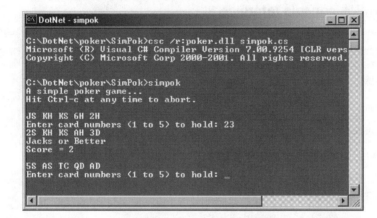

**Figure 3.4
Compiling and
running SimPok**

3.5   COMPOK: A COM-BASED POKER GAME

Before .NET came along, we might have developed and deployed our poker machine as a COM object. Doing so would have enabled us to create various clients which use COM automation to play video poker. Since COM and .NET will likely coexist for some time to come, .NET provides the ability for both to interoperate. For example, the assembly registration utility, *regasm.exe*, allows us to register a .NET assembly as a COM object. Let's explore this as a deployment option with a simple COM-based version of video poker.

3.5.1   Registering the poker assembly as a COM object

Copy *poker.dll* to the *C:\WINNT\system32* directory and then execute *regasm.exe* to register it in the registry, as shown in figure 3.5.

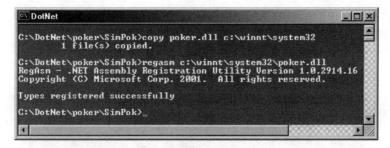

Figure 3.5   Registering the Poker.dll assembly

The *regasm.exe* utility reads the assembly metadata and makes the necessary entries in the registry to enable COM clients to create instances of the .NET types.

3.5.2   Console poker using COM and VBScript

Listing 3.5 presents a VBScript client which plays a COM-based version of our simple poker game.

> **Listing 3.5   The ComPok program**

```
' file:        compok.vbs
' description: VBScript poker game
' execute:     cscript compok.vbs

wscript.stdout.writeLine "A simple poker game..."
wscript.stdout.writeLine "Hit Ctrl-c at any time to abort"
wscript.stdout.writeLine

set machine = wscript.createObject("Poker.SimpleMachine")
do while true ' play forever

  set dealHand = machine.Deal()
  wscript.stdout.writeLine dealhand.Text

  wscript.stdout.write "Enter card numbers (1 to 5) to hold: "
  holdCards = wscript.stdin.readLine

  set drawHand = machine.Draw(dealHand, holdCards)
  wscript.stdout.writeLine drawHand.Text
  wscript.stdout.writeLine drawHand.Title
  wscript.stdout.writeLine "Score = " & drawHand.Score
  wscript.stdout.writeLine

loop
```

For our purposes, the most important line in the program is where we create a COM-based instance of the `SimpleMachine`:

```
set machine = wscript.createObject("Poker.SimpleMachine")
```

The fully qualified .NET type name, `Poker.SimpleMachine`, is used as the `ProgID` to identify the COM class in the registry.

We use the console version of the Windows Scripting Host to load and run this version of the poker game, as shown in figure 3.6.

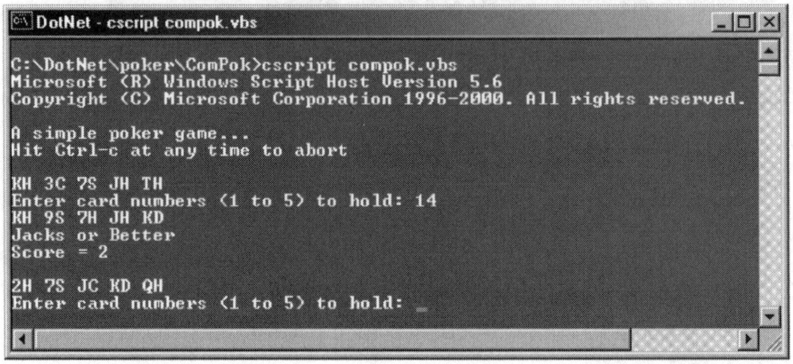

Figure 3.6   Running ComPok

3.5.3   RegAsm and the registry

When we run *regasm.exe*, all public types from the assembly are registered in the registry. To check this, run *regasm.exe* again, using the `/regfile:poker.reg` option to generate a registration file instead of updating the registry directly. (The *poker.reg* file can be used to install the component on another machine.) The file should contain an entry for `Poker.SimpleMachine` which looks something like:

```
[HKEY_CLASSES_ROOT
  \CLSID
    \{5F9EF3C3-6A12-3636-A11E-C450A65F3C0C}
      \InprocServer32]
@="C:\WINNT\System32\mscoree.dll"
"ThreadingModel"="Both"
"Class"="Poker.SimpleMachine"
"Assembly"="poker, Version=1.0.0.0,
                 Culture=neutral,
                 PublicKeyToken=null"
"RuntimeVersion"="v1.0.2904"
```

There should be a similar entry for `Poker.Hand`, but not for `Poker.Card` because the latter is internal to the assembly.

To unregister *poker.dll* enter:

```
regasm /unregister poker.dll
```

For readers who are familiar with COM+ services, .NET also provides a utility called `RegSvcs` which allows you to install a .NET assembly into a COM+ application. You'll find more information about this in the .NET and COM+ reference documentation.

3.6 *IEPOK: AN INTERNET EXPLORER POKER GAME*

Internet Explorer can download assemblies on demand and install them in the assembly download cache. This gives us the ability to install the poker engine directly from a Web page and to script a browser-hosted version of the game. So, before we leave our simple poker machine, let's create a more user-friendly interface by hosting the game inside Internet Explorer and providing a graphical interface similar to a real poker machine.

3.6.1 Downloading assemblies using Internet Explorer

We can deploy *poker.dll* on the Web server and can use the following `<object>` tag to install it directly from a Web page:

```
<object id=machine
        classid=http:poker.dll#Poker.SimpleMachine>
</object>
```

This causes Internet Explorer to download *poker.dll*, install it in the download cache, and instantiate a `SimpleMachine` object. In this example, the *poker.dll* assembly must be in the same virtual directory as the Web page. It is downloaded and activated without prompting the user, and without making any entries in the registry.

Let's explore this as a deployment option. First, we need to use Internet Services Manager to create a new virtual directory on the server. I called this directory *iepok* and mapped it to the local path *C:\DotNet\poker\IEPok*. Figure 3.7 shows the properties of this virtual directory.

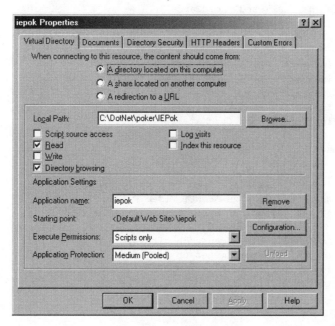

Figure 3.7
The IEPok virtual directory

3.6.2 Coding the IEPok application

Next, copy *poker.dll* to this new Web directory. We'll implement the Internet Explorer version of the game as the HTML file, *IEPok.html*, shown in listing 3.6. You'll find the GIF images of the playing cards in the download.

Listing 3.6   The IEPok.html file

```
<!-- file: IEPok.html -->
<html><head>

<object id=machine
        classid=http:poker.dll#Poker.SimpleMachine>
</object>
<script>
Hand = null;

function Cards() {
  if (Btn.value == "Deal") {
    Hand = machine.Deal();
    Hold1.checked = Hold2.checked = Hold3.checked =
         Hold4.checked = Hold5.checked = false;
    Btn.value = "Draw";
    Title.innerText = "Hold and Draw";
  } else { // draw cards...
    holdCards = "";
    if (Hold1.checked) holdCards += "1";
    if (Hold2.checked) holdCards += "2";
    if (Hold3.checked) holdCards += "3";
    if (Hold4.checked) holdCards += "4";
    if (Hold5.checked) holdCards += "5";
    Hand = machine.Draw(Hand, holdCards);
    Title.innerText = Hand.Title + "  (" + Hand.Score + ")";
    Btn.value = "Deal";
  }
  Card1.src="images/" + Hand.CardName(1) + ".gif";
  Card2.src="images/" + Hand.CardName(2) + ".gif";
  Card3.src="images/" + Hand.CardName(3) + ".gif";
  Card4.src="images/" + Hand.CardName(4) + ".gif";
  Card5.src="images/" + Hand.CardName(5) + ".gif";
}
</script></head>

<body>
<table rules="none" border=1 cellpadding="4" cellspacing="1">
  <tr><td align=center colspan=5>.NET Video Poker</td></tr>
  <tr><td id="Title" align=center colspan=5>Click Deal</td></tr>
  <tr>
    <td><img id="Card1" src="images/cb.gif" /></td>
    <td><img id="Card2" src="images/cb.gif" /></td>
    <td><img id="Card3" src="images/cb.gif" /></td>
    <td><img id="Card4" src="images/cb.gif" /></td>
    <td><img id="Card5" src="images/cb.gif" /></td>
```

```
    </tr>
    <tr>
      <td align=center><input type="checkbox" id="Hold1" /></td>
      <td align=center><input type="checkbox" id="Hold2" /></td>
      <td align=center><input type="checkbox" id="Hold3" /></td>
      <td align=center><input type="checkbox" id="Hold4" /></td>
      <td align=center><input type="checkbox" id="Hold5" /></td>
    </tr>
    <tr><td align=middle colSpan=5>
    <input type="button" value="Deal" id="Btn" onClick="Cards()"/>
    </td></tr>
  </table>
</body></html>
```

The <object> tag installs *poker.dll*. (Refer to chapter 2 for details on listing the contents of the download cache.) The remaining code is just standard HTML and JavaScript to create a table that displays 5 cards with checkboxes underneath. We use the same button for both dealing and drawing cards. All the user interface logic for the game is contained in the Cards JavaScript function. When the user clicks Deal/Draw, the program checks the button caption to see if it should deal or draw. If dealing, it simply deals a hand, clears the hold checkboxes, sets the button caption to Draw, and tells the user to hold and draw cards. If drawing, it examines the checkboxes to see which cards to hold, draws replacement cards, sets the button caption to Deal again, and tells the user the score. Refer to figure 3.8 to see how the game looks in the browser. The card images, which are available in the download for this book, are placed in the images subdirectory on the server. The image files follow the familiar two-character naming convention. For example, *qh.gif* is an image of the queen of hearts. Note that *cb.gif* is an image of the back of the cards.

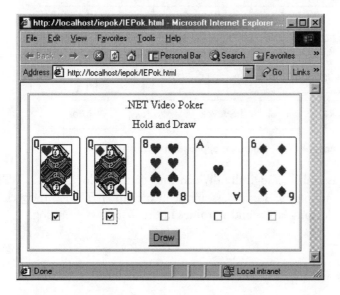

**Figure 3.8
Internet Explorer-hosted
video poker**

3.7 DESIGNING A COMPLETE GAME

In the next chapter, we'll expand our poker machine to record game histories and enforce payout control. To do so, we'll use SQL Server to store the data. It has become common to design so-called N-tier client/server systems which partition the application into separate layers. A typical design often involves three tiers, or layers: data, logic, and interface. Since we intend to develop multiple, distributed interfaces for our poker machine, this kind of partitioning is an absolute requirement. We don't want to restrict application access to just Windows or Web users when .NET provides the building blocks for wider deployment. With a little extra work, we can support users coming from Windows, the Web, UNIX via telnet, a mobile phone, a PDA, and, using either remoting or XML Web services, we can expose the poker engine to other developers who wish to build their own customized application front ends.

3.7.1 Video poker: the poker engine and its interfaces

Figure 3.9 shows an overview of the complete video poker application.

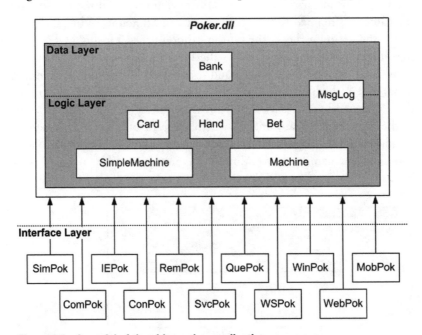

Figure 3.9   A model of the video poker application

The *poker.dll* assembly is logically divided into data and logic layers. We'll add the data layer, containing the Bank class, in the next chapter. The MsgLog class is just a utility class for logging errors and warnings in the Windows event log.

We've already developed the `Card`, `Hand`, and `SimpleMachine` classes. The full machine, a 3-tier application that supports betting and payout control, will be implemented in the `Machine` class, also in the next chapter.

Eleven versions of the poker game are shown:

- `SimPok`—The simple console-based poker game already seen in this chapter.
- `ComPok`—The VBScript/COM-based poker game already seen in this chapter.
- `IEPok`—The Internet Explorer-based poker game already seen in this chapter.
- `ConPok`—A 3-tier console poker game using SQL Server and ADO.NET.
- `RemPok`—A client/server poker game which uses .NET remoting services.
- `SvcPok`—A Windows service-based poker game.
- `QuePok`—A message queue-based poker game.
- `WSPok`—A client/server poker game which uses XML Web services.
- `WinPok`—A 3-tier Windows GUI poker game using Windows Forms, SQL Server, and ADO.NET.
- `WebPok`—A Web server-based, ASP.NET poker game.
- `MobPok`—A mobile poker game playable on a Web-enabled phone or PDA. We'll use .NET's Mobile Internet Toolkit to build this game.

In developing these game versions, we'll get a fairly complete tour of the different application models that .NET supports. We'll use the *poker.dll* assembly as a common poker engine behind each application.

3.8   SUMMARY

In this chapter, we introduced our case study and developed a simple, console-based poker game. We also saw how to expose the poker machine as a COM object, and how to download and install it inside Internet Explorer. We also laid out a model for a complete implementation of the poker machine which leverages the features of the .NET platform to gain maximum deployment.

In the next chapter, we'll explore ADO.NET and build the data layer for the poker machine. We'll also put the finishing touches to the poker engine assembly.

CHAPTER 4

Working with ADO.NET and databases

If you've programmed on the Windows platform for a while, you've probably encountered several different database access libraries such as Jet, ODBC, DAO, RDO, or ADO. ADO.NET, the latest incarnation of Microsoft ActiveX Data Objects, contains new features to bring ADO in line with connectionless Internet protocols, while retaining familiar ADO objects such as Connection and Command.

In this chapter, we explore the ADO.NET namespaces, and we program ADO.NET using C# to create the data layer of our video poker application. Familiarity with SQL databases and database objects, including tables and queries, is assumed. In addition, a basic understanding of XML will help when we discuss the ADO.NET DataSet.

Also in this chapter, we create the Poker.Bank class which encapsulates all of the application's data needs in a convenient package, while shielding the rest of the application from database or network errors. Finally, we create a reporting application, which uses XML/XSLT to report on machine statistics and profitability.

4.1 THE ADO.NET NAMESPACES

ADO.NET has several namespaces containing classes that represent database objects such as connections, commands, and datasets. Perhaps the most important of these classes is the new XML-enabled `DataSet` which provides a relational data store and a standard API independent of any underlying database management system. We'll look at the `DataSet` class in more detail in the following section. First we look at managed providers which provide the link between a `DataSet` and the underlying data store.

4.1.1 The OLE DB and SQL Server managed providers

Although a `DataSet` provides a stand-alone entity separate from the underlying store, in most cases it will get its data from a managed provider whose role is to connect, fill, and persist the `DataSet` to and from a data store. .NET offers two such providers embodied in the following two namespaces:

- `System.Data.SqlClient`—Used to talk directly to Microsoft SQL Server.
- `System.Data.OleDb`—Used to talk to any other provider that supports OLE DB (a COM-based API for accessing data).

For the most part, both namespaces provide the same important classes which represent the following major ADO.NET objects:

- `Connection`—Represents a connection to a data source.
- `Command`—Represents an executable SQL statement or stored procedure.
- `DataReader`—Facilitates the reading of a forward-only stream of rows from a database.
- `DataAdapter`—Represents a set of commands and a connection which can be used to fill a `DataSet` and update the underlying data store.

Depending on the provider used, these ADO.NET objects have different class names, as shown in table 4.1.

Table 4.1 The ADO.NET objects

ADO.NET Object	System.Data.SqlClient Class	System.Data.OleDb Class
Connection	SqlConnection	OleDbConnection
Command	SqlCommand	OleDbCommand
DataReader	SqlDataReader	OleDbDataReader
DataAdapter	SqlDataAdapter	OleDbDataAdapter

4.2 THE ADO.NET DATASET

The `DataSet` is the heart of ADO.NET. It contains a subset of an underlying database and contains both data and schema information. Unlike the legacy ADO `Recordset`, an ADO.NET `DataSet` can contain more than one table and also contains information about table relationships, the columns they contain, and any constraints that apply. Each table in a `DataSet` can contain multiple rows. Figure 4.1 is a diagram of a simple `DataSet`, called `myDataSet`, containing several tables.

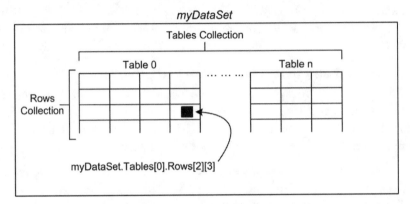

Figure 4.1   A DataSet containing a collection of tables

In the diagram, you can see that a `DataSet` has a `Tables` collection. In turn, each table has a `Rows` collection, and each row contains a collection of columns. Using indexing, we can access the fourth column of the third row of the first table as:

```
myDataSet.Tables[0].Rows[2][3]
```

Once data is retrieved from the database into a `DataSet` object, an application can disconnect from the database before processing the `DataSet`. This is an important feature of the ADO.NET `DataSet`. It gives us an in-memory, disconnected copy of a portion of the database which we can process without retaining an active connection to the database server. In the world of connectionless, Internet protocols, ADO.NET provides us with a workable solution for database access. Furthermore, because of the disconnected nature of ADO.NET, it is possible to use `DataSet`, `DataTable`, and other database-type objects, without using an underlying database management system (DBMS).

4.2.1   Creating and using a DataSet

The typical steps in creating and using a `DataSet` are:

- Create a `DataSet` object
- Connect to a database
- Fill the `DataSet` with one or more tables or views

- Disconnect from the database
- Use the DataSet in the application

4.2.2 A simple example

Listing 4.1 illustrates the creation of a DataSet by connecting to Microsoft's sample *Pubs* database (shipped with SQL Server and MSDE, the Microsoft Data Engine) and displaying the numbers of records in the *authors*, *publishers*, and *titles* tables.

Listing 4.1   Counting records in database tables

```
// file    : pubscount.cs
// compile : csc pubscount.cs

using System;
using System.Data;
using System.Data.SqlClient;

public class PubsCount {

  public static void Main() {

    // change the following connection string, as necessary...
    string con =
      @"server=(local)\NetSDK;database=pubs;trusted_connection=yes";

    DataSet ds = new DataSet("PubsDataSet");
    SqlDataAdapter sda;
    string sql;

    sql = "SELECT COUNT(*) AS cnt FROM authors";
    sda = new SqlDataAdapter(sql, con);
    sda.Fill(ds, "a_count");

    sql = "SELECT COUNT(*) AS cnt FROM titles";
    sda = new SqlDataAdapter(sql, con);
    sda.Fill(ds, "t_count");

    sql = "SELECT COUNT(*) AS cnt FROM publishers";
    sda = new SqlDataAdapter(sql, con);
    sda.Fill(ds, "p_count");

    int numAuthors = (int) ds.Tables["a_count"].Rows[0]["cnt"];
    int numTitles  = (int) ds.Tables["t_count"].Rows[0]["cnt"];
    int numPubs    = (int) ds.Tables["p_count"].Rows[0]["cnt"];

    Console.WriteLine(
      "There are {0} authors, {1} titles and {2} publishers.",
      numAuthors,
      numTitles,
      numPubs
    );
  }
}
```

In this example we connect to the *Pubs* database on the local machine using a trusted connection. If your setup is different, you'll need to change this connection string to run this example.

Next, we create a new `DataSet` object, `PubsDataSet`, to store our query results and we declare a reference to a `SqlDataAdapter` object which we'll use to execute commands against the underlying database and to fill the `DataSet` with results.

We build a string containing a SQL SELECT statement to count the number of records in the *authors* table and return the result as cnt. Then, we build a new `SqlDataAdapter` object passing the SELECT statement and connection string as arguments. We could explicitly create a connection object using the built-in `SQL-Connection` class (see "*Updating the database directly*" in this chapter). However, in this example we use the connection string and leave it to ADO.NET to create the connection under the covers.

Calling the `Fill` method on the `SqlDataAdapter` object makes the connection, executes the query, populates the `DataSet` by storing the results in a local table called a_count, and then disconnects. In this case the a_count table does not yet exist so ADO.NET creates it for us. Subsequent calls to `Fill` can append to, or refresh, this table.

We repeat the count process for the titles and publishers tables. We store the results of all three queries in a single `DataSet` object called ds. The structure of a `DataSet` is simple: it contains a collection of `DataTable` objects, each of which exposes a collection of `DataRow` objects.

Finally, we retrieve and display the record counts from the results `DataSet`. We could also use indexing to retrieve the author count:

```
int numAuthors = (int) ds.Tables[0].Rows[0][0];
```

Or we could create explicit references to the `DataTable` and `DataRow` objects as follows:

```
DataTable dt = ds.Tables["a_count"];
DataRow dr = dt.Rows[0];
int numAuthors = (int) dr["cnt"];
```

We can even access the results as elements in an XML document, as we'll see in the next section.

Figure 4.2 shows the result produced by compiling and running the *pubscount* program.

Figure 4.2   Compiling and running PubsCount

4.3   DATASETS AND XML

As we've seen, a DataSet can be processed as a collection of tables, each containing rows and columns. It can also be processed as an XML document.

4.3.1   The DataSet's GetXml and GetXmlSchema methods

We can display both the XML data and schema for the ds DataSet created in the pubscount program, as follows:

```
Console.WriteLine(ds.GetXml());          // display DataSet as XML
Console.WriteLine(ds.GetXmlSchema()); // display DataSet schema as XML
```

Listing 4.2 shows what the XML schema looks like.

Listing 4.2   DataSet XML schema

```
<xsd:schema id="PubsDataSet"
           targetNamespace=""
           xmlns=""
           xmlns:xsd="http://www.w3.org/2001/XMLSchema"
           xmlns:msdata="urn:schemas-microsoft-com:xml-msdata">

  <xsd:element name="PubsDataSet" msdata:IsDataSet="true">

    <xsd:complexType>
      <xsd:choice maxOccurs="unbounded">

        <xsd:element name="a_count">
          <xsd:complexType>
            <xsd:sequence>
              <xsd:element name="cnt"
                          type="xsd:int"
                          minOccurs="0" />
            </xsd:sequence>
          </xsd:complexType>
        </xsd:element>

        <xsd:element name="t_count">
          <xsd:complexType>
            <xsd:sequence>
              <xsd:element name="cnt"
                          type="xsd:int"
                          minOccurs="0" />
```

```
            </xsd:sequence>
          </xsd:complexType>
        </xsd:element>

        <xsd:element name="p_count">
          <xsd:complexType>
            <xsd:sequence>
              <xsd:element name="cnt"
                            type="xsd:int"
                            minOccurs="0" />
            </xsd:sequence>
          </xsd:complexType>
        </xsd:element>

      </xsd:choice>
    </xsd:complexType>

  </xsd:element>

</xsd:schema>
```

The XML schema, returned by the `GetXmlSchema` method, defines the structure of, and data types used in, the XML document returned by `GetXml`. In this example, it defines a single element, `PubsDataSet`, containing three elements, `a_count`, `t_count`, and `p_count`, each containing a single `cnt` element of type integer. Details of the XML schema namespace used to define these elements can be found on the World Wide Web Consortium's site at http://www.w3.org/2001/XMLSchema.

Listing 4.3 shows the XML produced by the `GetXml` method. It represents the data values in the `DataSet`, structured according to the above schema.

Listing 4.3 DataSet XML data

```
<PubsDataSet>
  <a_count>
    <cnt>23</cnt>
  </a_count>
  <t_count>
    <cnt>18</cnt>
  </t_count>
  <p_count>
    <cnt>8</cnt>
  </p_count>
</PubsDataSet>
```

We can persist (or save) a `DataSet` by saving both its schema and data as XML documents stored as text files, as follows:

```
ds.WriteXmlSchema("pubscount.schema");
ds.WriteXml("pubscount.data");
```

CHAPTER 4   WORKING WITH ADO.NET AND DATABASES

Then we can recreate the `DataSet` and reload its data as follows:

```
DataSet pubsDataSet = new DataSet("PubsDataSet");
pubsDataSet.ReadXmlSchema("pubscount.schema");
pubsDataSet.ReadXml("pubscount.data");
```

It is not strictly necessary to save and reload the schema. If we reload just the data without the schema information ADO.NET will use heuristics to infer the correct data types. However it is better to explicitly specify the schema if the information is available.

It should be clear from this example that we don't even need an underlying DBMS to create, store, and retrieve relational data using ADO.NET.

The tight integration of databases with XML suggests all sorts of interesting application design opportunities. We can stream relational data over the network as XML. We can traverse our database using an XML parser. We can embed a portion of our database directly in a document. We can probably throw away our proprietary report formatting tools and use XML with XSL, a style language for transforming XML, to create attractive reports with little coding effort.

Later in this chapter, we create a program which builds a simple XML document containing the elements of a report on the poker machine's statistics and profitability. The class uses an XSL transformation to convert the XML to HTML so that the report can be viewed online in a Web browser.

4.4   *UPDATING THE DATABASE USING A DATASET*

The underlying database can be updated directly by passing SQL `INSERT`/`UPDATE`/ `DELETE` statements, or stored procedure calls, through to the managed provider. It can also be updated using a `DataSet`. First let's look at updating the database by creating and updating an in-memory `DataSet` and then writing it back to the database. The steps are:

1. Create and fill the `DataSet` with one or more `DataTables`
2. Call `DataRow.BeginEdit` on a `DataRow`
3. Make changes to the row's data
4. Call `DataRow.EndEdit`
5. Call `SqlDataAdapter.Update` to update the underlying database
6. Call `DataSet.AcceptChanges` (or `DataTable.AcceptChanges` or `DataRow.AcceptChanges`)

Step 2 switches off validation constraints for the duration of the edit operation and step 4 turns them on again. This is necessary when making multiple changes to prevent an intermediate, inconsistent state from triggering the validation rules. Calls to `EndEdit` should be enclosed in a `try-catch` block since breaking a constraint raises an exception.

Step 5 updates the table in the underlying database while step 6 is not always necessary, as we'll see next.

4.4.1 Committing changes

Every `DataRow` has a `RowState` property which indicates the state of the `DataRow` in a `DataTable`. The `RowState` property takes its value from the `DataRowState` enumeration shown in Table 4.2.

Table 4.2   The System.Data.DataRowState enumeration

Value	Description
Added	The row has been added since the last call to `AcceptChanges`
Deleted	The row has been deleted from the table since the last call to `AcceptChanges`
Detached	The row is not attached to a `DataTable`
Modified	The row has been modified since the last call to `AcceptChanges`
Unchanged	The row is unchanged since the last call to `AcceptChanges`

Calling `DataTable.AcceptChanges` causes `Deleted` rows to disappear from the table while `Added` and `Modified` rows become `Unchanged`. We can also call `DataRow.AcceptChanges` on a particular `DataRow`. Similarly, calling `DataSet.AcceptChanges` causes `DataTable.AcceptChanges` to be called for every table which, in turn, calls `DataRow.AcceptChanges` for every row. This gives a high degree of granularity when it comes to controlling changes to a `DataSet`. Note that calling `AcceptChanges` on these `DataSet`-related objects is not the same as committing changes to the underlying database, such as when executing SQL's COMMIT TRANSACTION statement. Therefore, if the `DataSet` is to be discarded following the call to `Update`, the call to `AcceptChanges` is unnecessary as it has no effect on the underlying database. The `DataSet` also provides a `RejectChanges` method to roll back `DataSet` changes.

Listing 4.4 presents a program which takes the last name of the first author it finds called "White" in the *authors* table and changes it to "Black." In a production environment, we would wrap it in a `try-catch` block and check for errors before committing the changes to the database.

Listing 4.4   Using a DataSet to update a database

```
// file     : pubsedit.cs
// compile : csc pubsedit.cs

using System;
using System.Data;
using System.Data.SqlClient;

public class PubsEdit {
```

```
public static void Main() {
    // change the following connection string, as necessary...
    string con =
        @"server=(local)\NetSDK;database=pubs;trusted_connection=yes";

    DataSet ds = new DataSet("PubsDataSet");
    DataRow dr;
    SqlDataAdapter sda;
    string sql;

    // get an author...
    sql = "SELECT * FROM authors WHERE au_lname = 'White'";
    sda = new SqlDataAdapter(sql, con);
    sda.Fill(ds, "authors");
    dr = ds.Tables["authors"].Rows[0];

    // create a SqlCommandBuilder to ...
    // automatically generate the update command...
    SqlCommandBuilder scb = new SqlCommandBuilder(sda);

    // edit author row...
    dr.BeginEdit();
    dr["au_lname"] = "Black";
    dr.EndEdit();
    sda.Update(ds, "authors"); // update database
    ds.AcceptChanges(); // accept changes to DataSet
}
}
```

To delete a row, we can use `DataRow.Delete`. If the `RowState` property is `Added`, the row is physically removed, otherwise it is marked for deletion and removed when `AcceptChanges` is called. To insert a row use `DataTable.NewRow`. Remember, we are changing only the in-memory `DataSet` and that we must call `SqlDataAdapter.Update` to have changes reflected in the underlying database when using a managed provider.

There is more to the `DataSet` than we've seen here. The `DataSet` exposes a collection of `DataRelations` which models the column relationships between `DataTables`. It also models other schema information including constraints and it can raise events when certain changes to the `DataSet` occur.

4.5   *UPDATING THE DATABASE DIRECTLY*

To update the database directly, we can use the `SqlCommand` object, which allows us to execute SQL `INSERT`, `UPDATE`, and `DELETE` statements against a database. Listing 4.5 provides an example of a `DELETE` operation.

Listing 4.5 Using SqlCommand to update the database directly

```
// file    : pubsdelete.cs
// compile : csc pubsdelete.cs

using System;
using System.Data;
using System.Data.SqlClient;

public class PubsDelete {
  public static void Main() {
    SqlConnection con = new SqlConnection(
      @"server=(local)\NetSDK;database=pubs;trusted_connection=yes"
    );
    string sql = "DELETE FROM authors WHERE au_lname = 'Green'";
    SqlCommand cmd = new SqlCommand(sql, con);
    con.Open();
    int numRecsAffected = cmd.ExecuteNonQuery();
    con.Close();
    Console.WriteLine("{0} record(s) deleted.", numRecsAffected);
  }
}
```

In this example we create a `SqlConnection` object using the connection string. `SqlCommand.ExecuteNonQuery` executes the DELETE statement and returns the number of records affected (deleted).

We can execute stored procedures in this way too. However, if your stored procedure returns data you'll need to use a `DataSet` to access that data.

4.6 THE DATAREADER

The `DataReader` provides a read-only, forward-only stream of results from a database query or stored procedure. You should use a `DataReader` if it is desirable, and possible, to keep the connection to the database open while data is being processed. Listing 4.6 presents an example which displays the names of the authors in the Pubs database.

Listing 4.6 Using a DataReader

```
// file    : pubsreader.cs
// compile : csc pubsreader.cs

using System;
using System.Data;
using System.Data.SqlClient;

public class PubsReader {
  public static void Main() {
    SqlConnection con = new SqlConnection(
      @"server=(local)\NetSDK;database=pubs;trusted_connection=yes"
    );
    string sql = "SELECT * FROM authors";
```

```
      con.Open();
      SqlDataReader sdr = new SqlCommand(sql, con).ExecuteReader();
      while (sdr.Read()) {
        Console.WriteLine(sdr["au_fname"] + " " + sdr["au_lname"]);
      }
      con.Close();
    }
  }
```

4.7   *THE POKER.BANK CLASS*

Now it is time to use what we've learned about ADO.NET to implement the data
layer of our video poker machine. First, we need to create the application database.
If you have SQL Server installed on your local machine, or you have database creation privileges on a server elsewhere, then you can create a new database with the
script shown in listing 4.7. Otherwise, you'll have to seek the assistance of your local
database administrator.

Listing 4.7   Creating the poker database

```
--    file        :  pokdb.sql
--    description :  .NET Video Poker database creation script
--    execute     :  osql -E -S(local)\NetSDK -ipokdb.sql

-- DROP DATABASE poker

CREATE DATABASE poker
GO
USE poker

CREATE TABLE games (
  id INT IDENTITY(1,1) PRIMARY KEY,
  date_time DATETIME NOT NULL DEFAULT( getdate() ),
  hand CHAR(15) NOT NULL,
  score INT NOT NULL,
  bet INT NOT NULL)

INSERT INTO games(hand, score, bet)
  VALUES ('QC 7C QH KS QS ', 4, 1)

INSERT INTO games(hand, score, bet)
  VALUES ('QC JD 6H 5C KH ', 0, 1)

INSERT INTO games(hand, score, bet)
  VALUES ('KC 2C KD JD 6C ', 2, 1)

CREATE TABLE integers (
  name CHAR(30) PRIMARY KEY,
  value INT NOT NULL)

INSERT INTO integers(name, value) VALUES ('MinBet', 1)
INSERT INTO integers(name, value) VALUES ('MaxBet', 5)
INSERT INTO integers(name, value) VALUES ('StartCredits', 100)
INSERT INTO integers(name, value) VALUES ('TargetMargin', 25)
GO
```

The script starts by creating the poker database and the games table in which we'll store the results of every game played. This data will be used to drive the machine's payout control algorithm. We also insert three records into the table. These represent sample hands along with their scores and bet amounts. We'll use these records to test the data layer later in this chapter. We also create an integers table which we use as a convenient place to store machine configuration parameters, including the maximum and minimum bet amounts, the number of credits with which a player starts, and the target margin for the machine.

Save this script as *pokdb.sql* and use SQL Server's `osql` utility to execute it, as shown in figure 4.3.

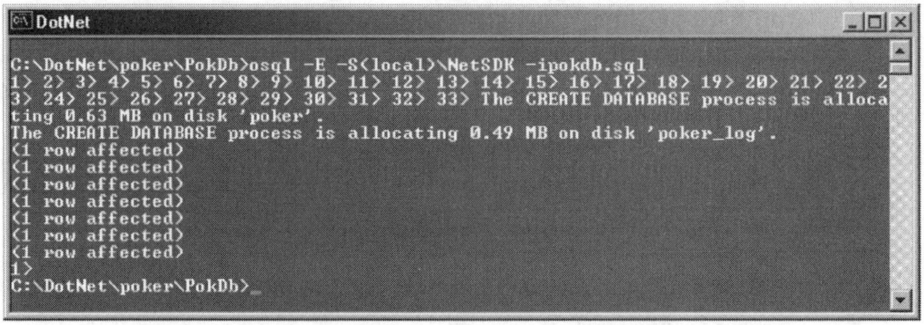

Figure 4.3   Creating the poker database

If all goes well, the database and tables should be created. Try selecting from the games table to check your work, as shown in figure 4.4.

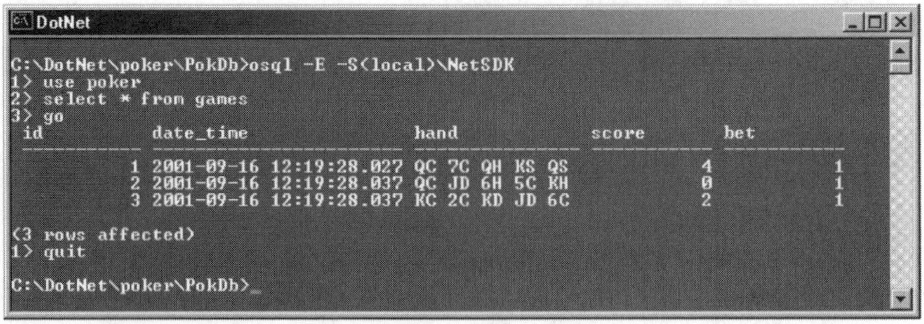

Figure 4.4   Selecting from the games table

The meanings of the columns in the games table are:

- `id`—This is an integer automatically generated by SQL Server to number the records in ascending sequence in the order they are created. We'll use this as a primary key since there are no other suitable candidate columns.
- `date_time`—This field is automatically generated by SQL Server and will contain the date and time the record was created.

- hand—This is a string representation of a poker hand. For example, "TD JD QD KD AD" denotes a royal flush in diamonds.
- score—This is the score assigned to the hand. Strictly speaking, it is not necessary to store the score since it depends on the hand and can be recomputed by the application. (In fact, doing so creates a non-key dependency of score on hand.) However, it is more convenient and efficient to store the score when it is available for free at the time the game is played and the record created. Omitting the score column would make it impossible to use SQL to compute the amount paid out and the profit.
- bet—The amount the player bet on this hand.

With the games table in place, we can use the following SQL statement to retrieve the total amounts taken in and paid out, and the profit for our poker machine:

```
SELECT
    SUM(bet) AS taken_in,
    SUM(score * bet) AS paid_out,
    SUM(bet) - SUM(score * bet) as profit
FROM games
```

4.7.1 Logging errors and warnings

Handling application errors in a sensible way can often be a frustrating task for which there are few firm rules. The poker machine's data layer is a potential source of errors. The database server will sometimes be unavailable, and occasionally the network connection may be broken. Unfortunately, many applications treat all errors as fatal when some are, in fact, recoverable.

For our poker machine, we need to decide on a robust error-handling strategy which will fit with our multi-interface design. We intend to implement multiple, local, and remote user interfaces including console, GUI, and Web versions. So we can't simply pop up error messages on the user's screen whenever there is a problem. Furthermore, we would like the application to be fault-tolerant so that it can recover from an error and continue whenever it makes sense to do so. For example, if SQL Server is unavailable, we'd like to continue playing without database support. There is a thin line between fault-tolerance and fault-concealment, so errors should be handled silently, but logged fully, and the log should be checked regularly. Listing 4.8 illustrates the approach.

> **Listing 4.8 Logging errors**

```
using System;
using System.Diagnostics;
namespace Poker {
  public class MsgLog {
    public MsgLog(string errMsg) {
      DateTime now = DateTime.Now;
      errMsg =  String.Format("{0} : {1}", now, errMsg);
```

```
      EventLog log = new EventLog("Application", ".", "Poker");
      log.WriteEntry(errMsg, EventLogEntryType.Error);
    }
  }
}
```

Now, we can use `MsgLog` to log errors with a one-liner such as:

```
new MsgLog("Oooops!  Something funny happened in method m, class c.");
```

To view the messages, select `Start|Programs|Administrative Tools |Event Viewer` from the Windows task bar, and click the application log in the left pane. (This is the procedure for Windows 2000 machines.) You should see something like the window in figure 4.5.

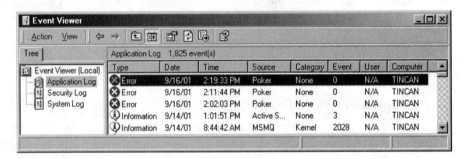

Figure 4.5   Windows event viewer with logged poker messages

In the Source column you'll see the name of the application that logged the message. Our log messages will identify themselves with the name Poker in this column. Double-click a message to view details of the error.

4.7.2   Creating the Poker.Bank class

The `Poker.Bank` class is the heart of the application's data layer. It provides the interface between the various poker applications and the database. The full source code for the `Bank` class is presented in listing 4.9. In the meantime, we'll go through the code in outline here. First, the constructor:

```
public class Bank {

  public Bank() {
    setConnectString();
    TargetMargin = GetParm("TargetMargin", 25);
    refresh();
  }

  ...

}
```

We don't want the application talking directly to the Bank class. When the application needs data, it should ask the Poker.Machine class, which asks the Poker.Bank class, which talks to the database directly. (We'll look at the Poker.Machine class soon.) This creates a nice layer of insulation around the database and allows the application to ignore database connectivity issues, or other errors.

The private setConnectString method looks for the connect string in the application configuration file. If not found, it defaults to a trusted connection to the *poker* database on the local host. We haven't looked at configuration files in sufficient detail yet, so we won't create one. Instead, the default will work for now.

```
private void setConnectString() {
  connectString = ConfigurationSettings.AppSettings["dsn"];
  if (connectString == null) connectString = "";
  if (connectString == "")
    connectString =
    @"server=(local)\NetSDK;database=poker;trusted_connection=yes";
}
```

The public Bank.GetParm method is used to retrieve the target margin from the SQL *integers* table. The target margin is the profit goal for the video poker machine. If the target margin equals 25, then the machine aims to keep 25% of the money taken in.

```
public int GetParm(string parmName, int defaultValue) {

  int parmValue = defaultValue;

  if (connectString == "") return parmValue;

  string sql =
    "SELECT value FROM integers WHERE name='" + parmName + "'";
  DataSet ds = new DataSet("PokerParm");
  SqlDataAdapter sda = new SqlDataAdapter(sql, connectString);

  try {
    sda.Fill(ds, "result");
    parmValue = (int) ds.Tables["result"].Rows[0][0];
  } catch (Exception e) {
    connectString = "";
    new MsgLog(
      String.Format("Bank.GetParm(): {0}", e.Message));
  }
  return parmValue;
}
```

The private refresh method executes the SQL statement, seen earlier, to retrieve the amounts taken in, paid out, and the profit:

```
...

public int TakenIn { get { return takenIn; } }
public int PaidOut { get { return paidOut; } }
```

```
public int Profit  { get { return profit;  } }

...

private void refresh() {
  if (connectString == "") return;
  string sql =
    "SELECT " +
      "SUM(bet) AS taken_in, " +
      "SUM(score * bet) AS paid_out, " +
      "SUM(bet) - SUM(score * bet) as profit " +
    "FROM games";

  SqlDataAdapter sda = null;
  try {
    sda = new SqlDataAdapter(sql, connectString);
    DataSet ds = new DataSet("PokerProfit");
    sda.Fill(ds, "stats");
    DataRow dr = ds.Tables[0].Rows[0];
    takenIn = (int) dr[0];
    paidOut = (int) dr[1];
    profit  = (int) dr[2];
    status = "Machine Stats (All Players)";
  } catch (Exception e) {
    new MsgLog(
      String.Format("Bank.refresh(): {0}", e.Message));
  }
}

...

private int    takenIn = 0;
private int    paidOut = 0;
private int    profit = 0;
```

Next comes the house margin property:

```
public double HouseMargin { get {
  if (takenIn == 0) return TargetMargin;
  return (double) profit * 100.0 / takenIn;
} }
```

This is a simple percentage profit calculation. If the database connection is unavailable, the target margin is returned instead. The effect of this default is an assumption, in the absence of data to the contrary, that the machine is meeting its profit target.

We use a public property called Delta to reflect the difference between the target and actual house margins:

```
public double Delta { get {
  return HouseMargin - TargetMargin;
} }
```

If `Delta` is positive, then the machine is meeting or exceeding its profit goal. The public `Bias` comes next. It drives our payout control algorithm. `Bias` is calculated as follows:

```
public int Bias { get {
   if (Delta >= 0.0) return 0;
   int bias = (int) Math.Round(Math.Abs(Delta));
   if (bias > 10) return 10;
   return bias;
} }
```

The public `SaveGame` method is used to store the result of a game:

```
public void SaveGame(string hand, int score, int bet) {

   if (connectString == "") return;

   SqlConnection conn = null;
   try {
      conn = new SqlConnection(connectString);
   } catch (Exception e) {
      new MsgLog(String.Format( "Bank.SaveGame(): {0} - {1}",
                                "Cannot create SqlConnection",
                                e.Message));

      return;
   }

   string sql =
      "INSERT INTO games(hand, score, bet) VALUES " +
      "('" + hand + "'," + score + "," + bet + ")";
   SqlCommand comm = null;
   try {
      comm = new SqlCommand(sql, conn);
   } catch (Exception e) {
      new MsgLog(String.Format( "Bank.SaveGame(): {0} - {1}",
                                "Cannot create SqlCommand",
                                e.Message));

      return;
   }

   try {
      conn.Open();
   } catch (Exception e) {
      new MsgLog(String.Format( "Bank.SaveGame(): {0} - {1}",
                                "Cannot open SqlConnection",
                                e.Message));

      return;
   }

   try {
      comm.ExecuteNonQuery();
   } catch (Exception e) {
      new MsgLog(String.Format( "Bank.SaveGame(): {0} - {1}",
                                "Cannot execute SqlCommand",
                                e.Message));
```

```
      return;
    }
    finally {
      if (conn.State == ConnectionState.Open) conn.Close();
    }

    refresh();
  }
```

■

Most of the code in the SaveGame method is there to provide meaningful error messages in the event of failure. The method takes a string representation of a poker hand, and integers representing the hand's score and the amount bet, and stores them in a record in the *games* table. Then it calls refresh to reload the statistics.

The complete Bank class is presented in listing 4.9.

Listing 4.9   The Poker.Bank class

```
namespace Poker {

  using System;
  using System.Configuration;
  using System.IO;
  using System.Data;
  using System.Data.SqlClient;

  public class Bank {

    public Bank() {
      setConnectString();
      TargetMargin = GetParm("TargetMargin", 25);
      refresh();
    }

    public readonly int TargetMargin;

    public int TakenIn  { get { return takenIn; } }
    public int PaidOut  { get { return paidOut; } }
    public int Profit   { get { return profit; } }

    public double HouseMargin { get {
      if (takenIn == 0) return TargetMargin;
      return (double) profit * 100.0 / takenIn;
    } }

    public double Delta { get {
      return HouseMargin - TargetMargin;
    } }

    public int Bias { get {
      if (Delta >= 0.0) return 0;
      int bias = (int) Math.Round(Math.Abs(Delta));
      if (bias > 10) return 10;
      return bias;
    } }
```

```csharp
public string Status { get {
  return status;
} }
public string Text { get {
    return "\n" +
    status + "\n" +
    "============================\n" +
    "Taken In        : " + takenIn + "\n" +
    "Paid Out        : " + paidOut + "\n" +
    "Profit          : " + profit + "\n" +
    "House Margin %  : " +
      String.Format("{0:00.00}", HouseMargin) + "\n" +
    "Target Margin % : " +
      String.Format("{0:00.00}", TargetMargin) + "\n" +
    "Delta           : " +
      String.Format("{0:00.00}", Delta) + "\n" +
    "Bias            : " + Bias + "\n";
} }

public override string ToString() {
  return Text;
}

public void SaveGame(string hand, int score, int bet) {

  if (connectString == "") return;

  SqlConnection conn = null;
  try {
    conn = new SqlConnection(connectString);
  } catch (Exception e) {
    new MsgLog(String.Format( "Bank.SaveGame(): {0} - {1}",
                              "Cannot create SqlConnection",
                              e.Message));

    return;
  }

  string sql =
    "INSERT INTO games(hand, score, bet) VALUES " +
    "('" + hand + "'," + score + "," + bet + ")";
  SqlCommand comm = null;
  try {
    comm = new SqlCommand(sql, conn);
  } catch (Exception e) {
    new MsgLog(String.Format( "Bank.SaveGame(): {0} - {1}",
                              "Cannot create SqlCommand",
                              e.Message));

    return;
  }

  try {
    conn.Open();
  } catch (Exception e) {
```

```
        new MsgLog(String.Format( "Bank.SaveGame(): {0} - {1}",
                                   "Cannot open SqlConnection",
                                   e.Message));
      return;
    }

    try {
      comm.ExecuteNonQuery();
    } catch (Exception e) {
      new MsgLog(String.Format( "Bank.SaveGame(): {0} - {1}",
                                   "Cannot execute SqlCommand",
                                   e.Message));
      return;
    }
    finally {
      if (conn.State == ConnectionState.Open) conn.Close();
    }

    refresh();
  }

  public int GetParm(string parmName, int defaultValue) {

    int parmValue = defaultValue;

    if (connectString == "") return parmValue;

    string sql =
      "SELECT value FROM integers WHERE name='" + parmName + "'";
    DataSet ds = new DataSet("PokerParm");
    SqlDataAdapter sda = new SqlDataAdapter(sql, connectString);

    try {
      sda.Fill(ds, "result");
      parmValue = (int) ds.Tables["result"].Rows[0][0];
    } catch (Exception e) {
      connectString = "";
      new MsgLog(
        String.Format("Bank.GetParm(): {0}", e.Message));
    }
    return parmValue;
  }

  private void setConnectString() {
    connectString = ConfigurationSettings.AppSettings["dsn"];
    if (connectString == null) connectString = "";
    if (connectString == "")
      connectString =
        @"server=(local)\NetSDK;" +
        @"database=poker;trusted_connection=yes";
  }

  private void refresh() {

    if (connectString == "") return;
```

```
                string sql =
                    "SELECT " +
                        "SUM(bet) AS taken_in, " +
                        "SUM(score * bet) AS paid_out, " +
                        "SUM(bet) - SUM(score * bet) as profit " +
                    "FROM games";

                SqlDataAdapter sda = null;
                try {
                    sda = new SqlDataAdapter(sql, connectString);
                    DataSet ds = new DataSet("PokerProfit");
                    sda.Fill(ds, "stats");
                    DataRow dr = ds.Tables[0].Rows[0];
                    takenIn = (int) dr[0];
                    paidOut = (int) dr[1];
                    profit  = (int) dr[2];
                    status = "Machine Stats (All Players)";
                } catch (Exception e) {
                    new MsgLog(
                        String.Format("Bank.refresh(): {0}", e.Message));
                }
            }

            // private static Bank bank = null;
            private string connectString = "";
            private string status = "Machine Stats Unavailable";
            private int    takenIn = 0;
            private int    paidOut = 0;
            private int    profit = 0;
        }
    }
```

4.7.3   Testing the Bank class

Let's test the Bank class by temporarily inserting the following Main into it:

```
public static void Main() {
    Bank b = new Bank();
    Console.WriteLine("TargetMargin: {0}", b.TargetMargin);
    b.SaveGame("5C 2D TH JD QD", 0, 5);
    Console.WriteLine(b);
}
```

Then compile the Bank class, together with the MsgLog class, and execute it, as shown in figure 4.6.

As you can see, I've already played (more than) a few hands. The actual profit is 42 and the house margin is 24.28%. This is less than the 25% target, and so bias is equal to one.

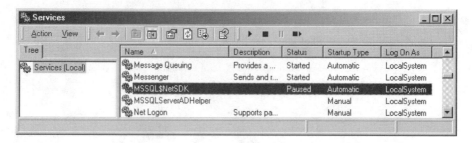

Figure 4.6 Displaying Bank data

Launch the Windows Services Manager and pause SQL Server. See figure 4.7.

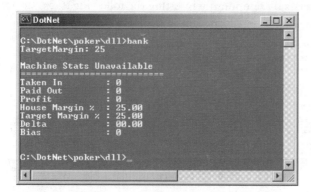

Figure 4.7 Pausing SQL Server

Then execute the program once again, as shown in figure 4.8.

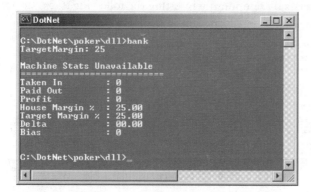

**Figure 4.8
Displaying Bank data when SQL
Server is paused**

Note that the program executes without error and we get the default property values. See figure 4.9 for the logged message.

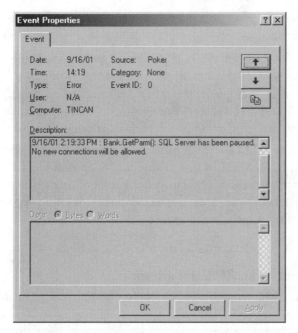

Figure 4.9
The Bank error message

Don't forget to start SQL Server again when you're done. Also, if you're editing the code as we go, you can delete the `Bank.Main` method which we inserted for testing purposes.

4.8 USING XML SERIALIZATION TO CREATE A REPORT

Before we leave the data layer, let's take the opportunity to use the functionality of the `Poker.Bank` class to create a reporting utility class, called `XmlRep`. We design it so that it generates the report in XML format. This gives us the flexibility to convert the report to HTML for display in a Web browser, or to send the XML to other applications for further processing.

We want the XML to look like the following:

```
<XmlRep>
    <TakenIn>303</TakenIn>
    <PaidOut>161</PaidOut>
    <Profit>142</Profit>
    <Bias>0</Bias>
    <HouseMargin>46.86</HouseMargin>
    <Delta>21.86</Delta>
</XmlRep>
```

This gives us the essential data necessary to evaluate the poker machine's performance. Because the report is in XML format, we can take advantage of the Framework to easily generate the report and to format it for display. We'll combine two important techniques to generate the report:

- *XML Serialization*—XML serialization provides a way of serializing (storing) a class instance into an XML document, and deserializing (loading) it back again. We've already seen an example of this when we serialized a `DataSet` to disk using its `GetXml` and `GetXmlSchema` methods. XML serialization goes further by supporting the serialization of any built-in or programmer-defined class.

- *XSL Transformation (XSLT)*—XSLT provides a standards-based way to transform the content of an XML document into a new document with a different structure. The transformation is specified using a set of rules. In our case, we'll use XSLT to transform the XML-formatted poker machine report into an HTML document for display in the browser.

We look at each of these two techniques in the following sections.

4.8.1   Serializing an object to an XML document

To prepare a class for XML serialization, you need to annotate its members with attributes from the `System.Xml.Serialization` namespace to identify them to the serializer. Listing 4.10 presents a simple `Person` class which serializes itself to a file called *person.xml*.

Listing 4.10   Serializing a simple class

```
// file    : person.cs
// compile : csc person.cs

using System;
using System.IO;
using System.Xml.Serialization;

[XmlRootAttribute]
public class Person {

  [XmlElementAttribute]
  public string FirstName;

  [XmlElementAttribute]
  public string LastName;

  public static void Main() {

    Console.WriteLine("generating person.xml");

    // create a new Person...
    Person p = new Person();
    p.FirstName = "Joe";
    p.LastName = "Bloggs";

    // serialize to disk...
    XmlSerializer sr = new XmlSerializer(typeof(Person));
    TextWriter tw = new StreamWriter("person.xml");
```

```
        sr.Serialize(tw, p);
        tw.Close();
    }
}
```

Annotating the `Person` class with `XmlRootAttribute` specifies that `<Person>` will be the root tag of the generated XML file. Using the `XmlElementAttribute` on members causes them to occur as elements in the XML file. The `Main` routine creates an instance of `Person` and then creates an `XmlSerializer` passing the type to be serialized as an argument. Next, it creates a `TextWriter` to write the instance to the file. If you open the generated XML file in Internet Explorer, you should see a page similar to the one shown in figure 4.10.

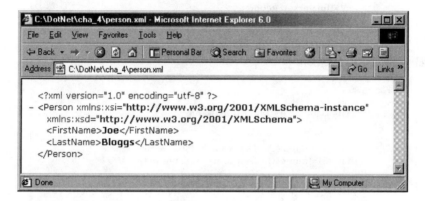

Figure 4.10 The serialized Person object

4.8.2   Performing an XSL transformation

Now that we've generated the *person.xml* file, let's transform it to HTML for display. First, we specify the XSLT rules and place them in the file *person.xsl*, shown in figure 4.11.

Unfortunately, XSLT is a complex and often confusing topic worthy of a book in its own right. However, the .NET SDK comes with several examples which you can study. In the meantime, we'll just note that this file has just two rules of the form:

```
<xsl:template match=" ... ">
```

The first rule matches the root document element, `Person`. When it matches, it generates a new HTML document with a suitable heading. It then calls `<xsl:apply-templates/>` to recursively apply the remaining rules. It wraps the result in a table and finishes by ending the HTML document. In this case, there is only one other rule. It matches either the `<FirstName>` or `<LastName>` tags and inserts their values into table cells.

Figure 4.11   The XSLT rules for transforming Person.Xml

To programmatically generate the transformation, we need a simple program which loads the XML file, transforms it using the XSLT rules, and writes the result to an HTML file. This program, *personrep.cs*, is shown in listing 4.11.

Listing 4.11   The XML to HTML transformation program

```
// file    : personrep.cs
// compile : csc personrep.cs

using System;
using System.IO;
using System.Xml;
using System.Xml.Xsl;
using System.Xml.XPath;
```

```
public class PersonRep {

  public static void Main() {

    Console.WriteLine("generating person.html");

    // load the XML document...
    XPathDocument xd =
      new XPathDocument(new XmlTextReader("Person.xml"));

    // create HTML output file...
    TextWriter tw = new StreamWriter("Person.html");

    // load the XSLT rules...
    XslTransform xt = new XslTransform();
    xt.Load("person.xsl");

    // perform the transformation...
    xt.Transform(xd, null, tw);
    tw.Close();
  }
}
```

We use `System.Xml.XPath.XPathDocument` to load the XML document. The
`XPathDocument` is designed for fast XML processing by XSLT. The transformation
is achieved by creating an `XslTransform` object and loading the XSLT rules into it.
Then we call its `Transform` method to write the HTML file, passing a suitable
`TextWriter` as the third argument. If you view the generated HTML source, you
should see something similar to figure 4.12.

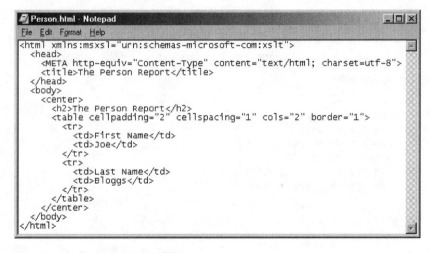

Figure 4.12   The generated HTML source

The report itself is shown in figure 4.13.

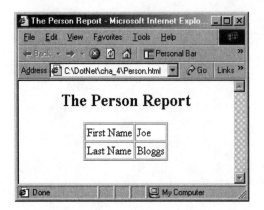

Figure 4.13
Viewing the person report

Although the result is not very exciting in this case, the combination of XML serialization and XSL transformation gives us a powerful way to automatically persist and transform application objects.

4.8.3   The XmlRep program

Now that we've explored XML serialization and XSL transformation, we have the skills to create a simple reporting application to display poker machine statistics in the browser. A good way to start would be to annotate certain members of the `Bank` class with XML serialization attributes. In the interest of clarity and simplicity, we won't do that here. Instead, we create a new `XmlRep` class as a wrapper around the Bank data, and serialize it. Then we transform it to HTML and launch the browser to view it. The complete program is shown in listing 4.12.

Listing 4.12   The XmlRep report program

```
// file        : xmlrep.cs
// description  : generate XML/HTML report for poker machine

namespace Poker {

  using System;
  using System.IO;
  using System.Xml;
  using System.Xml.Xsl;
  using System.Xml.XPath;
  using System.Xml.Serialization;
  using System.Diagnostics;

  [XmlRootAttribute]
  public class XmlRep {

    public XmlRep() {
      Bank b = new Bank();
      this.TakenIn = b.TakenIn;
      this.PaidOut = b.PaidOut;
      this.Profit = b.Profit;
      this.HouseMargin = Math.Round(b.HouseMargin, 2);
```

```csharp
      this.Delta = Math.Round(b.Delta, 2);
      this.Bias = b.Bias;
   }

   [XmlElementAttribute]
   public int TakenIn;

   [XmlElementAttribute]
   public int PaidOut;

   [XmlElementAttribute]
   public int Profit;

   [XmlElementAttribute]
   public int Bias;

   [XmlElementAttribute]
   public Double HouseMargin;

   [XmlElementAttribute]
   public Double Delta;

   public static void Main() {

      Console.WriteLine("Serializing data to report.xml...");
      XmlSerializer sr = new XmlSerializer(typeof(XmlRep));
      TextWriter tw = new StreamWriter("report.xml");
      sr.Serialize(tw, new XmlRep());
      tw.Close();

      Console.WriteLine("Creating report.html...");
      XPathDocument xd =
        new XPathDocument(new XmlTextReader("Report.xml"));
      tw = new StreamWriter("Report.html");
      XslTransform xt = new XslTransform();
      xt.Load("pokrep.xsl");
      xt.Transform(xd, null, tw);
      tw.Close();

      Console.WriteLine("Launching report in browser...");
      ProcessStartInfo si = new ProcessStartInfo();
      si.FileName = "Report.html";
      si.Verb = "open";
      Process pr = new Process();
      pr.StartInfo = si;
      pr.Start();

      Console.WriteLine("Done!");
   }
 }
}
```

The only thing that's new here is the code to launch the browser. To do that, we create an instance of `ProcessStartInfo` and set its public `FileName` property to `"Report.html"`. Then, we create a new process using this start-up information. This will launch whatever application is associated with *.html* files.

The XSLT rules used to transform the poker report are shown in figure 4.14.

Figure 4.14   The poker report XSL stylesheet

Finally, the generated report is shown in figure 4.15.

Figure 4.15
Browsing the poker machine report

NOTE This book was created as an XML document using a handful of custom tags. A simple C# program was used to apply XSLT rules to transform the manuscript into HTML for online review. Later, a further XSL transformation was used to prepare it for input to FrameMaker.

4.9 THE POKER.MACHINE CLASS

In the previous chapter, we created a `SimpleMachine` class to encapsulate the functionality of the basic poker machine. This time, we create `Poker.Machine` to bring together the full functionality of the client/server poker game. `Poker.Machine` deals and draws cards, implements payout control, saves games to the database, and provides play statistics. The full source code for the `Machine` class is presented in listing 4.13. In the meantime, we'll go through the code in outline here.

We implement `Machine` as a *singleton* class. This ensures that only a single instance of the class can be created and provides a convenient way to store program-wide global variables without passing arguments around:

```
public class Machine {

  public readonly int MinBet;
  public readonly int MaxBet;
  public readonly int StartCredits;
  public readonly int Bias;

  // private constructor...
  private Machine() {
    bank = new Bank();
    MinBet = bank.GetParm("MinBet", 1);
    MaxBet = bank.GetParm("MaxBet", 5);
```

```
    StartCredits = bank.GetParm("StartCredits", 100);
    Bias = bank.Bias;
}

public static Machine Instance {
  get {
    // allow just one instance...
    if (machine == null) machine = new Machine();
    return machine;
  }
}

...

private static Machine machine = null;
private Bank bank = null;

    ...
}
```

To enforce singleton mode, we make the constructor private and provide access to a
single instance of the poker machine through the static Instance property. As a
result, a caller will never need to explicitly create an instance of the
Poker.Machine class, allowing for the following type of application code:

```
int minBet = Machine.Instance.MinBet;
int maxBet = Machine.Instance.MaxBet;
int credits = Machine.Instance.StartCredits;
```

Payout control is implemented in the public Deal and Draw methods:

```
  ...

public Hand Deal() {
  Hand hand = new Hand();
  int bias = Bias;
  while (hand.Score > 0 && bias-- > 0)
    hand = new Hand();
  return hand;
}

public Hand Draw(Hand oldHand, string holdCards, int bet) {
  int bias = Bias;
  Hand newHand = new Hand(oldHand, holdCards);
  while (newHand.Score > 0 && bias-- > 0)
    newHand = new Hand(oldHand, holdCards);
  bank.SaveGame(newHand.ToString(), newHand.Score, bet);
  return newHand;
}

  ...
```

The payout management algorithm is simple. If bias is non-zero, the Deal method
will silently discard one or more scoring hands before finally dealing a hand. For
example, if bias is 3, the machine will make three attempts to deal a nonscoring

hand. If, on the third attempt, the new hand is a scoring hand, the machine will deal it anyway. The draw hand implements the same algorithm. When cards are drawn, the game is complete and is saved to the database.

The complete `Poker.Machine` class is presented in listing 4.13.

Listing 4.13   The Poker.Machine class

```
namespace Poker {

  using System;

  public class Machine {

    public readonly int MinBet;
    public readonly int MaxBet;
    public readonly int StartCredits;
    public readonly int Bias;

    // private constructor...
    private Machine() {
      bank = new Bank();
      MinBet = bank.GetParm("MinBet", 1);
      MaxBet = bank.GetParm("MaxBet", 5);
      StartCredits = bank.GetParm("StartCredits", 100);
      Bias = bank.Bias;
    }

    public static Machine Instance {
      get {
        // allow just one instance...
        if (machine == null) machine = new Machine();
        return machine;
      }
    }

    public Hand Deal() {
      Hand hand = new Hand();
      int bias = Bias;
      while (hand.Score > 0 && bias-- > 0)
        hand = new Hand();
      return hand;
    }

    public Hand Draw(Hand oldHand, string holdCards, int bet) {
      int bias = Bias;
      Hand newHand = new Hand(oldHand, holdCards);
      while (newHand.Score > 0 && bias-- > 0)
        newHand = new Hand(oldHand, holdCards);
      bank.SaveGame(newHand.ToString(), newHand.Score, bet);
      return newHand;
    }

    public Hand Draw(string handString, string holdCards, int bet) {
      return Draw(new Hand(handString), holdCards, bet);
    }
```

```
    public string Stats { get {
      return bank.Text;
    } }

    public static string PayoutTable { get {
        return "\n" +
        "Payout Table\n" +
        "============\n" +
        "Royal Flush    : 10\n" +
        "Straight Flush :  9\n" +
        "Four of a Kind :  8\n" +
        "Full House     :  7\n" +
        "Flush          :  6\n" +
        "Straight       :  5\n" +
        "Three of a Kind :  4\n" +
        "Two Pair       :  3\n" +
        "Jacks or Better :  2\n";
    } }

    private static Machine machine = null;
    private Bank bank = null;
  }
}
```

4.10   THE POKER.BET CLASS

We're almost ready to build the final version of the Poker DLL, which serves as the engine at the heart of the different poker applications in the remainder of the book. Before we do this, we create a simple helper class called Bet, which provides a convenient way to check the validity of placed bets and is shown in listing 4.14.

```
using System;
namespace Poker {
  public class Bet {
    public Bet(int bet, int credits, int minBet, int maxBet) {
      if (credits < minBet) {
        Message =
          "You don't have enough credits to bet...  Game over!";
        Amount = 0;
        return;
      }
      if (bet < minBet) {
        Message = String.Format(
          "You must bet the minimum... betting {0}.", minBet);
        Amount = minBet;
        Credits = credits - Amount;
        return;
      }
      maxBet = credits < maxBet ? credits : maxBet;
```

```
      if (bet > maxBet) {
        Message = String.Format(
          "You can only bet {0}... betting {0}.", maxBet);
        Amount = maxBet;
        Credits = credits - Amount;
        return;
      }
      Message = "";
      Amount = bet;
      Credits = credits - Amount;
    }
    public readonly int Amount;
    public readonly int Credits;
    public readonly string Message;
  }
}
```

The Bet class simply checks that the placed bet is no less than the minimum, or greater than the maximum allowable bet, and that the player has sufficient credits to cover it.

4.11   BUILDING THE POKER DLL

Now we can build the final version of the Poker DLL. To recap, the classes involved are:

- Bank
- Bet
- Card
- Hand
- Machine
- MsgLog
- SimpleMachine

Compile these classes, as shown in figure 4.16.

Figure 4.16   Compiling the poker DLL

4.12 ConPok: 3-tier Client/Server Poker

Now we can pull all the pieces together with a console poker game with full database support, statistics, and payout control. Listing 4.15 presents ConPok, the client/server console poker game.

Listing 4.15   ConPok: client/server console video poker

```csharp
// file     : ConPok.cs
// compile : csc /r:poker.dll conpok.cs

using System;
using System.Collections;
using System.Text;

using Poker;

class ConPok {

  public ConPok() {

    greeting();

    machine = Machine.Instance;
    uiBet = minBet = machine.MinBet;
    maxBet = machine.MaxBet;
    uiCredits = machine.StartCredits;

    // play until our opponent is wiped out!
    while (uiCredits >= minBet)
      nextGame();
    Console.WriteLine("*** Loser! ***   :-)");
  }

  private void greeting() {
    Console.WriteLine(
      "\nWelcome to the Console Version of Video Poker.");
    Console.WriteLine(
      "Cards are numbered 1 to 5 from left to right.");
    Console.WriteLine(
      "To hold cards, enter card numbers and hit enter.");
    Console.WriteLine(
      "Hit Ctrl-c at any time to abort.\n");
  }

  private void nextGame() {

    Console.WriteLine("Credits Remaining : {0}", uiCredits);
    Console.Write("Enter amount of bet : ");

    string reply = Console.ReadLine();
    int newBet;
    try {
      newBet = Int32.Parse(reply);
    }
    catch (Exception) {
```

```
      // use previous bet...
      newBet = uiBet;
    }

    Bet bet = new Bet(newBet, uiCredits, minBet, maxBet);
    uiBet = bet.Amount;
    uiCredits = bet.Credits;
    if (bet.Message.Equals(""))
      Console.WriteLine("Betting {0}...", uiBet);
    else
      Console.WriteLine(bet.Message + '\u0007'); // ring bell

    Hand dealHand = machine.Deal(); // deal
    Console.WriteLine("{0}", dealHand);

    Console.Write("Enter card numbers (1 to 5) to hold: ");
    string holdCards = Console.ReadLine();

    Hand drawHand =
      machine.Draw(dealHand.ToString(), holdCards, uiBet);

    int uiWin = drawHand.Score * uiBet;
    uiCredits += uiWin;
    string uiMsg =
      drawHand.ToString() + " - " + drawHand.Title + " " +
      "(Score=" + drawHand.Score + ", " +
      "Bet=" + uiBet + ", " + "Win=" + uiWin + ")";

    Console.WriteLine(uiMsg);

    Console.WriteLine(machine.Stats);
  }
  private Machine machine;
  private int minBet;
  private int maxBet;
  private int uiCredits;
  private int uiBet;
} // end Class ConPok

// action starts here...
public class Go {
  public static void Main() {
    ConPok cp = new ConPok();
  }
}
```

A makefile is provided in appendix B, which will build the console, and other versions, of the poker machine. Alternatively, to build ConPok alone, issue the following compiler command:

```
csc /r:poker.dll conpok.cs
```

Figure 4.17 shows `ConPok` in play.

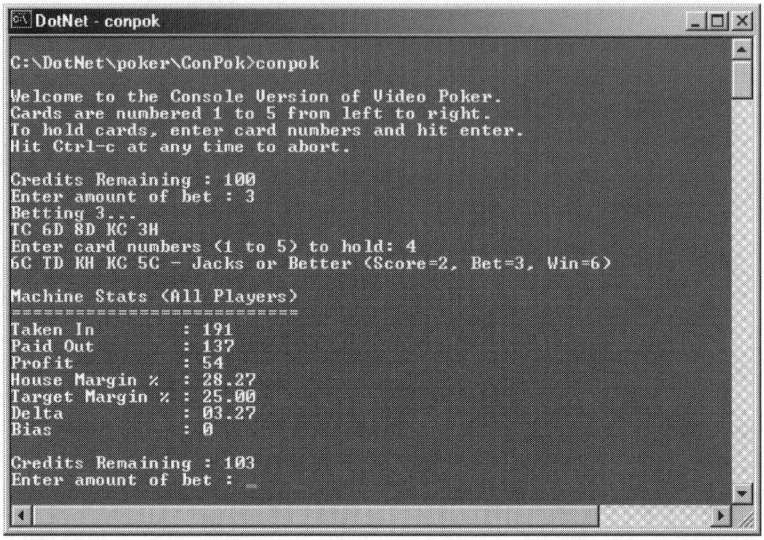

```
DotNet - conpok                                        _ |□| X|

C:\DotNet\poker\ConPok>conpok

Welcome to the Console Version of Video Poker.
Cards are numbered 1 to 5 from left to right.
To hold cards, enter card numbers and hit enter.
Hit Ctrl-c at any time to abort.

Credits Remaining : 100
Enter amount of bet : 3
Betting 3...
TC 6D 8D KC 3H
Enter card numbers (1 to 5) to hold: 4
6C TD KH KC 5C - Jacks or Better (Score=2, Bet=3, Win=6)

Machine Stats (All Players)
===========================
Taken In        : 191
Paid Out        : 137
Profit          : 54
House Margin %  : 28.27
Target Margin % : 25.00
Delta           : 03.27
Bias            : 0

Credits Remaining : 103
Enter amount of bet : _
```

Figure 4.17   Playing ConPok

4.13   SUMMARY

In this chapter, we coded and tested the data layer for the poker machine. In doing so, we examined the `DataSet` which is the centerpiece of ADO.NET. We learned how to use a `DataSet` to retrieve and process data from the database and how to persist both schema and data as XML documents. We saw how ADO.NET can operate without a managed provider. We also learned how to perform updates on an underlying database using the `DataSet` object and how to directly execute SQL `UPDATE/INSERT/DELETE` statements using the `SqlCommand` object.

We coded the data layer for our case study. In doing so we employed a fault-tolerant error handling strategy that records errors while ensuring that the poker machine remains playable even if SQL Server goes down.

We used XML and XSLT to create a flexible reporting mechanism so that reports can be read by users, or consumed in XML form by other applications. We finished by building a complete client-server console version of our case study application.

In the next chapter we explore .NET's remoting services, which provide us with the infrastructure to build distributed .NET applications. We build a remote version of the poker application and we also lay the necessary groundwork for our discussion of XML Web services in chapter 6.

CHAPTER 5

Developing remote services

In this chapter, we examine .NET's remoting infrastructure which supports the activation and use of remote objects across the network. The .NET remoting architecture offers a simple programming model which helps to make remote object invocation and use transparent to the client application. Developers can take advantage of this model to create distributed applications, or to expose application objects to remote clients.

.NET remoting can use TCP and HTTP channels to communicate between remote endpoints, and the channel services are pluggable so that alternative custom channels can be implemented. We'll explore both TCP and HTTP options. As usual, to illustrate the discussion, we'll use .NET's remoting services to implement a remote poker machine service. We'll create several versions of this service including one which operates as a Windows service (formerly known as an NT service).

Also, although not strictly part of .NET's remoting services, Microsoft Message Queuing (MSMQ) offers an alternative approach to developing distributed services. Therefore, as a bonus, this chapter includes an MSMQ-based version of our poker service.

5.1 INTRODUCTION TO REMOTING

The .NET remoting infrastructure allows developers to create applications which invoke methods across the network as though they were local to the application. This is made possible by the use of a proxy which acts as the local representative of the remote object. The proxy automatically forwards all remote method calls to the corresponding remote object and the results are returned to the calling client. To the client, this appears no different than invoking a method on a local object.

5.1.1 Remoting and application domains

Traditional Win32 applications were isolated from each other at run time by running each application in a separate process. Process boundaries ensured that memory and resources in one application were inaccessible to other applications, and that faults were isolated to the application in which they occurred. .NET avoids some of the overhead inherent in process switching by introducing a more lightweight unit of processing known as an application domain. Executing a .NET application causes the CLR to create an application domain into which it loads the application's assemblies and types. The Win32 process has not gone away. Instead a Win32 process can contain one or more managed application domains.

Under .NET, a remote object is an object which resides in a different application domain than the caller. A remote object need not necessarily reside on a remote machine, or even in a different process. .NET remoting simply allows objects to interact across application domains.

5.1.2 Marshaling objects

To make an object accessible outside its own application domain, the remoting infrastructure must provide a mechanism to transport objects, or object references, between domains. It does this using a technique known as marshaling which comes in two alternative forms:

- *Marshal by value*—Causes remoting services to make a copy of the object, serialize it, and transport it to the destination domain where it is reconstructed. This is the default for types passed as arguments to a remote method, and for types returned by that method. Objects which are passed by value must be serializable. For programmer-defined types, this may require implementing the `ISerializable` interface or marking the object with the `Serializable` attribute.

- *Marshal by reference*—Causes remoting services to create a reference to the remote object. This reference is returned to the calling domain to produce a proxy object. The proxy acts as a local representative of the remote object and transparently takes care of forwarding calls to, and receiving results from, the remote object. To facilitate this process, all remote objects must derive from `System.MarshalByRefObject`.

5.1.3 Hosting remote objects

A remote object must be hosted in a server application and the object is available only as long as the server is running. This server can be a minimal .NET managed executable which might do nothing more than register the object with .NET's remoting infrastructure. Remote objects can also be hosted in COM+ services, or in IIS. We'll look at an example of an IIS-hosted remote service later in this chapter.

It is the hosting server's job to make remote objects available on the network by registering them with the remoting infrastructure. To do so, it must uniquely identify each object using a URI (Uniform Resource Identifier, the generic term for URLs and URNs). The URI identifies each object by a unique name, scheme (i.e., channel), and endpoint (remote machine name/port). This information is used by clients to locate the remote object and invoke its services. Figure 5.1 depicts a remote service called `RemService`.

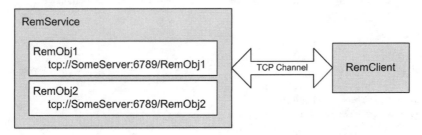

Figure 5.1 A remote service

This remote service resides on the *SomeServer* machine and listens on a TCP channel on port number *6789*. It hosts two remote objects, `RemObj1` and `RemObj2`. `RemObj1` is uniquely identified on the network by its URI, tcp://SomeServer:6789/-RemObj1. `RemObj2` is similarly identified.

5.1.4 Creating a remote service

Let's illustrate the discussion so far with a simple example. Listing 5.1 presents a remote service called *HelloService* which exposes an object called `HelloObj`. The program includes the code for both the server and the remote object which it hosts. The server could reside in a separate executable assembly but, for this example, we place both server and remote object together in a single assembly.

We have a lot of ground to cover as we explore the different features of the remoting infrastructure. We'll be creating several versions of HelloService, and several clients to test them. To keep the discussion short and manageable, our sample services will do little more than return a greeting to connecting clients.

Listing 5.1   Hello service hosting singleton HelloObj

```
// file:      helloservicest.cs
// compile:   csc helloservicest.cs

// Exposes HelloObj in Singleton mode over TCP

using System;
using System.Runtime.Remoting;
using System.Runtime.Remoting.Channels;
using System.Runtime.Remoting.Channels.Tcp;

// the remote HelloObj object...
public class HelloObj : MarshalByRefObject {

  public HelloObj() {
    Console.WriteLine("HelloObj activated...");
  }

  public string Greet(string name) {
    // lock out other clients while incrementing numGreet...
    lock(this) { numGreet++; }
    // greet...
    string greeting = "Hello, " + name + "!";
    Console.WriteLine("greeting #{0}: " + greeting, numGreet);
    return greeting;
  }

  private int numGreet = 0;
}

// the hosting service, HelloService...
public class HelloService {
  public static void Main(string[] args) {

    // register a channel...
    ChannelServices.RegisterChannel(new TcpChannel(6789));

    // register HelloObj with remoting services...
    Console.WriteLine("registering HelloObj as Singleton...");

    RemotingConfiguration.RegisterWellKnownServiceType(
      Type.GetType("HelloObj"),          // remote object type
      "HelloObj",                        // remote object name
      WellKnownObjectMode.Singleton);    // activation mode

    Console.WriteLine("waiting for remote calls...");
    Console.WriteLine("hit ENTER to exit...");
    Console.ReadLine();
  }
}
```

In listing 5.1, HelloObj provides a single public Greet method which displays a greeting on the server console and also returns the greeting to the client. It keeps count of the number of times Greet was invoked in the private integer field numGreet. To support marshaling by reference, we derive `HelloObj` from the `MarshalByRefObject` class.

The server is implemented in the `HelloService.Main` routine and simply registers the `HelloObj` object. The call to `ChannelServices.RegisterChannel` in `Main` registers a new TCP channel. Then we call `RemotingConfiguration.RegisterWellKnownServiceType` to register `HelloObj` with remoting services. The arguments include the type of the remote object, its name, and the mode in which the remote object should be activated. In this case, we specify that the object should be activated in `Singleton` mode which means that a single object is activated on the server and shared by multiple clients. We'll look more closely at this, and explore alternative activation modes, in more detail in the next section. Registration makes the object visible to clients. For example, a client on the same local machine will be able to connect to the object at tcp://localhost:6789/HelloObj.

Note that if you press ENTER to halt the server, the remote object will no longer be available to clients.

5.1.5   Creating the client

Listing 5.2 presents a client program which activates the remote object.

Listing 5.2   The HelloObj client

```
// file:     helloclient.cs
// compile:  csc /r:helloservicest.exe helloclient.cs

using System;
using System.Runtime.Remoting;
using System.Runtime.Remoting.Channels;
using System.Runtime.Remoting.Channels.Tcp;

class HelloClient {

  public static void Main(string[] args) {

    ChannelServices.RegisterChannel(new TcpChannel());

    HelloObj helloObjRef = (HelloObj)Activator.GetObject(
      typeof(HelloObj),
      "tcp://localhost:6789/HelloObj"
    );

    Console.WriteLine(helloObjRef.Greet("Joe Bloggs"));
    Console.WriteLine(helloObjRef.Greet("Mary Bloggs"));
  }
}
```

The client registers a new TCP channel and calls `Activator.GetObject`, passing the remote object type and its URI, to retrieve a reference to the remote object. Then it calls the `Greet` method and exits.

5.1.6 Testing the service

To test our work, first open a command window and compile and launch the server, as shown in figure 5.2.

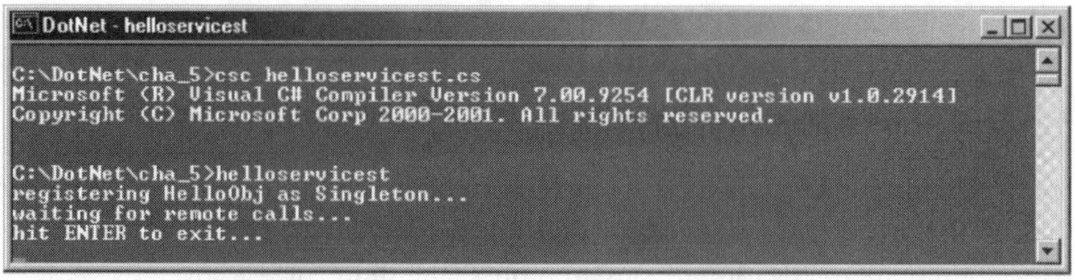

Figure 5.2 Running the HelloServiceSt service

Next, open a second command window, compile the client and execute it a number of times, as seen in figure 5.3.

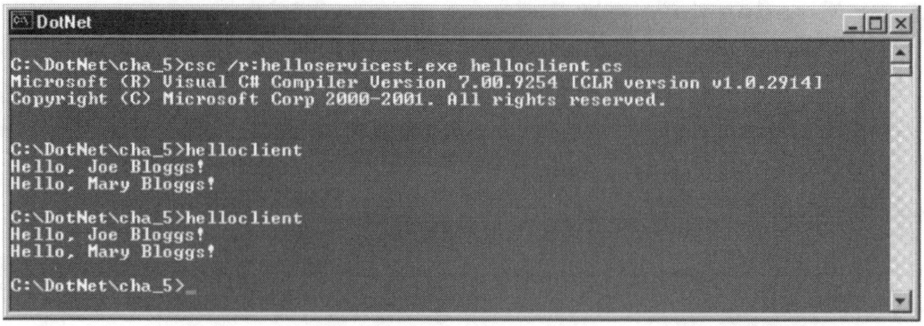

Figure 5.3 Running the HelloClient client

The /r:helloservicest.exe compiler option references the service assembly where the HelloObj type resides. This means that the remote server assembly must be available to the client at compile time. This won't always be possible. We'll look at alternative solutions to this problem later in the chapter.

Note the greetings returned from the remote object each time we invoked the client. Now return to the first command window and view the output from the server shown in figure 5.4.

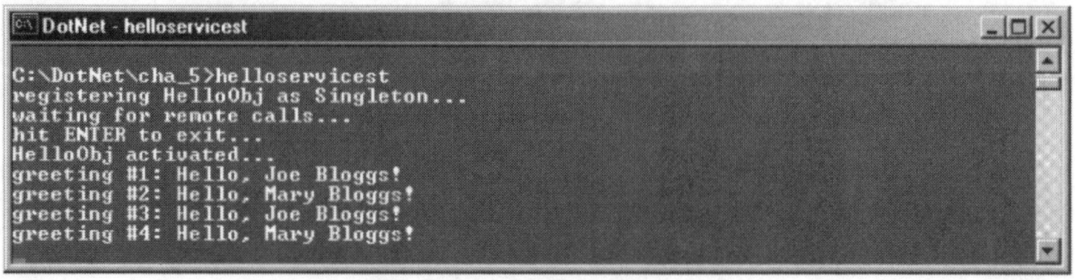

Figure 5.4 The output from the HelloServiceSt service

There are two important things to note here. First, we see that `HelloObj` was activated (i.e., its constructor executed) just once when the server was initially launched, and not when the client called `Activator.GetObject`. In this case, `HelloObj` is implemented as a server-activated object. We'll look more closely at server-activated objects in the following section.

Second, we can see that the greeting number has been incremented each time we executed the client program and called the `Greet` method. Obviously the remote object's state is being maintained on the server. If we open a third command window and run a second client against the server, the two clients will share the same object state, and the greeting count will reflect calls made by both. This is a consequence of activating the remote object in singleton mode.

5.2 IMPLEMENTING SERVER-ACTIVATED REMOTE OBJECTS

.NET remoting supports both server- and client-activated objects. We'll look at client-activated objects later in this chapter. The *helloservicest.exe* application registered `HelloObj` as a server-activated, singleton mode object. Server-activated objects can be `Singleton` or `SingleCall`:

- `Singleton`—A single instance of the object is activated by the server at start-up. It lives as long as the server executes, and its state is shared by all clients.
- `SingleCall`—The object is activated by the server on receipt of a method call and is discarded immediately thereafter. No state is maintained between calls.

Since both `Singleton` and `SingleCall` objects are activated by the server, they must provide a default, parameterless constructor for the server to call at activation time.

`Singleton` objects are appropriate where clients need to maintain and share state. An example might be a chat server where all clients share the community chat history. On the other hand, `SingleCall` objects live only as long as necessary to service a method call, and they do not share state. Therefore `SingleCall` objects can be more easily load-balanced across servers.

5.2.1 Coding a SingleCall HelloService

To illustrate the differences between `Singleton` and `SingleCall` objects, let's create a `SingleCall` version of the server. Copy *helloservicest.cs* to *helloservicesc.cs* and change the activation mode to `SingleCall`, as follows:

```
RemotingConfiguration.RegisterWellKnownServiceType(
    Type.GetType("HelloObj"),              // remote object type
    "HelloObj",                            // endpoint name
    WellKnownObjectMode.SingleCall);       // activation mode
```

5.2.2 Testing the SingleCall HelloService

Compile and launch this new version of the service. (Generally, you would recompile the client against the new service assembly. However, this is unnecessary here since both the HelloObj type and the service URI are unchanged.) When you execute the client a couple of times, you should see the server output shown in figure 5.5.

```
C:\DotNet - helloservicesc                                        _|□|x|

C:\DotNet\cha_5>csc helloservicesc.cs
Microsoft (R) Visual C# Compiler Version 7.00.9254 [CLR version v1.0.2914]
Copyright (C) Microsoft Corp 2000-2001. All rights reserved.


C:\DotNet\cha_5>helloservicesc
registering HelloObj as SingleCall...
waiting for remote calls...
hit ENTER to exit...
HelloObj activated...
HelloObj activated...
greeting #1: Hello, Joe Bloggs!
HelloObj activated...
greeting #1: Hello, Mary Bloggs!
HelloObj activated...
greeting #1: Hello, Joe Bloggs!
HelloObj activated...
greeting #1: Hello, Mary Bloggs!
```

Figure 5.5   Output from the HelloServiceSc service

This time, the server object is activated (i.e., its constructor executed) each time the client calls the Greet method. The number of greetings is always equal to one because the object is discarded after each method call, so state is not maintained. Note the extra activation at startup caused by the initial registration process.

5.3   CONFIGURING REMOTING

In the above example, we had to recompile the server to change the activation mode of HelloObj from Singleton to SingleCall. To avoid this, .NET remoting supports the use of configuration files for registering remote objects on the network. Our final version of HelloService, which we'll save as *helloservice.cs*, will use a configuration file to register HelloObj.

5.3.1 Using remoting configuration files

Listing 5.3 presents a sample configuration file called *helloservice.exe.http.singleton.config*, which registers HelloObj as a Singleton. This time we specify HTTP for the channel.

Listing 5.3   A remoting configuration file for HelloService

```
<!--
   file        : helloservice.exe.http.singleton.config
   description : server configuration file for HelloService
-->

<configuration>
```

```
<system.runtime.remoting>
  <application>

    <service>
      <wellknown
        type="HelloObj, HelloService"
        objectUri="HelloObj"
        mode="Singleton"
      />
    </service>

    <channels>
      <channel
        ref="http"
        port="6789"
      />
    </channels>

  </application>
 </system.runtime.remoting>
</configuration>
```

The format of the configuration file is identical to the application configuration files we saw in chapter 2. In this case, we'll be using multiple configuration files and we'll dynamically configure our remote service by passing the name of the configuration file as a command line argument at run time. The file in listing 5.3 is called *helloservice.exe.http.singleton.config* to remind us that it uses the `Singleton` mode of activation over an HTTP channel.

Inside the `<service>` tags we define a single well known object and specify the type using an attribute of the form `"typeName, assemblyName"`:

```
<wellknown
  type="HelloObj, HelloService"
  objectUri="HelloObj"
  mode="Singleton"
/>
```

We specify that `HelloObj` be activated in `Singleton` mode. This time, we use a HTTP channel:

```
<channel
    ref="http"
    port="6789"
/>
```

5.3.2   Coding HelloService

The new version of the service, which uses this configuration file, is presented in listing 5.4.

Listing 5.4 Using a configuration file with Hello server

```
// file:     helloservice.cs
// compile:  csc helloservice.cs

// Exposes HelloObj using a remoting configuration file

using System;
using System.Runtime.Remoting;

public class HelloObj : MarshalByRefObject {

  public HelloObj() {
    Console.WriteLine("HelloObj activated...");
  }

  public string Greet(string name) {
    lock(this) { numGreet++; }
    string greeting = "Hello, " + name + "!";
    Console.WriteLine("greeting #{0}: " + greeting, numGreet);
    return greeting;
  }

  private int numGreet = 0;
}

public class HelloService {
  public static void Main(string[] args) {

    Console.WriteLine("configuring remoting...");
    string configFile = "helloservice.exe.http.singleton.config";
    if (args.Length > 0) configFile = args[0];
    RemotingConfiguration.Configure(configFile);

    Console.WriteLine("waiting for remote calls...");
    Console.WriteLine("hit ENTER to exit...");
    Console.ReadLine();
  }
}
```

This new version of the server accepts the name of a configuration file as a command-line argument, and calls:

```
RemotingConfiguration.Configure(configFile);
```

This causes remoting services to configure the server using the information in the file.

5.3.3 Coding the new client

As we'll see in the next section, we can also use a configuration file to configure the client. For now, however, the following changes to the client will register an HTTP channel and communicate with our new server:

```
...
using System.Runtime.Remoting.Channels.Http;

...

ChannelServices.RegisterChannel(new HttpChannel());

HelloObj helloObjRef = (HelloObj)Activator.GetObject(
  typeof(HelloObj),
  "http://localhost:6789/HelloObj"
);

...
```

The choice of HTTP over TCP makes little practical difference in this example. By default, HTTP uses XML/SOAP to format the payload, while TCP uses binary formatting which yields better performance. However, HTTP is a better option for cross-Internet remoting where firewalls may block TCP communications, while TCP may suit intranet scenarios.

5.4   IMPLEMENTING CLIENT-ACTIVATED REMOTE OBJECTS

Both `Singleton` and `SingleCall` are examples of server-activated objects. .NET remoting also supports client-activated objects. Client-activated objects are analogous to common class instances where each caller gets its own copy of the object. For example, a remote chess-playing service might export client-activated objects which separately maintain the state of each client game on the server.

5.4.1   Configuring the service for client activation

To configure our service for client activation, we need only amend our configuration file, as shown in listing 5.5.

Listing 5.5   Configuring the service for client activation

```
<!--
  file        : helloservice.exe.http.ca.config
  description : server configuration file for HelloService
-->

<configuration>
  <system.runtime.remoting>
    <application>

      <service>
        <activated type="HelloObj, HelloService" />
      </service>

      <channels>
```

```
        <channel
          ref="http"
          port="6789"
        />

      </channels>

    </application>
  </system.runtime.remoting>
</configuration>
```

This is similar to our original configuration file, save for replacement of the
`<wellknown>` entry by an `<activated>` entry:

```
<activated type="HelloObj, HelloService" />
```

This registers the object for client activation.

5.4.2 Configuring the client for client activation

This time, we also use a configuration file with the client, as shown in Listing 5.6.

Listing 5.6 Client-activation configuration file for HelloService client

```
<!--
  file :          helloclient.exe.http.ca.config
  description : client configuration file for client activation
                of HelloObj over HTTP channel
-->

<configuration>
  <system.runtime.remoting>
    <application>

      <client url="http://localhost:6789">
        <activated type="HelloObj, HelloService" />
      </client>

      <channels>
        <channel
          ref="http"
        />
      </channels>

    </application>
  </system.runtime.remoting>
</configuration>
```

The `<client>` entry provides the URL of the service, the type name of the remote
object, and name of the assembly where it resides. The client uses this information to
locate and instantiate the remote object.

5.4.3 Coding the new client

Our new client is shown in listing 5.7. We'll be creating three versions of this client, so we'll save this version as *helloclientca1.cs*.

```
// file:     helloclientca1.cs
// compile:  csc /r:helloservice.exe helloclientca1.cs

using System;
using System.Runtime.Remoting;

class HelloClient {
  public static void Main(string[] args) {
    Console.WriteLine("starting HTTP Hello client...");
    string configFile = "helloclient.exe.http.ca.config";
    RemotingConfiguration.Configure(configFile);
    HelloObj helloObjRef = new HelloObj();
    for (int i = 0; i < 2; i++) {
      Console.WriteLine(helloObjRef.Greet("Joe Bloggs"));
      Console.WriteLine(helloObjRef.Greet("Mary Bloggs"));
    }
  }
}
```

Since the client configuration file contains all the information to locate the remote object, the client can simply use new to instantiate the object as if it were local to the client:

```
HelloObj helloObjRef = new HelloObj();
```

5.4.4 Testing the client-activated service

Compile the service, and then launch it passing the new configuration file name, as shown in figure 5.6.

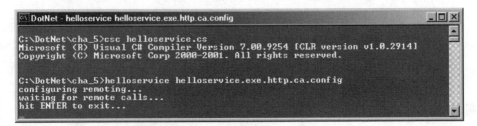

Figure 5.6 Running the client-activated HelloService service

Then, in a separate command window, compile the client and execute it a couple of times, as shown in figure 5.7.

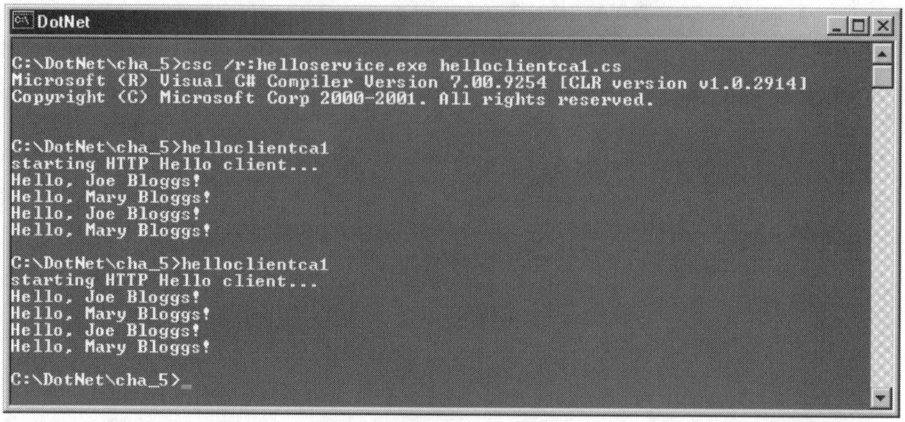

Figure 5.7   Running the client-activated HelloClient client

In the server window, you should see the results shown in figure 5.8.

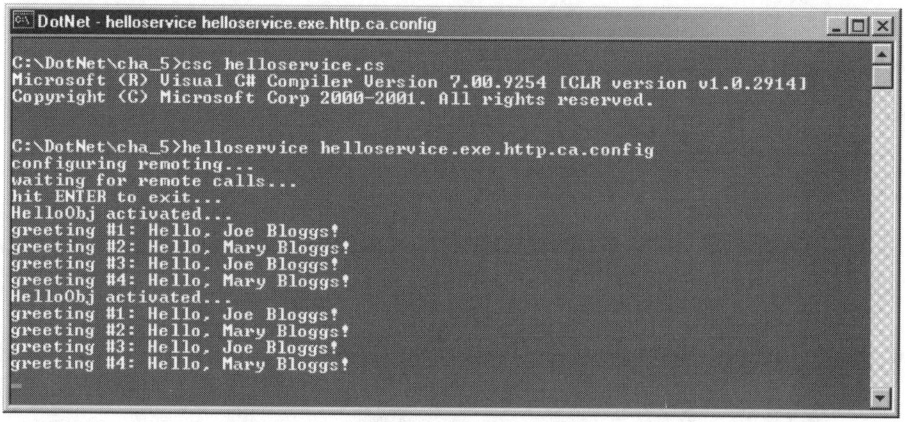

Figure 5.8   Output from the client-activated HelloService service

In this case, we can see that the object constructor ran when the client instantiated HelloObj. Thereafter, the client object was kept alive on the server, and serviced (four) calls by the client. In contrast to Singleton activation mode, executing the client a second time caused a fresh instance of the remote object to be created.

5.5   CLIENT ACTIVATION AND LEASING

We've seen how a Singleton object has just one instance which is activated at server startup, shared between clients, and lives as long as the server is running. In contrast, a SingleCall object is activated (i.e., its constructor is executed) each time a client invokes a method on it. When the method completes, the instance is discarded. In both cases, object lifetime is determined by the activation mode.

In contrast, client-activated objects require the server to create a fresh instance each time a client activates a new object, and the server must retain the state of each unique instance created by each client. If there are many clients, this can place a heavy burden on the server.

5.5.1 Understanding leasing

To manage the potential burden of many clients, remoting services implement a simple leased-based approach to client-activated object lifetime. When a client activates a new object, it obtains a time-based lease on it. The object instance is available to the client until the lease expires. Listing 5.8 presents a new version of the client, *helloclientca2.cs*, which displays the default lease information for the remote HelloObj reference.

Listing 5.8   Displaying lease information for client-activated remote objects

```
// file:      helloclientca2.cs
// compile: csc /r:helloservice.exe helloclientca2.cs

using System;
using System.Threading;
using System.Runtime.Remoting;
using System.Runtime.Remoting.Lifetime;

class HelloClient {

  public static void Main(string[] args) {

    Console.WriteLine("starting HTTP Hello client...");
    string configFile = "helloclient.exe.http.ca.config";
    RemotingConfiguration.Configure(configFile);
    HelloObj helloObjRef = new HelloObj();

    ILease lease = (ILease)helloObjRef.GetLifetimeService();

    while (true) {

      Console.WriteLine(helloObjRef.Greet("Joe Bloggs"));
      Console.WriteLine(helloObjRef.Greet("Mary Bloggs"));

      Console.WriteLine("CurrentState       : " +
        lease.CurrentState);
      Console.WriteLine("CurrentLeaseTime : " +
        lease.CurrentLeaseTime);
      Console.WriteLine("InitialLeaseTime : " +
        lease.InitialLeaseTime);
      Console.WriteLine("RenewOnCallTime  : " +
        lease.RenewOnCallTime);
      Console.WriteLine();

      Thread.Sleep(10000); // sleep for 10 seconds
    }
  }
}
```

The GetLifetimeService method is a member of the MarshalByRefObject class from which HelloObj derives. This allows us to get a reference to the lease and query its properties, as we do in this example. Once again, if not already running, start the server, as shown in figure 5.6.

Now compile and launch the new client as shown in figure 5.9. You can use CTRL+C to stop the client after a couple of iterations.

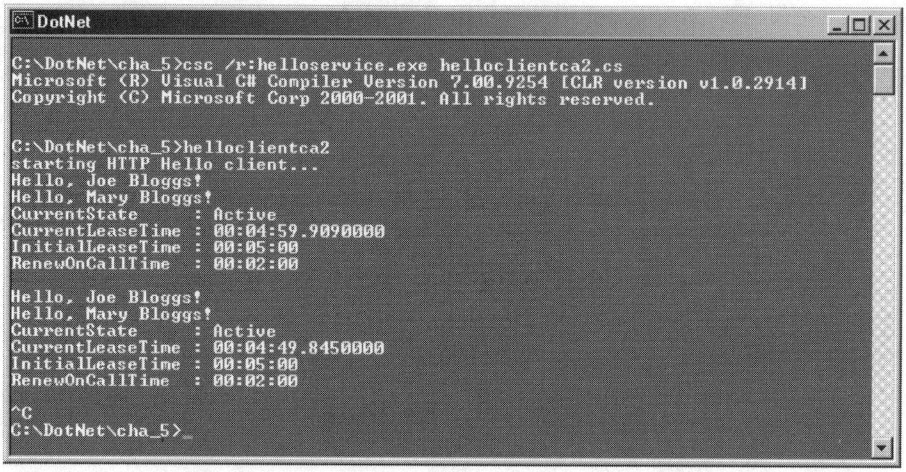

```
C:\DotNet\cha_5>csc /r:helloservice.exe helloclientca2.cs
Microsoft (R) Visual C# Compiler Version 7.00.9254 [CLR version v1.0.2914]
Copyright (C) Microsoft Corp 2000-2001. All rights reserved.


C:\DotNet\cha_5>helloclientca2
starting HTTP Hello client...
Hello, Joe Bloggs!
Hello, Mary Bloggs!
CurrentState      : Active
CurrentLeaseTime  : 00:04:59.9090000
InitialLeaseTime  : 00:05:00
RenewOnCallTime   : 00:02:00

Hello, Joe Bloggs!
Hello, Mary Bloggs!
CurrentState      : Active
CurrentLeaseTime  : 00:04:49.8450000
InitialLeaseTime  : 00:05:00
RenewOnCallTime   : 00:02:00

^C
C:\DotNet\cha_5>_
```

Figure 5.9   Displaying the lease information

Note the lease information. The CurrentState property indicates that the lease is active. Possible values for the CurrentState property are:

- Null (The lease is not initialized)
- Initial
- Active
- Renewing
- Expired

The InitialLeaseTime is 5 minutes by default, and this is the starting value for CurrentLeaseTime which is displayed above as 4:59.9090000 seconds. The program sleeps for 10 seconds before reinvoking the remote object's Greet method. By then, the value for CurrentLeaseTime has reduced to 4:49.8450000 seconds. The lease time continues to diminish toward expiration in this way. When it falls below the RenewOnCallTime, which is 2 minutes in this example, every subsequent method invocation resets the lease duration back to 2 minutes. In this way, provided the object is referenced at least once every 2 minutes (the RenewOnCallTime), the reference will remain alive. If the lease expires, a RemotingException will be raised stating that the service has disconnected.

5.5.2 Amending the lease

Both remote object and client can amend the lease. The remote object, which derives from `MarshalByRefObject`, can override the `MarshalByRefObject.InitializeLifetimeService` method and set values for the `InitialLeaseTime`, `RenewOnCallTime`, and so forth, before the lease becomes active. A better approach is to place these values in the server's configuration file. For example, the following entry in the server's configuration file sets the `InitialLeaseTime` to 24 hours (`1D`) and the `RenewOnCallTime`, for connecting clients, to 15 minutes (`15M`):

```
<configuration>
  <system.runtime.remoting>
    <application>

      <service>

        ...

      </service>

      <channels>

        ...

      </channels>

      <!-- set lease parameters -->
      <lifetime leaseTime = "1D"
                renewOnCallTime = "15M"
      />
    </application>
  </system.runtime.remoting>
</configuration>
```

However, increasing the lease duration on the server-side increases the lease duration for all clients, thus increasing the server burden. If a particular client requires a longer lease, this can be done by implementing a callback *sponsor* in the client.

5.5.3 Using a sponsor to amend lease duration

The client can register a callback sponsor by calling `ILease.Register` and passing a reference to an object that implements the `ISponsor` interface. The `ISponsor` interface requires a class to implement the `Renewal` method which returns a `TimeSpan` object containing the amount of time by which the lease should be extended. The `Renewal` method is invoked by the service when the lease is about to expire. Listing 5.9 presents another version of the client which uses a sponsor.

Listing 5.9   Implementing the ISponsor interface in the client

```
// file:     helloclientca3.cs
// compile: csc /r:helloservice.exe helloclientca3.cs

using System;
using System.Threading;
using System.Runtime.Remoting;
using System.Runtime.Remoting.Lifetime;

[Serializable]
class HelloSponsor : ISponsor {
  public TimeSpan Renewal(ILease lease) {
    Console.WriteLine("sponsor invoked by lease manager...");
    return new TimeSpan(1,0,0); // another hour
  }
}


class HelloClient {

  public static void Main(string[] args) {

    Console.WriteLine("starting HTTP Hello client...");
    string configFile = "helloclient.exe.http.ca.config";
    RemotingConfiguration.Configure(configFile);
    HelloObj helloObjRef = new HelloObj();

    ILease lease = (ILease)helloObjRef.GetLifetimeService();
    lease.Register(new HelloSponsor());

    while (true) {

      Console.WriteLine(helloObjRef.Greet("Joe Bloggs"));
      Console.WriteLine(helloObjRef.Greet("Mary Bloggs"));

      Console.WriteLine("CurrentState     : " +
        lease.CurrentState);
      Console.WriteLine("CurrentLeaseTime : " +
        lease.CurrentLeaseTime);
      Console.WriteLine("InitialLeaseTime : " +
        lease.InitialLeaseTime);
      Console.WriteLine("RenewOnCallTime  : " +
        lease.RenewOnCallTime);
      Console.WriteLine();

      Thread.Sleep(350000); // sleep for more than 5 minutes
    }
  }
}
```

This new client registers a sponsor with the lease manager. The HelloSponsor object implements the ISponsor interface by providing a public Renewal method which renews the lease for a further hour. The main routine sleeps for more than 5 minutes (the `InitialLeaseTime`) to ensure that the lease manager invokes the sponsor to see if the client would like to renew. (You'll have to wait.) Executing the client produces the output shown in figure 5.10.

```
C:\DotNet\cha_5>csc /r:helloservice.exe helloclientca3.cs
Microsoft (R) Visual C# Compiler Version 7.00.9254 [CLR version v1.0.2914]
Copyright (C) Microsoft Corp 2000-2001. All rights reserved.


C:\DotNet\cha_5>helloclientca3
starting HTTP Hello client...
Hello, Joe Bloggs!
Hello, Mary Bloggs!
CurrentState      : Active
CurrentLeaseTime  : 00:04:59.8490000
InitialLeaseTime  : 00:05:00
RenewOnCallTime   : 00:02:00

Hello, Joe Bloggs!
Hello, Mary Bloggs!
CurrentState      : Active
CurrentLeaseTime  : 00:59:09.9480000
InitialLeaseTime  : 00:05:00
RenewOnCallTime   : 00:02:00

^C
C:\DotNet\cha_5>_
```

Figure 5.10   Amending the lease—client view

Note that the sponsor is called before the loop executes for the second time. In the meantime, the `CurrentLeaseTime` has increased to 1 hour (59:09.9480000 minutes). Figure 5.11 presents the view from the service window.

```
C:\DotNet\cha_5>helloservice helloservice.exe.http.ca.config
configuring remoting...
waiting for remote calls...
hit ENTER to exit...
HelloObj activated...
greeting #1: Hello, Joe Bloggs!
greeting #2: Hello, Mary Bloggs!
sponsor invoked by lease manager...
greeting #3: Hello, Joe Bloggs!
greeting #4: Hello, Mary Bloggs!

C:\DotNet\cha_5>_
```

Figure 5.11   Amending the lease—service view

Implementing a sponsor does not guarantee that it will be successfully called in an Internet scenario where client and server are loosely coupled and the client sponsor may be unreachable. Also, using a sponsor requires that both client and server be running under the .NET runtime. This is not necessarily the case for our earlier examples. For example, a .NET remoting server which registers an object and exposes it on an HTTP channel could be called by a SOAP client running on a non-.NET platform.

5.6 HANDLING REMOTE EVENTS

So far our remoting examples, with the exception of the sponsor callback example, have followed a typical client/server pattern. However, an endpoint can be either client, or server, or both. Furthermore, a client can register a handler for an event raised by a remote object. For example, a chat server might raise an event when a member enters a chat room. A chat client, which registers a handler for this event, could update its user interface accordingly.

5.6.1 The EchoObj class

Let's look at an example of remote events. Listing 5.10 presents the code for the EchoObj class which contains an event member called ServerEchoEvent. The public Echo method accepts a string as an argument, creates a new EchoEventArgs object, and fires the event. A remote client can register a handler for ServerEchoEvent and invoke the Echo method to cause the event to be fired.

Listing 5.10   The EchoObj class

```
// file:     echoobj.cs
// compile: csc /target:library echoobj.cs

using System;

namespace Echo {

  public delegate void EchoEvent(object sender, EchoEventArgs e);

  [Serializable]
  public class EchoEventArgs : EventArgs {
    public EchoEventArgs(string message) {
      Message = message;
    }
    public string Message;
  }

  public class EchoObj : MarshalByRefObject {

    public EchoObj() {
      Console.WriteLine("EchoObj activated...");
    }

    public event EchoEvent ServerEchoEvent;

    public void Echo(string message) {
      Console.WriteLine("received message: " + message);
      if (ServerEchoEvent != null) // ensure handler is registered
        ServerEchoEvent(this, new EchoEventArgs(message));
    }
  }
}
```

5.6.2 The EchoService class

This time, we'll create a separate service application, *echoservice.exe*, to host the object and register it with remoting services. Listing 5.11 shows the service program.

Listing 5.11   The EchoService class

```
// file:     echoservice.cs
// compile: csc echoservice.cs

using System;
using System.Reflection;
using System.Runtime.Remoting;
using System.Runtime.Remoting.Channels;
using System.Runtime.Remoting.Channels.Http;

public class EchoService {
  public static void Main() {

    // register a channel...
    ChannelServices.RegisterChannel(new HttpChannel(6789));

    // register HelloObj with remoting services...
    Console.WriteLine("registering EchoObj as Singleton...");

    Assembly ass = Assembly.Load("echoobj");

    RemotingConfiguration.RegisterWellKnownServiceType(
      ass.GetType("Echo.EchoObj"),        // remote object type
      "EchoObj",                          // endpoint name
      WellKnownObjectMode.Singleton);     // activation mode

    Console.WriteLine("waiting for remote calls...");
    Console.WriteLine("hit ENTER to exit...");
    Console.ReadLine();
  }
}
```

5.6.3 The EchoClient class

Next, we create the simple client shown in listing 5.12.

Listing 5.12   The EchoClient class

```
// file:     echoclient.cs
// compile: csc /r:echoobj.dll echoclient.cs

using System;
using System.Runtime.Remoting;
using System.Runtime.Remoting.Channels;
using System.Runtime.Remoting.Channels.Http;
using System.Threading;
using Echo;
```

```
public class EchoHandler : MarshalByRefObject {
  public void Handler(object sender, EchoEventArgs e) {
    Console.WriteLine("echo callback: {0}", e.Message);
  }
}

public class EchoClient {
  public static void Main() {

    ChannelServices.RegisterChannel(new HttpChannel(0));
    EchoObj echoObjRef = (EchoObj)Activator.GetObject(
      typeof(EchoObj),
      "http://localhost:6789/EchoObj"
    );

    EchoHandler echoHandler = new EchoHandler();
    EchoEvent echoEvent = new EchoEvent(echoHandler.Handler);
    echoObjRef.ServerEchoEvent += echoEvent;

    echoObjRef.Echo("Hello!");
    echoObjRef.Echo("Goodbye!");

    Console.WriteLine("Press Enter to end...");
    Console.ReadLine();
    Console.WriteLine("Ending...");
    Thread.Sleep(2000); // give event time to fire

    echoObjRef.ServerEchoEvent -= echoEvent;
  }
}
```

As before, the client starts by registering a new HTTP channel and retrieving a reference to the remote object. The code:

```
EchoHandler echoHandler = new EchoHandler();
EchoEvent echoEvent = new EchoEvent(echoHandler.Handler);
echoObjRef.ServerEchoEvent += echoEvent;
```

creates a new instance of EchoHandler and registers its public Handler method as the handler for the remote ServerEchoEvent. Now EchoHandler too must derive from MarshalByRefObject so that remoting services can marshal its instance to register the handler. The client then calls the remote Echo method twice, unregisters the event handler, and ends.

5.6.4   Testing the EchoService

Compile and launch the remote object and service, as shown in figure 5.12.

Figure 5.12 Running EchoService

When you compile and execute the client, the client messages are echoed back from the remote object by the fired event as seen in figure 5.13.

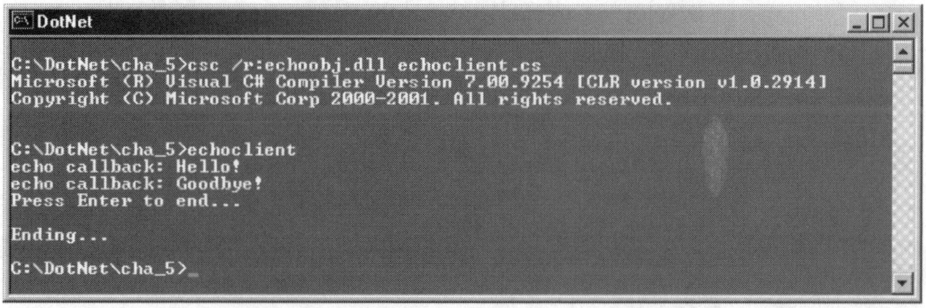

Figure 5.13 Testing EchoClient

The view from the service window is shown in figure 5.14.

Figure 5.14 Output from EchoService EchoClient

5.7 HOSTING OBJECTS IN INTERNET INFORMATION SERVER

So far, each of our remote objects has been hosted inside a dedicated server program, developed for that purpose. Next, we'll use IIS to host remote objects over HTTP. We explore this option with an example of a remote encoding service, hosted in IIS, which can encode strings in Base 64 format and decode them again. We'll also take this opportunity to illustrate the use of a separate interface assembly, against which client applications can be compiled.

5.7.1 Providing a public interface for a remote service

In all of our examples so far, the assembly containing the metadata for the remote object was required by the client at compile time. This is not always desirable or convenient, especially when client and service are developed by different parties. In such cases, a public interface to the object can be defined and made available to developers for use in developing client applications. This avoids the need to make the remote object assembly publicly available. In listing 5.13, we define the `RemoteEncoder.IStringEncoder` interface which provides public methods for both encoding and decoding strings.

Listing 5.13 An interface for an encoding object

```
// file:    istringencoder.cs
// compile: csc /target:library istringencoder.cs

namespace RemoteEncoder {

  public interface IStringEncoder {
    string Encode(string s);
    string Decode(string s);
  }
}
```

The remote encoding class will implement this interface and, at compile time, the client will reference the library containing the interface.

5.7.2 Coding the RemoteEncoder.Base64Service class

Next, we turn our attention to the remote encoding class itself. It will implement the `RemoteEncoder.IStringEncoder` interface to provide both `Encode` and `Decode` methods, as shown in listing 5.14.

Listing 5.14 The RemoteEncoder.Base64Service class

```
// file:    base64service.cs
// compile: csc /target:library
//              /r:istringencoder.dll
//              base64service.cs
```

```
using System;
using System.Text;

namespace RemoteEncoder {

  public class Base64Service : MarshalByRefObject, IStringEncoder {

    public string Encode(string s) {
      byte[] b = Encoding.ASCII.GetBytes(s);
      return Convert.ToBase64String(b);
    }

    public string Decode(string s) {
      byte[] b = Convert.FromBase64String(s);
      return Encoding.ASCII.GetString(b);
    }
  }
}
```

The purpose of the `RemoteEncoder.Base64Service` class is to encode and decode strings using Base 64 transfer encoding. Base 64 format is often used to encode nonprintable binary data as printable ASCII text and is a common format for encoding binary attachments. (It is also used in ASP.NET to encode the viewstate of a Web Form, as we'll see in chapter 8.) We use it here to encode and decode strings. For example, this can be a convenient way to obfuscate (but not encrypt) text in a URL or Web page.

The Encode method takes a string as an argument, transforms it to Base 64 format and returns the result. The Decode method reverses the procedure. Both methods use the built-in `Encoding` class from the `System.Text` namespace. Since it will be hosted in a remote server, we derive `Base64Service` from `MarshalByRefObject`. We also specify that it implements the `IStringEncoder` interface.

5.7.3   Coding the client

Listing 5.15 presents a client for our encoding service.

Listing 5.15   The RemoteEncoder.Base64Client class

```
// file:    base64client.cs
// compile: csc /r:istringencoder.dll base64client.cs

using System;
using System.Runtime.Remoting;
using System.Runtime.Remoting.Channels;
using System.Runtime.Remoting.Channels.Http;

namespace RemoteEncoder {

  class Base64Client {

    public static void Main(string[] args) {
```

```
ChannelServices.RegisterChannel(new HttpChannel());

IStringEncoder objRef = (IStringEncoder)Activator.GetObject(
  typeof(IStringEncoder),
  "http://localhost/RemoteEncoder/Base64Service.rem"
);

string s1 = "Mary had a little lamb.";
if (args.Length > 0) s1 = args[0];

Console.WriteLine("original : {0}", s1);

string s2 = objRef.Encode(s1);
Console.WriteLine("encoded  : {0}", s2);
Console.WriteLine("decoded  : {0}", objRef.Decode(s2));
      }
    }
}
```

We call `Activator.GetObject` to get a reference to the remote object. However, we don't refer to the remote object's type anywhere in the client program. Instead, we use the interface type `IStringEncoder`.

5.7.4   Compiling the Base64 string encoding application

Compile the `IStringEncoder` interface, and the `Base64Service` and `Base64-Client` classes, as shown in figure 5.15.

Figure 5.15 Compiling the string encoding application

As you can see, the *base64service.dll* library is not required to compile the client. Instead we reference the interface.

5.7.5   Deploying the StringEncoder service on IIS

To deploy the service on IIS, we need to create a virtual directory on the server. Call this directory *RemoteEncoder* and associate it with an appropriate physical directory.

Create a *bin* subdirectory and copy the interface assembly, *istringencoder.dll*, and the remote object assembly, *base64service.dll*, into it.

Next, we need to configure the remote service. In a Web scenario, the application configuration file is called *web.config* and is placed in the application's root directory. (We'll look at *web.config* in more detail in chapter 8.) Listing 5.16 presents a *web.config* file which exposes the object for `Singleton` mode activation.

Listing 5.16   The web.config configuration file

```
<!--
  file        : web.config
  description : IIS config file for RemoteEncoder.Base64Service
-->

<configuration>
  <system.runtime.remoting>
    <application>

      <service>
        <wellknown
          type="RemoteEncoder.Base64Service, Base64Service"
          objectUri="Base64Service.rem"
          mode="Singleton"
        />
      </service>

    </application>
  </system.runtime.remoting>
</configuration>
```

We specify `Base64Service.rem` as the `objectUri`. You must use an object URI that ends in *.rem* or *.soap* when hosting server-activated objects inside IIS.

5.7.6   Testing the IIS-hosted encoder

We don't need to do anything special to load the remote object into IIS. Instead, IIS does so automatically when it receives the first client request. Therefore, we need only launch the client, as shown in figure 5.16.

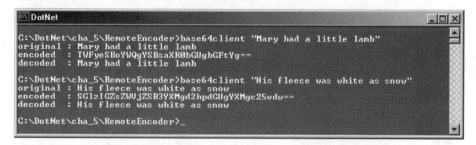

Figure 5.16   Testing Base64Service

5.8 REMPOK: A REMOTE POKER GAME

We return to our case study with a version of the poker machine which uses a RemPok-Service object to deal and draw cards. The service supports both server-activated Singleton mode and client-activated mode on either TCP or HTTP channels.

5.8.1 Developing the remote poker service

Listing 5.17 presents the service program called *RemPokService.cs*:

Listing 5.17   A remote poker machine service

```
// file    : RemPokService.cs
// compile : csc /r:poker.dll RemPokService.cs

namespace Poker {

  using System;
  using System.Runtime.Remoting;

  // use serializable GameResult struct to return game result...
  [Serializable]
  public struct GameResult {
    public string Hand;
    public int Score;
    public string Title;
  }

  public class RemPokService : MarshalByRefObject {

    public RemPokService() {
      Console.WriteLine("RemPokService activated...");
    }

    public string Deal() {
      string hand = new SimpleMachine().Deal().Text;
      Console.WriteLine("Dealing : {0}", hand);
      return hand;
    }

    public GameResult Draw(string oldHand, string holdCards) {
      GameResult g = new GameResult();
      Hand h = new SimpleMachine().Draw(oldHand, holdCards);
      g.Hand = h.Text;
      g.Score = h.Score;
      g.Title = h.Title;
      Console.WriteLine("Drawing : {0}  ({1})", g.Hand, g.Title);
      return g;
    }

    public static void Main(string[] args) {

      // get the default application configuration file name...
      string configFile =
        AppDomain.CurrentDomain.SetupInformation.ConfigurationFile;
```

```
        // configure remoting...
        Console.WriteLine("using " + configFile + "...");
        RemotingConfiguration.Configure(configFile);

        Console.WriteLine("waiting for remote calls...");
        Console.WriteLine("hit ENTER to exit...");
        Console.ReadLine();
    }
  }
}
```

The game is similar to versions seen earlier. The most notable difference is the addition of a serializable `GameResult` structure to return the game result to the client. This provides a neat way of packaging the hand, score, and title fields for transmission to the calling client.

The `Main` routine retrieves the default configuration file name, as follows:

```
string configFile =
    AppDomain.CurrentDomain.SetupInformation.ConfigurationFile;
```

In this case, this should return `RemPokService.exe.config`, which we'll look at next. Then the program configures remoting.

5.8.2 The remote poker machine configuration file

Listing 5.18 shows the configuration file for the remote service.

Listing 5.18   The remote poker machine configuration file

```
<!--
  file        : RemPokService.exe.config
  description : server configuration file for remote poker service
-->

<configuration>
  <system.runtime.remoting>
    <application>
      <service>

        <!-- server-activated singleton -->
        <wellknown
          type="Poker.RemPokService, RemPokService"
          objectUri="RemPokService"
          mode="Singleton"
        />

        <!-- client-activated -->
        <activated
          type="Poker.RemPokService, RemPokService"
        />

      </service>
      <channels>
```

```
            <!-- TCP channel -->
            <channel
              ref="tcp"
              port="6789"
            />

            <!-- HTTP channel -->
            <channel
              ref="http"
              port="8085"
            />

          </channels>
        </application>
      </system.runtime.remoting>
    </configuration>
```

The configuration file specifies both server-activated singleton and client-activated modes. It also specifies both TCP and HTTP channels. We'll use command-line switches with the client program to choose the operational activation mode and channel at run time.

5.8.3 The RemPok poker client

Listing 5.19 shows the poker client.

Listing 5.19 The RemPok poker client

```
// file:          rempok.cs
// description:    a remote poker machine client
// compile:        csc /r:rempokservice.exe rempok.cs

namespace Poker {

  using System;
  using System.Runtime.Remoting;
  using System.Runtime.Remoting.Channels;
  using System.Runtime.Remoting.Channels.Tcp;
  using System.Runtime.Remoting.Channels.Http;
  using System.Runtime.Remoting.Activation;

  class RemPok {

    public static void Main(string[] args) {

      string argLine = String.Join(" ", args).ToLower() + " ";

      string uri = "";
      if (argLine.IndexOf("/tcp") >= 0) {
        Console.WriteLine("starting TCP RemPok client...");
```

```
        ChannelServices.RegisterChannel(new TcpChannel());
        uri += "tcp://localhost:6789";
      } else {
        Console.WriteLine("starting HTTP RemPok client...");
        ChannelServices.RegisterChannel(new HttpChannel());
        uri += "http://localhost:8085";
      }

      if (argLine.IndexOf("/ca") >= 0) {
        Console.WriteLine("client activation...");
      } else {
        Console.WriteLine("server activation...");
        uri += "/RemPokService"; // append well-known endpoint name
      }

      new RemPok(argLine, uri); // start game
    }

    public RemPok(string argLine, string uri) {
      this.argLine = argLine;
      this.uri = uri;
      Console.WriteLine("A remote poker game...");
      Console.WriteLine("Hit Ctrl-c at any time to abort.\n");
      while (true) nextGame(); // play
    }

    private void nextGame() {
      RemPokService service = getService();
      string dealHand = service.Deal(); // deal hand
      Console.WriteLine(dealHand); // display it
      Console.Write("Enter card numbers (1 to 5) to hold: ");
      string holdCards = Console.ReadLine();

      // draw replacement cards...
      GameResult res = service.Draw(dealHand, holdCards);
      Console.WriteLine(res.Hand);
      Console.WriteLine(res.Title);
      Console.WriteLine("Score = {0}\n", res.Score);
    }

    private RemPokService getService() {

      if (argLine.IndexOf("/ca") >= 0) {
        object[] constructorArguments = new object[0];
        object[] activationAttributes = new object[1];
        activationAttributes[0] = new UrlAttribute(uri);
        return (RemPokService)Activator.CreateInstance(
          typeof(RemPokService),
          constructorArguments,
          activationAttributes
        );
      } else {
```

```
        return (RemPokService)Activator.GetObject(
          typeof(Poker.RemPokService),
          uri
        );
      }
    }

    private string argLine = null;
    private string uri = null;
  }
}
```

The /tcp command line switch instructs the client to use a TCP channel. Otherwise, HTTP is the default. Likewise, the /ca switch causes the client to use client
activation when instantiating the remote object. Otherwise, the default is server activation in Singleton mode, with /RemPokService appended to the URL.

The RemPok.getService method takes care of remote object activation. For
server activation, it uses the familiar Activator.GetObject method to retrieve
a reference to the remote object. This time, for client activation, we use Activa-
tor.CreateInstance to create a new object reference. As arguments, we pass the
remote object type, an empty array of constructor arguments, and an array of activation arguments containing just one element representing the URL of the object to
be activated.

5.8.4 Testing the remote poker machine

To test the application, we first compile and execute the poker service, as shown in
figure 5.17.

Figure 5.17   Running RemPokService

Then, try compiling the client and starting it in different modes, on different channels, as shown in figure 5.18.

```
DotNet - rempok /ca                                          _|□|×|

C:\DotNet\poker\RemPok>csc /r:rempokservice.exe rempok.cs
Microsoft (R) Visual C# Compiler Version 7.00.9254 [CLR version v1.0.2914]
Copyright (C) Microsoft Corp 2000-2001. All rights reserved.


C:\DotNet\poker\RemPok>rempok
starting HTTP RemPok client...
server activation...
A remote poker game...
Hit Ctrl-c at any time to abort.

4C 5S JS 3C AC
Enter card numbers (1 to 5) to hold: 5
TD 5D 4H 5C AC
No Score
Score = 0

QC 5C QD TD 7D
Enter card numbers (1 to 5) to hold: ^C
C:\DotNet\poker\RemPok>
C:\DotNet\poker\RemPok>
C:\DotNet\poker\RemPok>rempok /ca
starting HTTP RemPok client...
client activation...
A remote poker game...
Hit Ctrl-c at any time to abort.

4D QD TS 5S AC
Enter card numbers (1 to 5) to hold: _
```

Figure 5.18   Testing RemPokService—client view

In the service window, you should see the output shown in figure 5.19.

```
DotNet - rempokservice                                       _|□|×|

C:\DotNet\poker\RemPok>rempokservice
using RemPokService.exe.config...
waiting for remote calls...
hit ENTER to exit...
RemPokService activated...
Dealing : 4C 5S JS 3C AC
Drawing : TD 5D 4H 5C AC   (No Score)
Dealing : QC 5C QD TD 7D
RemPokService activated...
Dealing : 4D QD TS 5S AC
_
```

Figure 5.19   Testing RemPokService—service view

5.9   SVCPOK: A REMOTE POKER GAME AS A WINDOWS SERVICE

As we've seen, a remote object must be hosted by a server and is available only as long as the server is running. In our examples so far, with the exception of the IIS-hosted service, we've started and stopped the server manually. This would be unacceptable in a production environment. Instead, we need the server to start automatically when the machine is booted and to run forever. We can do this with a Windows service.

A Windows service runs in its own session, typically with no user interface, instead using the event log for recording errors and warnings. Windows services can be started automatically when the machine is booted. They can also be started, stopped, paused, and resumed by an administrator using the Services Control Manager. Windows services run in the security context of a specific user account which typically differs from the logged-on user or default account.

Coding a Windows service involves defining methods to handle the start, stop, pause, continue, and any custom commands. We do this by deriving our service class from `System.ServiceProcess.ServiceBase` and overriding the appropriate protected instance methods:

- `OnStart`—Executes when a start command is sent to the service. This can happen automatically when the machine is booted or the service may be started manually by an administrator using the Services Control Manager. Typically, you would add code here to open a connection to a database or perform some other initialization of the service. In our case, we'll use it to configure remoting and load any remote objects.

- `OnStop`—Executes when a stop command is sent to the service. We might add code here to release resources and close connections.

- `OnPause`—Executes when a pause command is sent to the service.

- `OnContinue`—Executes when a continue command is issued to resume a paused service.

- `OnShutdown`—Executes when the system is shutting down.

5.9.1 Coding the poker Windows service

In our case, we're interested in only the `OnStart` method since, when the service stops, the remote object will no longer be available. Also, we don't need the ability to pause and resume the poker machine so we'll disable these commands. The `PokerService` will look like:

```
public class PokerService : ServiceBase {

  public PokerService() {
    CanPauseAndContinue = false;
    CanStop = true;
    ServiceName = "PokerService";
  }

  protected override void OnStart(string[] args) {
    ChannelServices.RegisterChannel(new HttpChannel(6789));

    RemotingConfiguration.RegisterWellKnownServiceType(
      new SvcPokService().GetType(),      // remote object type
      "SvcPokService",                    // remote object name
      WellKnownObjectMode.Singleton);     // activation mode
  }

  public static void Main() {
    ServiceBase.Run(new PokerService());
  }
}
```

In `OnStart` we configure remoting, as before. In `Main`, we call `Service-Base.Run` to launch the service.

We use the installer utility, *installutil.exe*, to install the service. (You'll need to be logged on as administrator to do this.) This utility looks for installer classes, marked with the `RunInstallerAttribute(true)` attribute, in a given assembly and executes the installation code in the constructor:

```
[RunInstallerAttribute(true)]
public class PokerServiceInstaller : Installer {

  public PokerServiceInstaller() {

    ServiceProcessInstaller processInstaller =
      new ServiceProcessInstaller();
    processInstaller.Account = ServiceAccount.LocalSystem;

    ServiceInstaller serviceInstaller = new ServiceInstaller();
    serviceInstaller.StartType = ServiceStartMode.Manual;
    serviceInstaller.ServiceName = "PokerService";

    Installers.Add(serviceInstaller);
    Installers.Add(processInstaller);
  }
}
```

We name the installer class `PokerServiceInstaller` and we derive it from the `System.Configuration.Install.Installer` class. The constructor creates a new `ServiceProcessInstaller` which is used to install the service named `PokerService`. We specify that the service will be started manually and run under the local system account. To have the service started automatically at boot time, we would specify `ServiceStartMode.Automatic`.

Listing 5.20 presents *SvcPokService.cs* containing the new poker machine together with the `PokerService` and `PokerServiceInstaller` classes.

Listing 5.20 A Windows service-based poker machine

```
// file:    SvcPokService.cs
// compile: csc /r:poker.dll SvcPokService.cs

namespace Poker {

  using System;
  using System.ServiceProcess;
  using System.Runtime.Remoting;
  using System.Configuration.Install;
  using System.ComponentModel;
  using System.Runtime.Remoting.Channels;
  using System.Runtime.Remoting.Channels.Http;

  // use serializable GameResult struct to return game result...
  [Serializable]
  public struct GameResult {
```

```
    public string Hand;
    public int Score;
    public string Title;
}

public class SvcPokService : MarshalByRefObject {

    public string Deal() {
        string hand = new SimpleMachine().Deal().Text;
        Console.WriteLine("Dealing : {0}", hand);
        return hand;
    }

    public GameResult Draw(string oldHand, string holdCards) {
        GameResult g = new GameResult();
        Hand h = new SimpleMachine().Draw(oldHand, holdCards);
        g.Hand = h.Text;
        g.Score = h.Score;
        g.Title = h.Title;
        Console.WriteLine("Drawing : {0}  ({1})", g.Hand, g.Title);
        return g;
    }
}

public class PokerService : ServiceBase {

    public PokerService() {
        CanPauseAndContinue = false;
        CanStop = true;
        ServiceName = "PokerService";
    }

    protected override void OnStart(string[] args) {
        ChannelServices.RegisterChannel(new HttpChannel(6789));

        RemotingConfiguration.RegisterWellKnownServiceType(
            new SvcPokService().GetType(),      // remote object type
            "SvcPokService",                    // remote object name
            WellKnownObjectMode.Singleton);     // activation mode
    }

    public static void Main() {
        ServiceBase.Run(new PokerService());
    }
}

[RunInstallerAttribute(true)]
public class PokerServiceInstaller : Installer {

    public PokerServiceInstaller() {

        ServiceProcessInstaller processInstaller =
            new ServiceProcessInstaller();
        processInstaller.Account = ServiceAccount.LocalSystem;

        ServiceInstaller serviceInstaller = new ServiceInstaller();
        serviceInstaller.StartType = ServiceStartMode.Manual;
```

```
        serviceInstaller.ServiceName = "PokerService";

        Installers.Add(serviceInstaller);
        Installers.Add(processInstaller);
    }
  }
}
```

5.9.2   Installing the poker Windows service

We compile *svcpokservice.cs* and install it as a Windows service using the *installutil.exe* utility, as shown in figure 5.20.

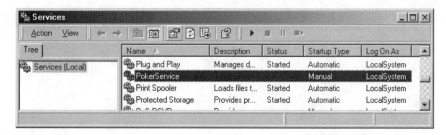

Figure 5.20   Installing SvcPokService—service view

`Installutil` performs a transacted two-phase installation and will roll back in the event of an error. Launch the Services Control Manager and you should see `PokerService` listed among the installed services, as shown in figure 5.21.

Figure 5.21   The PokerService Windows service

Double-click `PokerService` to view its properties shown in figure 5.22.

From the properties window, you can issue commands to start and stop the service. You can also change the `Startup` type to automatic or disabled, change the local system account under which the service runs, and specify recovery steps if the service fails. In this case, we just want to start the service, so click Start. The service should start up and the Stop button should be enabled. (We disabled the Pause and Resume options in the `PokerService` class.)

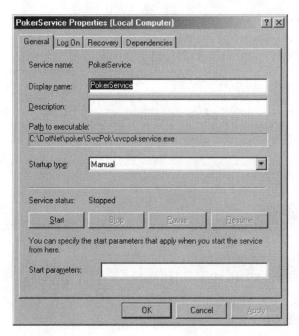

Figure 5.22
The PokerService properties

5.9.3 Creating the client

The client program, shown in listing 5.21, is essentially the same as the RemPok client we saw earlier and is presented here for completeness. This version dispenses with the configuration file and configures remoting directly instead.

Listing 5.21   The SvcPok client

```
// file:          SvcPok.cs
// description:    a client for the Windows service poker machine
// compile:        csc /r:SvcPokService.exe;poker.dll SvcPok.cs

namespace Poker {

  using System;
  using System.Runtime.Remoting;
  using System.Runtime.Remoting.Channels;
  using System.Runtime.Remoting.Channels.Http;

  class SvcPok {

    public static void Main(string[] args) {
      Console.WriteLine("starting HTTP SvcPok client...");
      ChannelServices.RegisterChannel(new HttpChannel());
      string url = "http://localhost:6789/SvcPokService";
      SvcPokService service = (SvcPokService)Activator.GetObject(
        typeof(Poker.SvcPokService),
        url
      );
```

       CHAPTER 5   DEVELOPING REMOTE SERVICES

```
      new SvcPok(service); // start game
    }

    public SvcPok(SvcPokService service) {
      this.service = service;
      Console.WriteLine("A Windows service-based poker game...");
      Console.WriteLine("Hit Ctrl-c at any time to abort.\n");
      while (true) nextGame(); // play
    }

    private void nextGame() {

      string dealHand = service.Deal(); // deal hand
      Console.WriteLine(dealHand); // display it
      Console.Write("Enter card numbers (1 to 5) to hold: ");
      string holdCards = Console.ReadLine();

      GameResult res = service.Draw(dealHand, holdCards);
      Console.WriteLine(res.Hand);
      Console.WriteLine(res.Title);
      Console.WriteLine("Score = {0}\n", res.Score);
    }

    private SvcPokService service = null;
  }
}
```

Once again, if you want the service to be started automatically when the machine boots, use the Services Control Manager to change the startup type to automatic. Finally, to uninstall the service, execute `installutil /u svcpokservice.exe`.

5.10 QUEPOK: A MESSAGE QUEUE-BASED POKER GAME

Our final example of a remote machine is based on MSMQ. While not strictly part of .NET's remoting services, MSMQ offers an alternative means of communicating with a remote application by sending and receiving messages. MSMQ guarantees message delivery. If the remote application is unavailable, messages are stored in a queue and remain there until the application comes back up. This can provide a more robust solution than regular remoting when the application is suited to the request/response messaging model. Also, several related messages can be combined into a single transaction to ensure that they are delivered in order, and only once, and are successfully retrieved from their queue by the remote application. If an error occurs, the entire transaction is rolled back.

Message queues can be categorized into public, private, and system.

- *Public queues*—MSMQ enables computers to participate in a message queuing network and to send and receive messages across the network. A public queue is a message queue that is visible throughout the network and can potentially be accessed by all participant machines.

- *Private queues*—A private message queue is visible only on the local machine and can be accessed only by applications which know the full path or name of the queue.

- *System queues*—System queues can be journal queues which store copies of messages, dead letter queues which store copies of undelivered or expired messages, and report queues which contain message routing information. An application can specify which system queues it needs depending on its journaling, acknowledgement, and audit requirements.

We use the `System.Messaging.MessageQueue` class to work with message queues. For example, the following code creates a private queue for sending `Poker.Hand` objects:

```
using System.Messaging;

...

string qPath = @".\Private$\PokerHandQueue";
if (!MessageQueue.Exists(qPath))
  MessageQueue.Create(qPath); // create the queue
MessageQueue q = new MessageQueue(qPath); // instantiate a queue object
```

We create a queue specifying its path and we access it by instantiating a queue object. The general syntax for a queue's path is `machineName\queueName` for a public queue and `machineName\Private$\queueName` for a private queue. You can use "." a period to represent the local machine and you can change a queue's `Path` property at runtime:

```
// access local private Poker.Hand queue...
q.Path = @".\Private$\PokerHandQueue";

// access public Poker.Hand queue on myMachine...
q.Path = @"myMachine\PokerHandQueue";
```

We set the queue's `Formatter` property so that we can send and receive our own user-defined types. For example, the following code creates a `XmlMessageFormatter` to format the queue to store an XML-encoded representation of the `Poker.Hand` type:

```
...

q.Formatter =
  new XmlMessageFormatter(new string[]{"Poker.Hand"});

...

// receive a Poker.Hand object...
Poker.Hand pokerHand = (Poker.Hand)q.Receive().Body;

...

// send a Poker.Hand object...
q.Send(pokerHand);
```

5.10.1 Designing an MSMQ-based poker service

The design of our message queue-based poker machine is simple and is illustrated in figure 5.23. We'll create a service which will read DEAL and DRAW requests from its incoming queue and respond appropriately using each client's unique incoming queue.

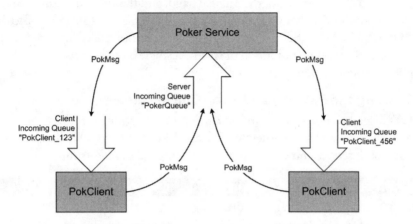

Figure 5.23   A remote service

All request and response messages will use a PokMsg class which contains fields to store the client queue's ID, the DEAL/DRAW command, the hand, the cards to hold, and the hand's title and score. Table 5.1 presents a sample of the four messages exchanged during a single poker game.

Table 5.1   Sample PokMsg messages

PokMsg Member:	QID	Command	Hand	HoldCards	Title	Score
1: Client Deal Request:	"PokClient_123"	"DEAL"	-	-	-	-
2: Service Deal Response:	-	-	"8D 7D AH TD 2S"	-	-	-
3: Client Draw Request:	"PokClient_123"	"DRAW"	"8D 7D AH TD 2S"	"3"	-	-
4: Service Draw Response:	-	-	"7S 7C AH JD JC"	-	"Two Pair"	3

The client creates a PokMsg object and sets its QID field to "PokClient_123" and its Command field to "DEAL". The QID is the name of the client queue the service should use when responding to the client's request. Each client will generate its own unique random QID by appending a random number to "PokClient_". In this example, the generated client queue name is `"PokClient_123"`. The service will use a single queue for all incoming requests.

The service responds by dealing a hand, storing its string representation in `Pok-Msg.Hand`, and sending it to the client. The client sends a new request with the same QID, a `"DRAW"` command, the original hand, and the string of cards to hold. The service responds by drawing cards, setting the new value for `PokMsg.Hand`, setting the `Title` and `Score` fields, and returning the result to the client. As you can see, the different messages do not use all the fields. A single message format is used here to simplify the presentation of the example.

5.10.2 Creating the PokMsg and PokerQueue classes

Let's begin by creating our own private local `PokerQueue` message queue which can send, receive, and store a new user-defined `PokMsg` type. We'll use these classes to build both service and client programs. Listing 5.22 presents the code.

Listing 5.22 The PokMsg and PokerQueue classes

```
// file: PokerQueue.cs
// compile: csc /target:library PokerQueue.cs

using System;
using System.Messaging;

namespace Poker {

  public class PokMsg {
    public string QID;
    public string Command;
    public string Hand;
    public string HoldCards;
    public string Title;
    public int Score;
  }

  public class PokerQueue {

    public PokerQueue (string qPath) {
      QPath = @".\Private$\" + qPath;
      // create and instantiate queue...
      if (!MessageQueue.Exists(QPath)) MessageQueue.Create(QPath);
      q = new MessageQueue(QPath);

      // format queue for storing the PokMsg type...
      // from the pokerqueue.dll assembly
      q.Formatter =
        new XmlMessageFormatter(
          new string[]{"Poker.PokMsg, pokerqueue"}
        );
    }

    public void Send(PokMsg msg) {
      q.Send(msg); // send a PokMsg object
```

```
    }

    public PokMsg Receive() {
        return (PokMsg)q.Receive().Body; // receive a PokMsg object
    }

    public void Kill() {
        q.Purge(); // zap messages (not strictly necessary)
        MessageQueue.Delete(QPath); // delete the queue
    }

    private string QPath;
    private MessageQueue q;
  }
}
```

5.10.3 Creating the QuePokService service

The message queue-based poker service, shown in listing 5.23, creates the service's incoming PokerQueue, and a SimpleMachine poker engine, and loops indefinitely responding to incoming "DEAL" and "DRAW" requests.

> **Listing 5.23 The QuePokService service**

```
// file:     QuePokService.cs
// compile:  csc /r:PokerQueue.dll;poker.dll QuePokService.cs

using System;

namespace Poker {

  public class QuePokService {

    public static void Main () {

      PokerQueue inQ = new PokerQueue("PokerServer");
      SimpleMachine machine = new SimpleMachine();

      Console.WriteLine("waiting for messages...");
      while(true) {

        PokMsg pokMsg = inQ.Receive();
        Console.WriteLine(
          "received : {0} : {1}",
          pokMsg.QID, pokMsg.Command
        );

        PokerQueue outQ = new PokerQueue(pokMsg.QID);

        if (pokMsg.Command.Equals("DEAL")) {
          pokMsg.Hand = machine.Deal().Text;
          outQ.Send(pokMsg);
          continue;
        }

        if (pokMsg.Command.Equals("DRAW")) {
```

```
            Hand h = machine.Draw(pokMsg.Hand, pokMsg.HoldCards);
            pokMsg.Hand = h.Text;
            pokMsg.Title = h.Title;
            pokMsg.Score = h.Score;
            outQ.Send(pokMsg);
          }
        }
      }
    }
}
```

When the service receives a message, it extracts the QID and uses it to create a reference to the outgoing queue for sending its response to the client.

5.10.4   Creating the QuePok client

The QuePok client, shown in listing 5.24, is similarly simple.

Listing 5.24   The QuePok client

```
// file:        QuePok.cs
// description: a MSMQ poker machine client
// compile:     csc /r:PokerQueue.dll QuePok.cs

namespace Poker {

  using System;

  class QuePok {

    public static void Main(string[] args) {
      new QuePok(); // start game
    }

    public QuePok() {
      inQPath = "PokClient_" + new System.Random().Next(1, 1000000);
      inQ = new PokerQueue(inQPath);
      outQ = new PokerQueue("PokerServer");
      pokMsg = new PokMsg();
      pokMsg.QID = inQPath;
      Console.WriteLine("A message queue-based poker game...");
      while (!gameOver) nextGame(); // play
    }

    private void nextGame() {

      pokMsg.Command = "DEAL";
      outQ.Send(pokMsg);
      pokMsg = inQ.Receive();

      Console.WriteLine(pokMsg.Hand); // display it
      Console.Write(
        "Enter card numbers (1 to 5) to hold, or Q to exit: "
      );
```

```
        string command =
          pokMsg.HoldCards =
            Console.ReadLine().Trim().ToUpper();

        if (command.Equals("Q")) {
          inQ.Kill();
          gameOver = true;
          return;
        }

        pokMsg.Command = "DRAW";
        outQ.Send(pokMsg);
        pokMsg = inQ.Receive();

        Console.WriteLine(pokMsg.Hand); // the hand
        Console.WriteLine(pokMsg.Title); // the title
        Console.WriteLine("Score = {0}\n", pokMsg.Score); // the score
      }

    private bool gameOver = false;
    private string inQPath;
    private PokerQueue inQ;
    private PokerQueue outQ;
    private PokMsg pokMsg;
  }
}
```

Typically, queues live forever in the system until deleted. Therefore, this time, we tell the user to enter "Q" to end the client and we call `inQ.Kill()` to delete the queue from the system.

5.10.5   Compiling and testing the QuePok service

Compile both client and service, as shown in figure 5.24.

Now, launch the service in one window and a few clients in their own windows. The output in the service window is shown in figure 5.25.

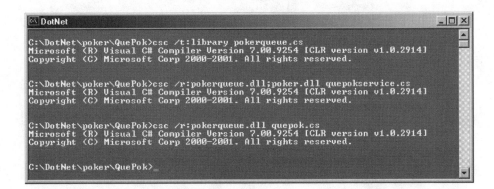

Figure 5.24   Compiling the QuePok application

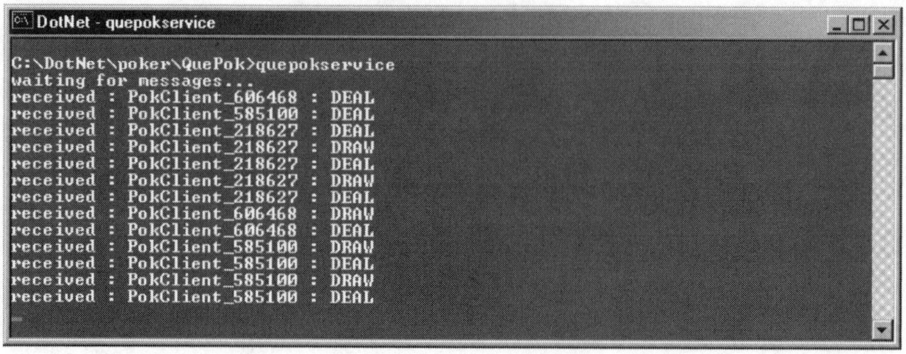

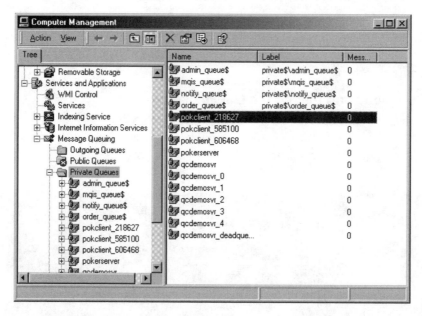

Figure 5.25 The QuePokService output

In this case, the service is communicating with three clients, each with its own unique response queue. If you stop the service, the clients will continue to run without error. However, they will block while waiting for a response from the service. Restarting the service will allow the clients to proceed and no messages will be lost. This is one of the key reliability features of the message queuing architecture. If you open the Computer Management window, found under Administrative Tools in Windows 2000, you can view the new poker message queues in the system, as in figure 5.26.

Figure 5.26 Viewing message queues

5.11 SUMMARY

Remoting services open the way for the creation of powerful distributed applications without requiring the developer to work with complex protocols or a special interface description language. In this chapter, we looked at both server- and client-activated remote objects and how to configure services and clients for both. For client-activated objects, we explored the leasing mechanism used by remoting to manage remote object lifetime.

We developed a remote version of our poker game which supports `Singleton` and client-activated modes of operation over both TCP and HTTP channels. We also created a remote poker machine which runs as a Windows service.

Finally, we explored an alternative to remoting services when we developed a remote, message queue-based version of our poker machine. In the next chapter, we build on our knowledge of .NET remoting when we explore XML Web services.

Developing XML Web services

XML Web services are one of the most talked-about features of the .NET platform. Many see a future where businesses expose applications to customers as Web services using a pay-per-use model and where the systems of different companies interact with one another across the Web. The Universal Description, Discovery, and Integration (UDDI) project, initiated by Microsoft, IBM, and others, supports these goals by allowing companies to publish information about the Web services they produce in a universal registry that will be accessible by all.

Perhaps the most attractive feature of Web services is that, unlike DCOM or CORBA, they are founded on universal, nonproprietary standards including XML and HTTP. Web services are not exclusive to .NET. On the contrary, one of their strengths is that they offer a model that is platform independent. However, .NET includes several tools and a degree of support which simplify the development of Web services by automating many of the tasks involved and shielding the developer from many of the technical details.

In this chapter, we explore XML Web services by developing sample services and client applications. We learn how to manage state within a Web service and how to emulate remoting's singleton, single-call, and client-activated modes. We also explore Web service discovery and learn how to use UDDI to publish services to potential customers. As usual, we'll round out the discussion by returning to our case study and presenting a poker machine Web service.

6.1 INTRODUCTION TO XML WEB SERVICES

A Web service is an application that exposes a programming interface to remote callers over the Web. Unlike alternative remoting models, such as DCOM and CORBA, Web services offer a simple, scalable model based on industry standards such as XML/ SOAP. SOAP, in turn, uses HTTP as the transport layer to move structured type information across the Internet. (SOAP version 1.1 opened the possibility of using other Internet protocols as transport layers.)

SOAP messages are essentially one-way transmissions, but can be combined to create a request/response conversation model suited to remote method invocation. SOAP data is encapsulated for transmission in a SOAP envelope which is basically an XML document containing the structured data to be transmitted.

Developing XML Web services and clients does not necessarily require an understanding of SOAP, although it doesn't hurt. Using ASP.NET, developing the service can be as simple as coding a C#, or Visual Basic .NET class and deploying it on IIS. Microsoft IIS and the ASP.NET infrastructure look after compiling the source, building a WSDL contract which describes the service, forwarding client calls to the service, and returning results. (We'll look at ASP.NET in more detail in chapter 8.) The .NET SDK, and Visual Studio .NET, both provide tools to query the WSDL contract, and generate a proxy class to be used in compiling client applications.

6.2 CREATING A FIRST WEB SERVICE

Without further delay, let's create our first Web service. We'll develop a simple service that accepts the caller's name and returns a greeting. We'll be installing our Web services on IIS, so we'll need a virtual directory on the Web server. Call this new virtual directory *ws* (for Web services) and remember to assign it permission to execute scripts.

6.2.1 Creating the service

Web services are stored on the server in files with a *.asmx* extension. These files are a bit like *.asp* files and can contain server directives and C# code. You can also use the `CodeBehind` directive to place the C# code in a separate file, as Visual Studio .NET does when you create a new Web service project. We don't bother to do this for the simple examples shown here.

Once again, we'll use our old friend `HelloService`. While not very exciting, its simplicity will allow us to cover more ground within the confines of a single chapter. We'll be creating several versions of `HelloService`, so we'll call the first version `HelloService1` and store it as *helloservice1.asmx*. Listing 6.1 contains the code for this first version.

Listing 6.1   The HelloService1 Web service

```
<%@ WebService Language="C#" Class="HelloService1" %>

// file:          helloservice1.asmx
// description:   hello web service - basic version

using System.Web.Services;

[WebService(
  Description="A greeting Web service",
  Namespace="http://manning.com/dotnet/webservices"
)]

public class HelloService1 : WebService {

  [WebMethod(Description="Greet by name.")]
  public string Greet(string name) {
    if (name == "") name = "Stranger";
    return "Hello, " + name + "!";
  }
}
```

The first line in the file identifies the application as a Web service coded in C# and contained in the class `HelloService1`. The `WebService` attribute assigns a description for the Web service and a default XML namespace for schemas generated for the service. This attribute is not strictly necessary and your service will work without it. However, it allows you to specify a name for the service which is not constrained by the naming rules of the CLR. In this example, we just accept the default class name, `HelloService1`. You should assign a unique namespace when you are publicly exposing your Web service to callers. This will disambiguate your service from other services on the Web which have the same name. You can use your company's Internet domain name as part of the XML namespace, as I have done in this example. Note that, although this may look like a URL, it does not point to an actual resource on the Web.

The `HelloService1` class is derived from `System.Web.Services.Web-Service`. Doing so provides access to the ASP.NET `Context` property and makes available the familiar ASP.NET objects including `Request`, `Response`, and `Session`. We'll use some of these objects later when we consider how to maintain state between service invocations.

Public methods which clients can call must be annotated with the `WebMethod` attribute. This attribute has several optional properties including the `Description` property which we set in this case.

6.2.2 Testing the service

Save this file to the server, launch Internet Explorer and go to the URL. By default, you should see a page similar to that shown in figure 6.1.

Figure 6.1
Browsing the Hello service

ASP.NET provides these default pages to allow you to browse Web service descriptions. The page in figure 6.1 is generated by the *DefaultWsdlHelpGenerator.aspx* page, which is shipped with .NET. You can change this default by editing the `<web-Services>` section of the machine-wide configuration file, *machine.config*, typically installed at *C:\WINNT\Microsoft.NET\Framework\<version>\CONFIG*. See figure 6.2.

```
2839
2840        <webServices>
2841            <protocols>
2842                <add name="HttpSoap" />
2843                <add name="HttpPost" />
2844                <add name="HttpGet" />
2845                <add name="Documentation" />
2846            </protocols>
2847            <soapExtensionTypes>
2848            </soapExtensionTypes>
2849            <soapExtensionReflectorTypes>
2850            </soapExtensionReflectorTypes>
2851            <soapExtensionImporterTypes>
2852            </soapExtensionImporterTypes>
2853            <wsdlHelpGenerator
2854                href="DefaultWsdlHelpGenerator.aspx" />
2855            <serviceDescriptionFormatExtensionTypes>
2856            </serviceDescriptionFormatExtensionTypes>
2857        </webServices>
2858
```

Figure 6.2   The default WSDL help generator setting

Returning to the page in figure 6.1, click the *Greet* link and you should be presented with a page containing a textbox where you can enter your name, and a button to invoke the `Greet` method. See figure 6.3.

Figure 6.3
Browsing the Hello service

Enter your name and click the button. If your name is Joe Bloggs, you should see a page similar to that shown in figure 6.4.

Figure 6.4
Invoking the Hello service

The result is an XML document containing the greeting string returned by the service. Note the XML namespace name in the response. Also, the URL of the returned page is http://localhost/ws/helloservice1.asmx/Greet?name=Joe+Bloggs. This is simply the URL of the virtual directory followed by the name of the file where the service resides, followed by the method name and arguments. This is the familiar URL string for a HTTP GET request. Next, we'll code a C# client program which also uses HTTP GET to invoke the service.

CHAPTER 6   DEVELOPING XML WEB SERVICES

6.3 CREATING AN HTTP GET CLIENT

A simple HTTP GET client is shown in listing 6.2. It calls `WebRequest.Create` to create a `WebRequest` object and issue an HTTP GET command to the service. An `XmlDocument` object is used to capture the returned document and extract the result.

Listing 6.2 An HTTPGET client for HelloService1

```
// file:    helloget.cs
// compile: csc helloget.cs

using System;
using System.Net;
using System.IO;
using System.Xml;

class HelloGet {
  public static void Main(string[] args) {

    // build URL...
    string url =
      "http://localhost/ws/helloservice1.asmx/Greet?name=";
    string argLine = String.Join(" ", args);
    if (argLine.Length > 0) url += argLine;

    // create Web request...
    WebRequest req = WebRequest.Create(new Uri(url));
    WebResponse resp = req.GetResponse();

    // get reply...
    StreamReader sr = new StreamReader(resp.GetResponseStream());
    XmlDocument xd = new XmlDocument();
    xd.LoadXml (sr.ReadToEnd());

    // display returned value...
    Console.WriteLine(xd.DocumentElement.InnerText);
  }
}
```

The HTTP client program takes an optional user's name as a parameter and builds a URL to invoke the service's `Greet` method. It uses the built-in `System.Net.WebRequest` class to invoke the HTTP request and the `System.Net.WebResponse` to retrieve the result which is, as we saw in figure 6.4, an XML document. Then it displays the text of the root document element which, in this case, is the greeting string returned by `HelloService1`.

Compiling and executing this client produces the output shown in figure 6.5.

Although this client is perfectly useful in its current form, there are better ways to build a client to interact with a Web service, as we'll see soon. First, we take a look at WSDL which is an XML language for describing Web services.

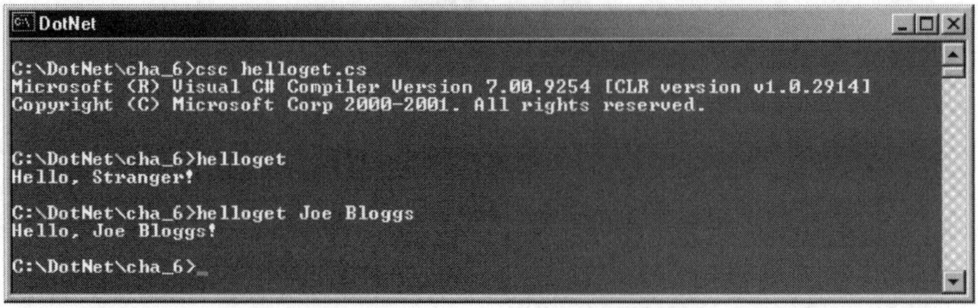

Figure 6.5   Testing HelloService1

6.4   USING *WSDL* TO DESCRIBE A *WEB SERVICE*

Remember that Web services are not exclusive to .NET. Other vendors have their own vision of an interconnected business-to-business marketplace based on the Web service model. (For an IBM-centric view, check out http://www.ibm.com/developer-works/webservices.) Since Web services provide a nonproprietary, open model, they must be based on common standards. WSDL is one such standard, and is the product of a collaborative effort of Microsoft, IBM, and others.

WSDL provides a means of describing Web services. These descriptions may be stored with the service itself or published in the UDDI registry which we mentioned earlier and to which we'll return later in this chapter. The good news is that .NET's Web service infrastructure will automatically generate the necessary WSDL to fully describe .NET services. This is yet another benefit of the self-describing nature of .NET types based on metadata and reflection. Even better, .NET provides tools that can consume WSDL descriptions of services and use these descriptions to generate proxy classes for use in client applications. So in the .NET world, the developer can choose to remain ignorant of WSDL, and even SOAP, and still benefit from the ability to create feature-rich Web services and clients.

To retrieve the WSDL for `HelloService1`, point your browser to http://local-host/ws/helloservice1.asmx?WSDL. The WSDL listing comes to more than 100 lines of XML, so we won't show it in full here. It consists of a `<definitions>` section containing subsections for types, messages, portTypes, bindings, and services.

6.4.1   WSDL types

The `<types>` section defines two complex types, `Greet` and `GreetResponse`, as string types. These correspond to the argument passed to `HelloService1` and the response returned, respectively. The generated WSDL looks like:

```
<types>
  <s:schema
    attributeFormDefault="qualified"
    elementFormDefault="qualified"
    targetNamespace="http://manning.com/dotnet/webservices">
```

```
            <s:element name="Greet">
              <s:complexType>
                <s:sequence>
                  <s:element
                    minOccurs="1"
                    maxOccurs="1"
                    name="name"
                    nillable="true"
                    type="s:string" />
                </s:sequence>
              </s:complexType>
            </s:element>
            <s:element name="GreetResponse">
              <s:complexType>
                <s:sequence>
                  <s:element
                    minOccurs="1"
                    maxOccurs="1"
                    name="GreetResult"
                    nillable="true"
                    type="s:string" />
                </s:sequence>
              </s:complexType>
            </s:element>
            <s:element name="string" nillable="true" type="s:string" />
          </s:schema>
        </types>
```

WSDL supports a rich set of common types in accordance with the draft standard for the XML Schema Definition Language. These include signed and unsigned integer and floating-point types, boolean and string types, and arrays of same. The SOAP version of a service supports the serialization of complex types built from these underlying simple types.

6.4.2   WSDL messages

A message can be compared to an envelope containing information moving from a source to a destination. In our example, `HelloService1` defines a single `Greet` method which, when called, responds by returning a result. Both the call and the response are messages. Therefore the round-trip involves two messages.

The generated WSDL specifies support for three protocols:

- *HttpGet*—Uses HTTP GET to invoke service. See listing 6.2 for a sample client.
- *HttpPost*—Uses HTTP POST to invoke the service.
- *Soap*—Uses SOAP to invoke the service.

With two messages involved in a single round-trip method invocation, and three supported protocols, the generated WSDL defines six messages:

- GreetSoapIn—Greet method call via SOAP.
- GreetSoapOut—Greet method response via SOAP.
- GreetHttpGetIn—Greet method call via HTTP GET.
- GreetHttpGetOut—Greet method response via HTTP GET.
- GreetHttpPostIn—Greet method call via HTTP POST.
- GreetHttpPostOut—Greet method response via HTTP POST.

SOAP is a superior message format because of its ability to represent complex types. Therefore, from now on, we'll work with SOAP only. The generated WSDL for the SOAP messages looks like:

```
<message name="GreetSoapIn">
  <part name="parameters" element="s0:Greet" />
</message>
<message name="GreetSoapOut">
  <part name="parameters" element="s0:GreetResponse" />
</message>
```

The GreetSoapIn and GreetSoapOut messages encapsulate the sent Greet and returned GreetResponse types seen above.

6.4.3 WSDL portTypes

Next come the <portType> entries. This time, we confine ourselves to the SOAP entry:

```
<portType name="HelloService1Soap">
  <operation name="Greet">
    <documentation>Greet by name.</documentation>
    <input message="s0:GreetSoapIn" />
    <output message="s0:GreetSoapOut" />
  </operation>
</portType>
```

A <portType> section contains a set of one or more <operation> entries, each of which represents a single round-trip method invocation and return. In this case, the Greet operation involves sending a GreetSoapIn message and receiving a GreetSoapOut message in reply. Both messages must be defined in the prior <message> sections.

6.4.4 WSDL bindings

Next we look at the <binding> entries. Once again, we confine ourselves to the SOAP-related entry:

```
<binding name="HelloService1Soap" type="s0:HelloService1Soap">
  <soap:binding
    transport="http://schemas.xmlsoap.org/soap/http"
    style="document" />
  <operation name="Greet">
```

CHAPTER 6 DEVELOPING XML WEB SERVICES

```
    <soap:operation
      soapAction="http://manning.com/dotnet/webservices/Greet"
      style="document" />
    <input>
      <soap:body use="literal" />
    </input>
    <output>
      <soap:body use="literal" />
    </output>
  </operation>
</binding>
```

A <binding> entry binds an operation to a protocol. In this example, it specifies that the Greet operation, http://manning.com/dotnet/webservices/Greet, is available via SOAP-encoded format over the HTTP transport. (Since version 1.1, SOAP can be used with other transports.)

6.4.5   WSDL services

The <service> entry represents a set of ports, where a port represents a defined binding at a specific location:

```
<service name="HelloService1">
  <documentation>A greeting Web service</documentation>
  <port name="HelloService1Soap"
    binding="s0:HelloService1Soap">
    <soap:address
      location="http://localhost/ws/helloservice1.asmx" />
  </port>
  <port name="HelloService1HttpGet"
    ...
  </port>
  <port name="HelloService1HttpPost"
    ...
  </port>
</service>
```

6.5   CODING A SOAP CLIENT

The WSDL standard for describing Web services means that we can query a service description and discover information about it. For example, listing 6.3 presents a simple program which queries a service at a given URL and displays the service name, description, and ports.

Listing 6.3   Querying a service description

```
// file:    wsdldesc.cs
// compile: csc wsdldesc.cs

namespace WsdlServices {

  using System;
```

```
using System.Xml;
using System.Web.Services.Description;

class WsdlDesc {

  public static void Main(string[] args) {

    string url;
    if (args.Length > 0)
      url = args[0];
    else
      url = "http://localhost/ws/helloservice1.asmx?WSDL";

    ServiceDescription desc = ServiceDescription.Read(
      new XmlTextReader(url)
    );

    Console.WriteLine("url             : {0}", url);
    foreach (Service s in desc.Services) {
      Console.WriteLine("service name : {0}", s.Name);
      Console.WriteLine("description  : {0}", s.Documentation);
      Console.Write("ports          : ");
      foreach (Port p in s.Ports) {
        Console.Write("{0} ", p.Name);
      }
      Console.WriteLine();
    }
  }
}
```

The `System.Web.Services.Description.ServiceDescription` class provides an object-oriented model of a WSDL document which we can use to inspect or create WSDL documents. Compiling this program and executing it against the `HelloService1` service results in the output shown in figure 6.6.

Figure 6.6 Retrieving the description of HelloService1

Conceivably, we could use this technique to code a utility which can query a service description and automatically generate the code to build the necessary SOAP messages and call the service. However, we don't need to do so because .NET's *wsdl.exe* can do the work for us.

6.5.1 Generating the Web service proxy

The developer tools provided with the .NET SDK and Visual Studio .NET, remove the need for the developer to work at the SOAP level. Instead, clients make calls against a proxy object derived from the `System.Web.Services.Protocols.SoapHttpClientProtocol` and .NET takes care of setting up, formatting, and transmitting messages. The proxy class can be generated automatically using the command-line utility, *wsdl.exe*, as shown in figure 6.7.

Figure 6.7   Generating the HelloService1 proxy

By default, this generates the file, *HelloService1.cs*, in the current directory. Note the optional `/namespace:Hello` switch which causes *wsdl.exe* to place the generated proxy class in the `Hello` namespace. The `http://localhost/ws/helloservice1.asmx?WSDL` argument tells the utility to use the WSDL description at the specified URL. By default, *wsdl.exe* generates C# code. However, you can specify the language of your choice using the `/language` switch. For example, use `/language:VB` for Visual Basic.

HelloService1.cs is shown in listing 6.4.

Listing 6.4   The HelloService1.cs proxy

```
//------------------------------------------------------------
// <autogenerated>
//     This code was generated by a tool.
//     Runtime Version: 1.0.2914.16
//
//     Changes to this file may cause incorrect behavior and will
//     be lost if the code is regenerated.
// </autogenerated>
//------------------------------------------------------------

//
// This source code was auto-generated by wsdl, Version=1.0.2914.16.
//
namespace Hello {
  using System.Diagnostics;
```

```csharp
using System.Xml.Serialization;
using System;
using System.Web.Services.Protocols;
using System.Web.Services;

[System.Web.Services.WebServiceBindingAttribute(
  Name="HelloService1Soap",
  Namespace="http://manning.com/dotnet/webservices")]
public class HelloService1 :
  System.Web.Services.Protocols.SoapHttpClientProtocol {

    [System.Diagnostics.DebuggerStepThroughAttribute()]
    public HelloService1() {
        this.Url = "http://localhost/ws/helloservice1.asmx";
    }

    [System.Diagnostics.DebuggerStepThroughAttribute()]
    [System.Web.Services.Protocols.SoapDocumentMethodAttribute(
      "http://manning.com/dotnet/webservices/Greet",
      RequestNamespace="http://manning.com/dotnet/webservices",
      ResponseNamespace="http://manning.com/dotnet/webservices",
      Use=
        System.Web.Services.Description.SoapBindingUse.Literal,
      ParameterStyle=
        System.Web.Services.Protocols.SoapParameterStyle.Wrapped)]
    public string Greet(string name) {
        object[] results = this.Invoke("Greet", new object[] {
                    name});
        return ((string)(results[0]));
    }

    [System.Diagnostics.DebuggerStepThroughAttribute()]
    public System.IAsyncResult BeginGreet(
      string name,
      System.AsyncCallback callback,
      object asyncState) {
        return this.BeginInvoke("Greet", new object[] {
                    name}, callback, asyncState);
    }

    [System.Diagnostics.DebuggerStepThroughAttribute()]
    public string EndGreet(System.IAsyncResult asyncResult) {
        object[] results = this.EndInvoke(asyncResult);
        return ((string)(results[0]));
    }
  }
}
```

The generated file contains the `Hello.HelloService1` proxy class which is derived from `System.Web.Services.Protocols.SoapHttpClientProtocol`. It contains the following methods:

- HelloService1—The default constructor simply stores the URL of the service. Url is a public read/write property.

- Greet—This is the method we call to invoke the service synchronously. It calls SoapHttpClientProtocol's protected Invoke method. It passes the name of the remote method and the name argument, storing the returned string in the first element of the results array and returning it to the caller. As you can see, this arrangement shields the developer from the details of the underlying SOAP/XML/HTTP processing required to actually make the remote call.

- BeginGreet—This is the method we call to invoke the service asynchronously. In a loosely coupled, widely distributed environment such as the Web, we cannot be guaranteed that remote calls will return promptly, or at all. Using asynchronous calls will prevent the client from blocking while waiting for a response, and allow it to proceed with other tasks. We'll look at an example of asynchronous Web service invocation later in this chapter.

- EndGreet—This method is called to retrieve the result of an asynchronous request.

6.5.2 Coding the client

Now that we have a proxy class, we need to create a client which uses it to invoke the service. Listing 6.5 presents a client, *helloclient1.cs*, for this purpose.

Listing 6.5   A test client

```
// file:      helloclient1.cs
// compile:  csc /out:helloclient1.exe
//              helloclient1.cs helloservice1.cs

namespace Hello {

  using System;

  class HelloClient1 {
    public static void Main(string[] args) {
      HelloService1 h = new HelloService1();
      string name = "";
      if (args.Length > 0) name = args[0];
      Console.WriteLine(h.Greet(name));
    }
  }
}
```

The client creates an instance of HelloService1 and invokes its Greet method in the ordinary way. The fact that the object represents a remote Web service makes no difference since the local proxy takes care of marshaling the call.

6.5.3 Compiling and executing the client

To invoke the service, we compile the client, together with the generated proxy, and execute it, as shown in figure 6.8.

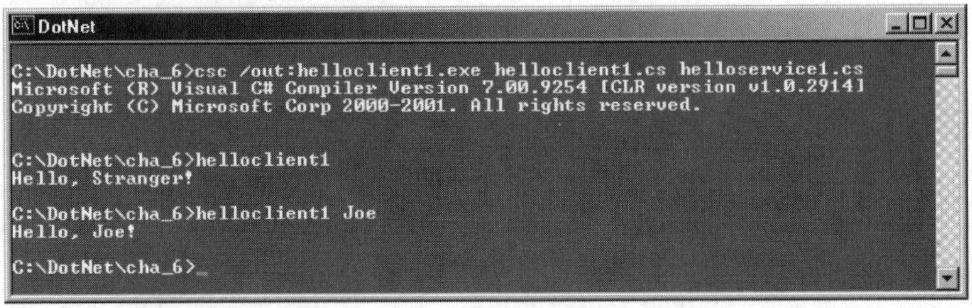

```
C:\DotNet\cha_6>csc /out:helloclient1.exe helloclient1.cs helloservice1.cs
Microsoft (R) Visual C# Compiler Version 7.00.9254 [CLR version v1.0.2914]
Copyright (C) Microsoft Corp 2000-2001. All rights reserved.


C:\DotNet\cha_6>helloclient1
Hello, Stranger!

C:\DotNet\cha_6>helloclient1 Joe
Hello, Joe!

C:\DotNet\cha_6>
```

Figure 6.8   Testing the Hello client

The client should execute as expected, with no discernible evidence that a remote Web service invocation is involved. In a wide-area scenario, where the service is physically distant from the client, you might find that occasionally the client is unable to connect and will time out, generating a System.Net.WebException in the process. You can trap this exception and attempt a recovery strategy. One strategy would be to increase the time-out value and/or try an alternative URL where a backup service is installed:

```
string response = "";
try {
  // invoke the service...
  response = hs.Greet(name);
} catch (System.Net.WebException) {
  // try backup URL...
  hs.Url = "http://backup_machine/ws/helloservice1.asmx";
  // and double the timeout...
  hs.Timeout *= 2;
  // and try again...
  response = hs.Greet(name);
}
```

6.5.4 Creating an asynchronous client

The previous example used a synchronous call to invoke the Greet method. This means that the client will block until the method returns or times out. We can use the asynchronous methods of the generated proxy class to allow the client to proceed with other tasks while waiting for a response from the service. Listing 6.6 illustrates the asynchronous approach.

Listing 6.6   Invoking Web methods asynchronously

```
// file:    helloclient1a.cs
// compile: csc /out:helloclient1a.exe
//              helloclient1a.cs helloservice1.cs

namespace Hello {

  using System;
  using System.Threading;
  using System.Runtime.Remoting.Messaging;
  using System.Web.Services.Protocols;

  class HelloClient1a {

    public static void Main(string[] args) {
      string name = "";
      if (args.Length > 0) name = args[0];
      new HelloClient1a(name);
    }

    public HelloClient1a(string name) {
      HelloService1 hs = new HelloService1();
      AsyncCallback ac = new AsyncCallback(this.GreetCallback);
      IAsyncResult ar = hs.BeginGreet(name, ac, hs);

      while (waitingOnReply) Thread.Sleep(500);
      Console.WriteLine("Done!");
    }

    private void GreetCallback(IAsyncResult ar) {
      HelloService1 hs = (HelloService1) ar.AsyncState;
      string reply = hs.EndGreet(ar);
      Console.WriteLine("callback: " + reply);
      waitingOnReply = false;
    }

    private bool waitingOnReply = true;
  }
}
```

This time the program uses the BeginGreet method, provided in the generated *helloservice1.cs* file, to invoke the service. We pass the Web method argument, an AsyncCallback object, and a reference to the service, as arguments. The client then sleeps until the callback method executes. The callback method retrieves the service reference and calls EndGreet to retrieve the returned result.

6.6   *THE WEBMAILSERVICE EXAMPLE*

Web services provide a simple, standardized way of exposing application or server functionality to any client that can talk XML and HTTP. Let's look at a realistic example of a useful Web service. Listing 6.7 presents a simple Web service that clients can use to send email via SMTP.

Listing 6.7   An SMTP mail Web service

```
<%@ WebService Language="C#" Class="WebMailService" %>

// file:         WebMailService.asmx
// description:  SMTP mail Web service

using System;
using System.Web.Services;
using System.Web.Mail;

[WebService(
  Description="An SMTP mail Web service",
  Namespace="http://manning.com/dotnet/webservices"
)]

public class WebMailService : WebService {

  [WebMethod(Description="Send an SMTP mail message")]
  public string Send(string from,
                     string to,
                     string subject,
                     string cc,
                     string bcc,
                     string body) {
    try {
      MailMessage msg = new MailMessage();
      msg.From = from;
      msg.To = to;
      msg.Subject = subject;
      msg.Cc = cc;
      msg.Bcc = bcc;
      msg.Body= body;
      // set SMTP server here, if necessary
      // SmtpMail.SmtpServer = "smtp.server.com";
      SmtpMail.Send(msg);
      return "OK";
    } catch (Exception e) {
      return "ERROR : " + e.Message;
    }
  }
}
```

This example uses the `System.Web.Mail.MailMessage` class to construct a mail message and send it using the static `SmtpMail.Send` method. To a client, the service exposes a single method which can be used to send an email:

```
WebMailService wms = new WebMailService();
wms.Send(fromStr, toStr, subjectStr, ccStr, bccStr, bodyStr);
```

If you browse this service at http://localhost/ws/webmailservice.asmx?op=Send you should get a ready-made page for sending simple emails as shown in figure 6.9. (You'll need to have SMTP configured on the server to use this service.)

Figure 6.9
The WebMailService
page

This simple example illustrates one of the benefits of Web services. In just a few lines of code, we have provided a simple platform independent interface to the Windows SMTP mail service.

6.7 *MANAGING SERVICE STATE*

Web services provide a stateless model similar to the `SingleCall` activation mode which we explored in the previous chapter when we looked at remoting. Therefore, when a client invokes a remote method, the server automatically constructs the relevant object, executes the method, returns any results, and discards the object. This is in keeping with the stateless nature of the HTTP protocol. In this section, we explore ways of maintaining state between method calls and we see how to emulate singleton and client-activated modes of operation.

6.7.1 Creating a stateful Web service

Web services can make use of ASP.NET's state management capabilities to augment services with the ability to store session- and application-based state information. We can use these features to emulate something akin to remoting's singleton and client-activated models. Listing 6.8 presents a new version of our earlier sample service, *helloservice2.asmx*, which stores session state between requests. This version counts the number of times the service is invoked, and the number of times the Greet method is called by an individual client.

Listing 6.8   Saving session state in a Web service

```
<%@ WebService Language="C#" Class="HelloService2" %>

// file:         helloservice2.asmx
// description:  hello web service with session state info

using System.Web.Services;

[WebService(
  Description="A stateful greeting Web service",
  Namespace="http://manning.com/dotnet/webservices"
)]

public class HelloService2 : WebService {

  public HelloService2() {
    if (newSession) {
      newSession = false; // no longer a new session
      numInst = 0;        // no instances so far
      numGreet = 0;       // no greetings yet either
    }
    numInst++;
  }

  [WebMethod(
    Description="Greet by name.",
    EnableSession= true
  )]
  public string Greet(string name) {
    numGreet++;
    if (name == "") name = "Stranger";
    return "Hello, " + name + "!";
  }

  [WebMethod(
    Description="Get number of greetings.",
    EnableSession= true
  )]
  public int NumGreet() {
    return numGreet; // return private property
  }

  [WebMethod(
    Description="Get number of times constructor invoked.",
    EnableSession= true
  )]
  public int NumInst() {
    return numInst; // return private property
  }
```

```
    private bool newSession {
      // wraps Session["newSession"] in a private property
      get {
        if (Session["newSession"] == null) return true;
        return (bool) Session["newSession"];
      }
      set {
        Session["newSession"] = value;
      }
    }
  private int numGreet {
    // wraps Session["numGreet"] in a private property
    get {
      return (int) Session["numGreet"];
    }
    set {
      Session["numGreet"] = value;
    }
  }
  private int numInst {
    // wraps Session["numInst"] in a private property
    get {
      return (int) Session["numInst"];
    }
    set {
      Session["numInst"] = value;
    }
  }
}
```

The new service uses the Session property to reference the HttpSessionState
object for the current session. For convenience, we wrap session variables inside private class properties:

```
private bool newSession {
  // wraps Session["newSession"] in a private property
  get {
    if (Session["newSession"] == null) return true;
    return (bool) Session["newSession"];
  }
  set {
    Session["newSession"] = value;
  }
}
```

This allows us to use the more natural:

```
if (newSession) ...
```

instead of:

```
if (Session["newSession"]) ...
```

Since the constructor is called every time the service is invoked, we need to check that this is indeed a new session before we initialize the session variables:

```
public HelloService2() {
  if (newSession) {
    newSession = false; // no longer a new session
    numInst = 0;        // no instances so far
    numGreet = 0;       // no greetings yet either
  }
  numInst++;
}
```

The private `numInst` property records the number of times the class is instantiated, while the `numGreet` property counts the number of times the `Greet` Web method is invoked. The public `NumInst` and `NumGreet` Web methods return these values to the client. Note that the `WebMethod` attribute must set `EnableSession=true` for each method that uses session data. We'll use cookies in the client to take advantage of this.

6.7.2   Creating the stateful client

The new client is presented in listing 6.9.

Listing 6.9   Enabling session state in the client

```
// file:    helloclient2.cs
// compile: csc /out:helloclient2.exe
//              helloclient2.cs helloservice2.cs

namespace Hello {

  using System;
  using System.Net;

  class HelloClient2 {

    public static void Main(string[] args) {

      HelloService2 h = new HelloService2();

      string argLine = String.Join(" ", args).ToLower() + " ";
      if (argLine.IndexOf("/state") >= 0)
        h.CookieContainer = new CookieContainer(); // enable state
      else
        h.CookieContainer = null; // stateless

      for (int i = 0; i < 3; i++) {
        Console.WriteLine(h.Greet("Mary"));
        Console.WriteLine("Num. Greet.: {0}", h.NumGreet());
        Console.WriteLine("Num. Inst.: {0}", h.NumInst());
      }
    }
  }
}
```

This client accepts an optional command-line /state switch to turn on stateful execution. If this switch is set, the client enables the use of cookies with the service, as follows:

```
h.CookieContainer = new CookieContainer(); // enable state
```

This creates a new cookie container which enables client and service to retain state information by enabling cookies for the session.

6.7.3 Testing the stateful service

Once again, we use *wsdl.exe* to generate the service proxy which we compile into the client, as shown in figure 6.10.

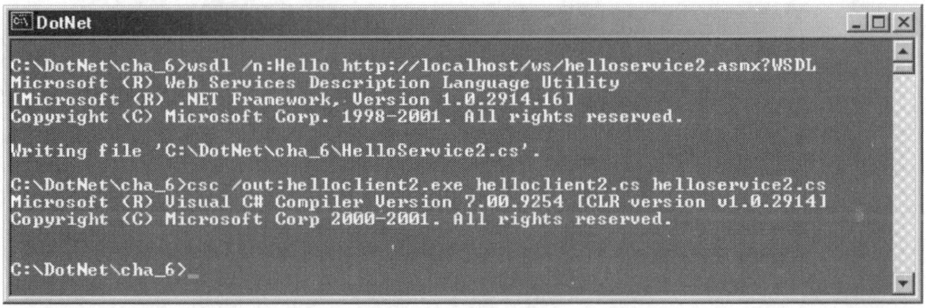

Figure 6.10 Building the stateful service

Now, let's execute the client, first without cookies, and then with cookies enabled. See figure 6.11.

With cookies disabled, the count of the number of times the Greet method was invoked is always zero, while the count of the number of times the service was invoked

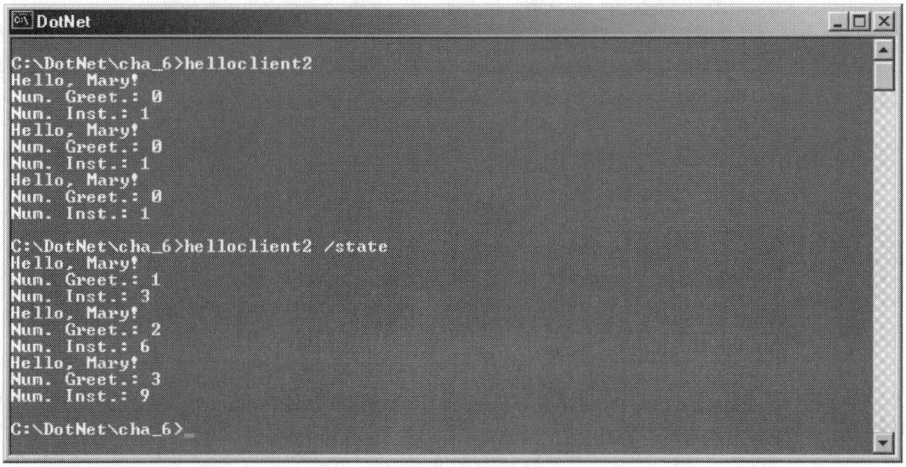

Figure 6.11 Testing the stateful service

is always one. (The `NumInst` call necessarily invokes the service.) Setting the `/state` switch enables cookies causing the correct count to be returned. This essentially emulates remoting's client-activated behavior which we explored in the previous chapter.

6.7.4 Example: logging into a Web service

You could use the stateful approach to provide application-level login/logout for a service. Listing 6.10 presents a `StringCaseService` service which requires the client to login in order to call the `ToUpper` and `ToLower` Web methods. In contrast, the `GetLength` method can be executed without logging in.

Listing 6.10 StringCaseService

```
<%@ WebService Language="C#" Class="StringCaseService" %>

// file:        stringcaseservice.asmx
// description: A web service to change string case.
//              Requires user to login first.
using System.Web.Services;
using System.Security;

[WebService(
  Description="A web service to change case.  Requires login.",
  Namespace="http://manning.com/dotnet/webservices"
)]

public class StringCaseService : WebService {

  [WebMethod(
    Description="Login with username and password.",
    EnableSession= true
  )]
  public bool Login(string username, string password) {
    loggedIn = false; // logout existing user, if any
    if (username == "jbloggs" && password == "secret")
      loggedIn = true;
    return loggedIn;
  }

  [WebMethod(
    Description="Logout.",
    EnableSession= true
  )]
  public void Logout() {
    loggedIn = false; // logout existing user
  }

  [WebMethod(
    Description="Uppercase a string. Must be logged in to call.",
    EnableSession= true
  )]
  public string ToUpper(string s) {
    requireLogin();
```

```
    return s.ToUpper();
  }

  [WebMethod(
    Description="Lowercase a string. Must be logged in to call.",
    EnableSession= true
  )]
  public string ToLower(string s) {
    requireLogin();
    return s.ToLower();
  }

  [WebMethod(
    Description="Return string length."
  )]
  public int GetLength(string s) {
    // login not necessary...
    return s.Length;
  }

  private void requireLogin() {
    if (!loggedIn)
      throw new SecurityException("Client not logged in!");
  }

  private bool loggedIn {
    get {
      if (Session["loggedIn"] == null) return false;
      return (bool) Session["loggedIn"];
    }
    set {
      Session["loggedIn"] = value;
    }
  }
}
}
```

This time we have a single private `loggedIn` property which we set to `true` when the client successfully logs in. Those methods that require the client to log in, namely `ToUpper` and `ToLower`, call `requireLogin` before doing any work. The latter raises a `SecurityException` if the client is not logged in. A client for this service is shown in listing 6.11.

Listing 6.11   StringCaseClient

```
// file:    stringcaseclient.cs
// compile: csc /out:stringcaseclient.exe
//              stringcaseservice.cs stringcaseclient.cs

namespace StringCase {

  using System;
  using System.Net;
```

```
class StringCaseClient {

  public static void Main(string[] args) {

    StringCaseService scs = new StringCaseService();
    scs.CookieContainer = new CookieContainer(); // enable state

    string s = "Hello";

    Console.WriteLine("length of {0} : {1}", s, scs.GetLength(s));
    Console.WriteLine(
      "logging in mmouse:secret : {0}",
      scs.Login("mmouse", "secret")
    );
    Console.WriteLine(
      "logging in jbloggs:secret : {0}",
      scs.Login("jbloggs", "secret")
    );
    Console.WriteLine("ToUpper {0} : {1}", s, scs.ToUpper(s));
    Console.WriteLine("ToLower {0} : {1}", s, scs.ToLower(s));
    Console.WriteLine("Logging out...");
    scs.Logout();
    Console.WriteLine("Logged out.");

    // following call will raise a client-side SoapException...
    Console.WriteLine("ToLower {0} : {1}", s, scs.ToLower(s));
  }
 }
}
```

Once again we enable cookies to support session state. We execute GetLength
before we log in. Next, we make an unsuccessful login attempt, followed by a success-
ful login. Then we call ToUpper and ToLower before we log out. Finally, we
attempt to call ToLower again after we have logged out.

To test the client, execute *wsdl.exe* to generate the proxy. Then compile and execute
the client. The program should end in an exception because we tried to invoke the
ToLower method after the client logged out.

> **NOTE** When implementing a scheme such as this, the service should be exposed
> via a Secure Sockets Layer (SSL) connection to prevent the username and
> password being sent in clear text. Also, note that you cannot secure just the
> Login Web method with SSL, while leaving other service methods unse-
> cured. Instead, you must implement the Login function as a separate se-
> cured service.

6.7.5 Maintaining state without cookies

If you're implementing application-level security to authenticate users of your Web
service, you could avoid using cookies by using a user's identity to generate a key for
the duration of a session:

CHAPTER 6 DEVELOPING XML WEB SERVICES

```
[WebMethod(Description="Login to Web service.")]
public string Login(string username, string password) {
  if (isSubscriber(username, password)) {
    string key = genKey(username,
                        Context.Request.UserHostAddress,
                        DateTime.Now.ToString()
                        );
    addKey(key, username);
    return key;
  }
  return "";
}
```

The Login method checks that the caller is a current subscriber. If so, it calls gen-Key to generate a session key using the caller's username, IP address, and the current time. (The current time could be used to expire a session after a certain time has elapsed.) Thereafter, the caller must include the key as the first parameter in each method invocation:

```
[WebMethod(Description="Greet by name.")]
public string Greet(string key, string name) {
  if (!validKey(key))
    throw new SecurityException ("Invalid session key!");
  return "Hello, " + name + "!";
}
```

Each secured Web method should check the key and throw an exception if the key is invalid. For example, we might design genKey to perform a cryptographic hash on the generated key using a secret password known only to our Web service. (Coding genKey is left as an exercise.) The validKey key-validation routine would first recompute the hash and immediately reject the key if the hash does not compute. Only after the hash successfully computes, should the key be looked up in our database and the username retrieved.

Finally, you might wish to create a Logout method to delete the session key from storage:

```
[WebMethod(Description="Logout of Web service.")]
public void Logout(string key) {
  if (!validKey(key))
    throw new SecurityException ("Invalid session key!");
  delKey(key);
}
```

6.7.6   Emulating singleton activation

Before we close our discussion of stateful Web services, let's quickly see how we can emulate a singleton service. The solution is simple. We use ASP.NET's application-level, instead of session-level, storage. Listing 6.12 presents a third version of our HelloService. This version counts the number of times the Greet method has been called by all clients since the service was launched.

Listing 6.12   Storing application-level state in a Web service

```
<%@ WebService Language="C#" Class="HelloService3" %>

// file:        helloservice3.asmx
// description: hello web service with application state info

using System.Web.Services;

[WebService(
  Description="A stateful greeting Web service",
  Namespace="http://manning.com/dotnet/webservices"
)]

public class HelloService3 : WebService {

  [WebMethod(Description="Greet by name.")]
  public string Greet(string name) {
    numGreet++;
    if (name == "") name = "Stranger";
    return "Hello, " + name + "!";
  }

  [WebMethod(Description="Get number of greetings.")]
  public int NumGreet() {
    return numGreet;
  }

  private int numGreet {
    get {
      if (Application["numGreet"] == null) return 0;
      return (int) Application["numGreet"];
    }
    set {
      Application.Lock();
        if (Application["numGreet"] == null)
          Application["numGreet"] = 0;
        Application["numGreet"] = value;
      Application.UnLock();
    }
  }
}
}
```

This time we use ASP.NET's `Application` object to store the data. In effect, the `numGreet` property can be looked upon as a static property of the service, shared by all instances.

We won't bother to create a test client in this case. Instead, you can use your browser to test the service at http://localhost/ws/helloservice3.asmx. Launch several instances of the browser and note how the number of greetings is shared by all clients.

6.8   *ENABLING WEB SERVICE DISCOVERY*

The process of locating Web services and retrieving their WSDL contracts is known as *Web service discovery.* Discovery can be facilitated by storing a so-called DISCO file with the service, or at an appropriate URL such as in a UDDI registry. The DISCO file is a regular XML document which provides links to the WSDL contract and associated documentation.

6.8.1 Generating a DISCO document

The XML Web services infrastructure will automatically generate a bare-bones DISCO file for your service. Point your browser to http://localhost/ws/-helloservice1.asmx?DISCO to generate the DISCO document shown in figure 6.12.

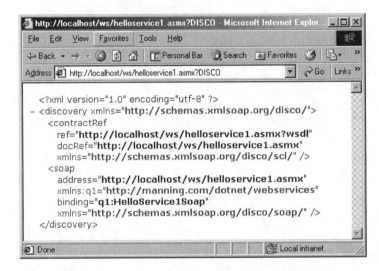

Figure 6.12
Browsing a DISCO document

In this case, the DISCO document provides a link to the WSDL contract and a docRef documentation link to the service itself. It also provides the address and binding information for the service.

You can also generate and save a DISCO document for your service using the *disco.exe* utility, as shown in figure 6.13.

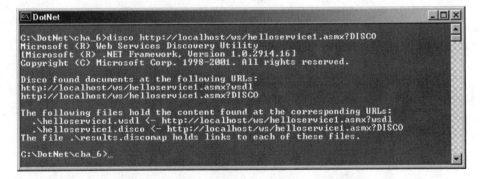

Figure 6.13   Generating a DISCO document

This generates three files in the local directory:

- *helloservice1.wsdl*—The service's WSDL contract.
- *helloservice1.disco*—The service's discovery document.
- *results.discomap*—A discovery client results file containing links to both the contract and the discovery document, as shown in listing 6.13.

Listing 6.13   results.discomap

```
<?xml version="1.0" encoding="utf-8"?>
<DiscoveryClientResultsFile
  xmlns:xsi="http://www.w3.org/2001/XMLSchema-instance"
  xmlns:xsd="http://www.w3.org/2001/XMLSchema">

 <Results>
  <DiscoveryClientResult
    referenceType=
      "System.Web.Services.Discovery.ContractReference"
    url="http://localhost/ws/helloservice1.asmx?wsdl"
    filename="helloservice1.wsdl" />
  <DiscoveryClientResult
    referenceType=
      "System.Web.Services.Discovery.DiscoveryDocumentReference"
    url="http://localhost/ws/helloservice1.asmx?DISCO"
    filename="helloservice1.disco" />
 </Results>

</DiscoveryClientResultsFile>
```

6.8.2   Creating a default.disco file

DISCO documents can point to other DISCO documents, thus building a discovery hierarchy. For example, we could store a master DISCO document at a root URL such as http://www.MyCompany.com/default.disco. Then, using the Framework's System.Web.Services.Discovery.DiscoveryDocument class, we could enumerate all the public services at the site. Listing 6.14 presents a *default.disco* document which references some of the sample Web services we have developed so far.

Listing 6.14   A sample default.disco file

```
<?xml version="1.0" encoding="utf-8"?>
<discovery
  xmlns:xsi="http://www.w3.org/2001/XMLSchema-instance"
  xmlns:xsd="http://www.w3.org/2001/XMLSchema"
  xmlns="http://schemas.xmlsoap.org/disco/">

 <discoveryRef
   ref="http://localhost/ws/helloservice1.asmx?DISCO" />
 <discoveryRef
   ref="http://localhost/ws/helloservice2.asmx?DISCO" />
```

```
    <discoveryRef
      ref="http://localhost/ws/helloservice3.asmx?DISCO" />

</discovery>
```

6.8.3   Processing a default.disco file

Listing 6.15 is a short program which extracts references to other DISCO files from
this DISCO file. For each extracted reference, the program retrieves the new DISCO
file and displays the contract reference.

Listing 6.15   Processing the default.disco file

```
// file:    alldisco.cs
// compile: csc alldisco.cs

namespace WsdlServices {

  using System;
  using System.Xml;
  using System.Web.Services.Discovery;

  class WsdlDesc {

    public static void Main(string[] args) {

      string url;
      if (args.Length > 0)
        url = args[0];
      else
        url = "http://localhost/ws/default.disco";

      DiscoveryDocument desc = DiscoveryDocument.Read(
        new XmlTextReader(url)
      );

      Console.WriteLine("default : {0}", url);
      // get each discovery reference...
      foreach (object o in desc.References) {
        if (o is DiscoveryReference) {
          DiscoveryReference d = (DiscoveryReference) o;
          Console.WriteLine("========================");
          // get the WSDL contract...
          discover(d.Url);
        }
      }
    }

    public static void discover(string url) {
      // get WSDL contract at this URL...
      DiscoveryDocument desc = DiscoveryDocument.Read(
        new XmlTextReader(url)
      );
      Console.WriteLine("url     : {0}", url);
      foreach (object o in desc.References) {
        if (o is ContractReference) {
          ContractReference c = (ContractReference) o;
```

```
        Console.WriteLine("Ref      :  {0}", c.Ref);
        Console.WriteLine("DocRef :  {0}", c.DocRef);
      }
    }
  }
}
}
```

We call `DiscoveryDocument.Read` to load the DISCO document from the supplied URL. Then we look through any discovery references, retrieve them in turn, and display details of their contracts. Compiling and executing this program produces the output shown in figure 6.14.

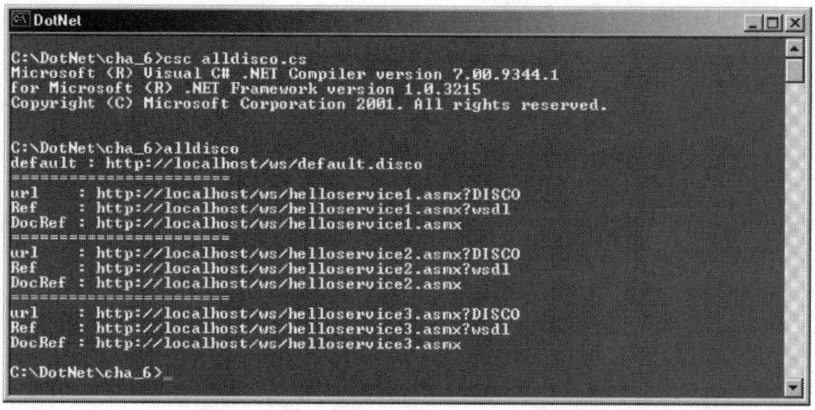

Figure 6.14   Processing the default.disco file

The combination of DISCO, WSDL, and .NET's proxy generation ability gives us a robust framework for the automatic discovery and inspection of Web services and for the creation of client applications which use those services.

6.9   USING UDDI TO ADVERTISE A WEB SERVICE

The UDDI specification represents the combined efforts of several technology companies to produce a global Internet-based registry of businesses and the services they provide. The idea is that business partners will be able to efficiently discover each other and interact through published, standards-based services.

In chapter 1, we considered the example of a loan department in a bank using Web services to communicate with business partners. The department produced a Web service to allow a collection agency to hook its own applications into the bank's loan system and extract delinquent accounts as required. The loan department also acted as consumer of a credit agency Web service which provided real-time credit reports on the bank's loan applicants. These are examples of business partners using Web service technology to communicate with each other's applications in a standardized, platform-independent way. UDDI is designed to help such partners discover and interact with one another.

Some of the functionality of UDDI is similar to the Yellow Pages. If you know the service you want, you can search the UDDI registry to find potential providers of that service. You can tailor your search to specific companies, industries, or geographical areas. Alternatively, you might simply use the UDDI registry to retrieve contact information for a particular company. In either case, you can search manually using a Web browser, or automatically using a SOAP-based client application. The UDDI registry API is itself exposed as a Web service to facilitate programmatic searching. (This would be a case of invoking a service to find a service.)

UDDI is a comprehensive standard worthy of a book in its own right. However, at the time of writing, it has yet to be widely adopted by business, and the public UDDI test and production registries appear largely unused. Therefore, we'll examine UDDI only briefly here. We'll take a look at the public Microsoft UDDI registry. We'll also use the UDDI SDK to write a client application which can interact with a UDDI registry, search for businesses and services, and retrieve service descriptions.

Of course, you don't have to publish your Web service. In fact, it is likely that many custom Web services will be used by other in-house departments, or that they will be specialized to the individual requirements of unique business engagements. Such services will be of no interest to the larger marketplace and should not be published. (Of course, this does not preclude the use of private UDDI registries to serve closed communities.)

6.9.1   Searching the UDDI registry

At the time of writing, there were two beta UDDI implementations:

- http://uddi.microsoft.com
- http://www.ibm.com/services/uddi

From both sites you can navigate the registry, search for businesses and services, and, with the proper authorization, publish your own services. Also, Microsoft and IBM provide both test and production registries. The former can be used in the development and test of UDDI clients.

If you visit http://uddi.microsoft.com, and click the Search link, you should be presented with a search form similar to that shown in figure 6.15.

The list box on the right allows you to search the registry by categories such as business name or location, service type, and several important international and North American standardized categories:

- *SIC codes*—Standard Industrial Classification codes were developed by the U.S. Department of Labor to classify industries. These are numerical codes with associated alphanumeric descriptions and they cover everything from Irish potatoes, SIC 0134, to antitank rocket launchers, SIC 3489. Categories are classified into hierarchical groups of related industries.

- *NAICS codes*—North American Industry Classification System codes were developed jointly by the U.S., Mexico, and Canada, to replace the SIC classification system. Like SIC, NAICS is a hierarchical, numerical system for classifying industries and business sectors.

- *UNSPSC*—Universal Standard Products and Services Classification is a system of 8-digit numerical codes which provide a hierarchical classification system. They are divided into four 2-digit elements which specify the segment, family, class, and commodity to which the product or service belongs. For example, 25.10.18.01 denotes motorcycles, while scooters are 25.10.18.02 and mopeds are 25.10.18.03.

- *ISO 3166 Geographic Taxonomy*—This is an international standard for the representation of geographic areas using codes for individual countries and their subdivisions. For example, California is US-CA, while IT-MI is the Italian province of Milano. You can use this code to narrow a UDDI registry search by geographic area.

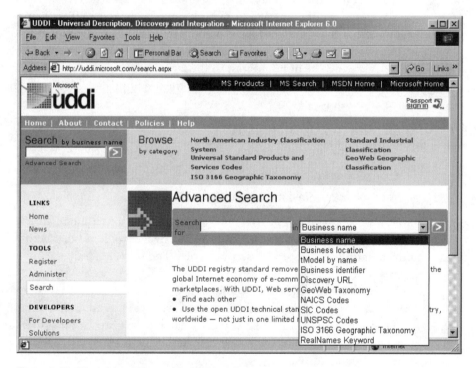

Figure 6.15   Searching Microsoft's UDDI registry

If you are familiar with the standardized codes, they typically offer the ability to perform a much more tightly focused search than regular keywords.

Let's explore a client application that can interact with the UDDI registry. First, we need to install Microsoft's UDDI SDK.

6.9.2   Installing the UDDI SDK and test registry

At the time of writing, the UDDI .NET SDK, *Microsoft.UDDI.SDK.v1.5.2.exe*, was available as a separate download from http://uddi.microsoft.com/developer. Downloading and installing the SDK should create the *C:\Program Files\Microsoft UDDI SDK* directory containing the *Microsoft.Uddi.Sdk.dll* assembly.

> **NOTE**   When I installed the SDK, the UDDI assembly was not automatically installed in the global assembly cache. You can do this yourself (see chapter 2) or copy it to your working directory for now.

In addition to the UDDI assembly, the SDK can install a private registry on your machine which requires Microsoft SQL Server or MSDE to host the data. We won't use the private registry for our example.

6.9.3   Creating a simple inquiry client using the UDDI SDK

We begin with a simple client which searches the UDDI test registry. The URL of the inquiry service for Microsoft's test registry is http://test.uddi.microsoft.com/inquire. Listing 6.16 presents the code for a simple program which will search the registry for business names beginning with a certain string.

Listing 6.16   Searching the UDDI registry by business name

```
// file    : uddifindbus.cs
// compile : csc /r:microsoft.uddi.sdk.dll uddifindbus.cs
// note    : make sure microsoft.uddi.sdk.dll is installed...
//            in global cache, or copy to working directory

namespace UddiTest {

  using System;
  using Microsoft.Uddi;          // from UDDI SDK
  using Microsoft.Uddi.Api;      // from UDDI SDK
  using Microsoft.Uddi.Business; // from UDDI SDK

  public class FindBus {

    public static void Main(string[] args) {

      Inquire.Url = "http://test.uddi.microsoft.com/inquire";

      FindBusiness fb = new FindBusiness();
      if (args.Length == 0)
        fb.Name = "Joe";
      else
        fb.Name = args[0];
      Console.WriteLine("searching for {0}...", fb.Name);

      fb.MaxRows = 5; // no more than 5 businesses
      BusinessList bl = fb.Send(); // get the list
      foreach(BusinessInfo bi in bl.BusinessInfos) {
        Console.WriteLine("=================================");
        Console.WriteLine(bi.Name); // the business name
```

```
        foreach(Description d in bi.Descriptions) {
          Console.WriteLine(d.Text); // the business description
        }
      }

      Console.WriteLine("Done!");
    }
  }
}
```

To start, we reference the `Microsoft.Uddi` namespaces. In the `Main` routine we set the static `Url` property of the `Microsoft.Uddi.Inquire` class to point to the URL of the inquiry service. We'll be searching businesses by name, so we create a new `FindBusiness` class and store a partial business name in its `Name` property. We use the `Send` method to perform the search and capture the result in a `BusinessList`. Then we loop through the list to display the results, as shown in figure 6.16.

Figure 6.16   Finding a business

As you can see, we got just three results including a suspiciously familiar provider of video poker services.

6.9.4   More on UDDI

The previous introduction just scratches the surface of UDDI. The UDDI API provides full support for registering and administering business entities, and services, and for searching the registry. For more information on the emerging UDDI standard try the following sites:

- *http://www.uddi.org*—The UDDI program management team's site
- *http://uddi.microsoft.com/developer*—Microsoft's UDDI developer site
- *http://www.ibm.com/services/uddi/*—IBM's UDDI site

Before we move on, note that the UDDI inquiry API is itself exposed as a Web service. This allows us to dispense with the proprietary SDK and generate a proxy for use in developing our own UDDI clients. This is a good example of the power of the Web services model.

6.10 *WSPok*: THE *WEB SERVICE-BASED POKER GAME*

Like all other versions, the Web service-based version of the poker game will use the same *poker.dll* assembly. Our Web service will provide Web methods to deal and draw cards.

Create a virtual directory called *wspok* on your Web server and associate it with a suitable working directory. We'll create our Web service, *wspokservice.asmx*, in this directory. Also create a *bin* subdirectory and place the *poker.dll* assembly in it.

6.10.1 Creating the WSPokService poker Web service

Our poker Web service will be just a few lines of code to wrap the public `Simple-Machine.Deal` and `SimpleMachine.Draw` methods. Also, like the remoting version, *rempokservice.cs*, we'll use a `GameResult` struct to return the game result. Listing 6.17 presents the poker Web service, *wspokservice.asmx*.

Listing 6.17   The poker Web service

```
<%@ WebService Language="C#" Class="WSPokService" %>

// file:         WSPokService.asmx
// description:  poker machine web service

using System.Web.Services;
using Poker;

[WebService(
  Description="A Poker Web service",
  Namespace="http://manning.com/dotnet/webservices"
)]

public class WSPokService : WebService {

  [WebMethod(Description="Deal a poker hand.")]
  public string Deal() {
    return new SimpleMachine().Deal().Text;
  }

  [WebMethod(Description="Draw cards.")]
  public GameResult Draw(string oldHand, string holdCards) {
    GameResult g = new GameResult();
    Hand h = new SimpleMachine().Draw(oldHand, holdCards);
    g.Hand = h.Text;
    g.Score = h.Score;
    g.Title = h.Title;
    return g;
```

```
  }
}
public struct GameResult {
  public string Hand;
  public int Score;
  public string Title;
}
```

The `WebService` attribute contains a description and a unique namespace for the service, while the `WSPokService` class provides the familiar `Deal` and `Draw` methods. Browsing the service should produce the page shown in figure 6.17.

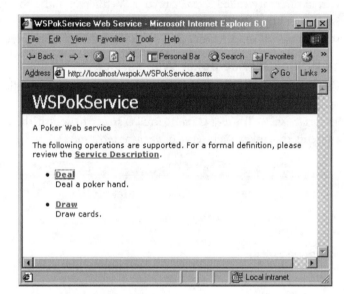

**Figure 6.17
Browsing the
WSPokService
poker Web service**

6.10.2 Creating the WSPok client

As usual, run the *wsdl.exe* utility to generate the client proxy:

```
wsdl /namespace:Poker http://localhost/wspok/wspokservice.asmx
```

This will generate the *wspokservice.cs* file containing definitions for both the `Poker.WSPokService` and `Poker.GameResult` classes.

All that remains is to code the simple client shown in listing 6.18.

Listing 6.18   The WSPok client

```
// file    : WSPok.cs
// compile : csc /out:WSPok.exe WSPokService.cs WSPok.cs

namespace Poker {

  using System;
```

```
class WSPok {

  public static void Main() {
    new WSPok(); // start game
  }

  public WSPok() {
    Console.WriteLine("A WebService-based poker game...");
    Console.WriteLine("Hit Ctrl-c at any time to abort.\n");
    service = new WSPokService(); // create poker service
    while (true) nextGame(); // play
  }

  private void nextGame() {

    string dealHand = service.Deal(); // deal hand
    Console.WriteLine(dealHand); // display it
    Console.Write("Enter card numbers (1 to 5) to hold: ");
    string holdCards = Console.ReadLine();

    // draw replacement cards...
    GameResult res = service.Draw(dealHand, holdCards);
    Console.WriteLine(res.Hand);
    Console.WriteLine(res.Title);
    Console.WriteLine("Score = {0}\n", res.Score);
  }

  private WSPokService service;
  }
}
```

This is almost identical to previous simple console-based versions of the game. This time, however, most of the heavy work takes place on the Web server.

6.10.3 Testing the poker Web service

To test the service, compile and run the client, as shown in figure 6.18.

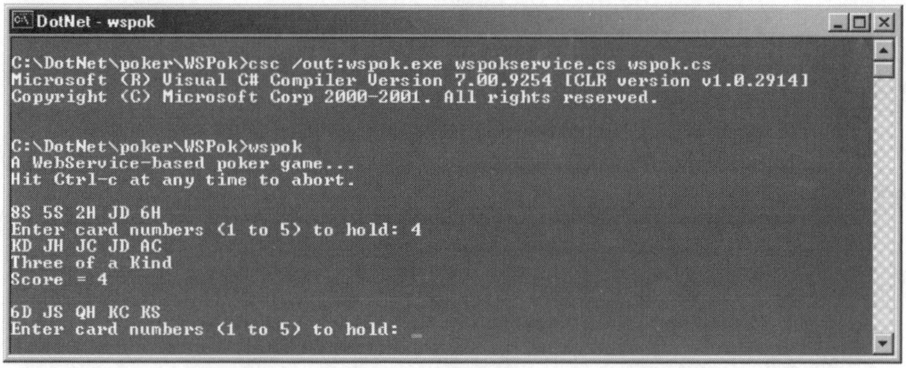

Figure 6.18   Testing WSPokService

6.11 SUMMARY

We've come a long way in this chapter. We started by presenting Web services and noting the advantages of this technology over previous alternatives such as DCOM and CORBA. By being founded on simple, open standards, Web services provide a simple model for interconnecting applications across the Internet.

We developed simple services and built both synchronous and asynchronous clients to invoke these services. We looked at WSDL contracts and generated proxies using the *wsdl.exe* utility. We also examined important techniques for maintaining state across method calls.

We explored DISCO and UDDI and saw how these initiatives are designed to help potential clients discover services. Finally, as usual, we put our knowledge to work by implementing a poker Web service and client.

Although, at the time of writing, Web services are in their infancy, there can be little doubt that this technology will be a hit with developers. It provides the means to leverage the Internet as a huge repository of callable services and a way to expose application functionality to a potentially vast audience. Most importantly, it achieves this using simple, open standards.

In the next chapter, we examine Windows Forms which provide a new model for building traditional Windows GUI applications.

CHAPTER 7

Creating the Windows Forms user interface

Windows Forms is Microsoft's new forms-based programming model for creating Windows GUI applications. In the past Windows developers have used C/SDK or MFC, or Visual Basic, to build Windows applications. Each approach had its own special advantages, disadvantages, quirks, and limitations. Using C with the Windows SDK, a simple "Hello, World!" program took almost 100 lines of code. The drudgery was somewhat alleviated by the introduction of Visual C++ 1.0 and the Microsoft Foundation Classes (MFC) which provided a class library for the automation of many tedious programming tasks. At the same time, Visual Basic programmers enjoyed a highly productive drag-drop environment for creating GUI applications, although those applications were limited in their access to the underlying operating system. Windows Forms provides a new unified model that is fully integrated into the .NET Framework, independent of the programming language, and almost as simple as the Visual Basic approach.

So far, we have avoided using Windows Forms in our examples. The code required to set up a form, position controls, and hook up event handlers, tends to obscure the point of even simple examples. However, Windows Forms programming is not difficult and much of the tedious work can be avoided by using the automated wizards, and drag-drop designer, provided by Visual Studio .NET. On the other hand, this automation makes it more difficult for the beginner to learn the programming model. We compromise in this section by hand-coding our simple examples and the Windows Forms version of our poker game, WinPok. Then we revisit WinPok and recreate the GUI using Visual Studio .NET.

7.1 BEGINNING WINDOWS FORMS DEVELOPMENT

Creating a simple Windows Forms application involves creating the form to represent the main application window, adding any necessary controls such as buttons, menus, check boxes, and labels, and displaying the form on the screen. Let's explore some simple examples.

7.1.1 Creating a simple form

Listing 7.1 presents a bare-bones Windows Forms application. It just displays a window, centers it on the screen, and shows a message in the title bar.

Listing 7.1 A first Windows Form

```
// file    : firstform.cs
// compile : csc /t:winexe firstform.cs

using System.Windows.Forms; // for the Form class

namespace MyForms {

  public class FirstForm : Form {

    public static void Main() {
      // create form and start Windows message loop...
      Application.Run(new FirstForm());
    }

    public FirstForm() {
      Text = "My First Form"; // title bar text
      Width = 200;            // form width
      Height = 100;           // form height
      CenterToScreen();       // display center screen
    }
  }
}
```

The form represents the application's main window. Use the /t:winexe switch to tell the compiler that you are building a Windows Forms application. If you don't, you'll see

Figure 7.1
Displaying a basic form

an ugly console window behind your form when you execute the program. Figure 7.1 shows the form displayed by this simple program.

You typically create a Windows Forms application by deriving a new class from the `System.Windows.Forms.Form` class. Then, to execute the application, create an instance of your new form class and call `Application.Run` passing the class instance. This shows the form and begins running a standard Windows message loop on the current thread. (We'll look at the Windows message loop later in this chapter when we explore `WndProc`.) In the form's constructor, you typically set up the GUI by creating controls such as buttons, menus, check boxes, text boxes, and labels. In this example, we just set the form's title bar text, its width and height, and we center it on the screen. All are public instance properties of the base `Form` class.

`Application.Run` is one of several static members provided by the `Application` class to start and stop an application, process Windows messages, provide information about the application, and so forth. For example, to end an application, you can call `Application.Exit`, and to allow messages to proceed while your program is busy looping, you can call `Application.DoEvents`. The `Application` class also provides convenient static properties for retrieving the application name and version.

7.1.2 Adding controls to a form

Listing 7.2 presents a second version of our simple form. This version contains a button which displays the current time in the form's title bar when clicked.

Listing 7.2 Adding a button control

```
// file    : secondform.cs
// compile : csc /t:winexe secondform.cs

using System;
using System.Windows.Forms;

namespace MyForms {

  public class SecondForm : Form {

    public static void Main() {
      // create form and start Windows message loop...
      Application.Run(new SecondForm());
    }

    public SecondForm() {

      // set up the form...
      Width = 250;              // form width
      Height = 100;             // form height
      CenterToScreen();         // display form center screen
```

```
    // set up the button...
    Button b = new Button();    // create button
    b.Text = "Show Time";       // set button text
    b.Width = 100;              // set button width
    b.Top = 20;                 // set top coordinate
    b.Left = 30;                // set left coordinate

    // set up click event handler...
    b.Click += new EventHandler(clickHandler);

    // add the control to the form...
    Controls.Add(b);
  }
  private void clickHandler(object sender, EventArgs e) {
    // user has clicked button, so...
    // display current time...
    Text = String.Format("Click Time: {0:T}", DateTime.Now);
  }
 }
}
```

Figure 7.2
Responding to button clicks

This time, we create a button, set its text and width, and specify its top and left coordinates relative to the top, left corner of its containing form. We set up a handler for button clicks using the `System.EventHandler` delegate and we pass the name of our event handler, `clickHandler` as its constructor argument. The `clickHandler` event must have the signature shown. Its first parameter identifies the object that fired the event, while the second `EventArgs` parameter, which is unused here, is sometimes used by other event types to pass additional information about the event. Clicking the button causes the current time to be displayed in the form's title bar, as shown in figure 7.2.

Most control events use the generic `EventHandler` delegate and `EventArgs` class. However, some events, such as the mouse events, use their own classes which inherit from the `EventHandler` and `EventArgs` classes. For example, the `MouseDown` event uses the `MouseEventHandler` delegate and `MouseEvent-Args` class:

```
public class MouseForm : Form {

  ...

  public MouseForm() {
    Text = "My Mouse Form";
    Width = 400;
    MouseDown += new MouseEventHandler(mouseDownHandler);
  }
```

CHAPTER 7   CREATING THE WINDOWS FORMS USER INTERFACE

```
private void mouseDownHandler(object sender, MouseEventArgs e) {
   Text = String.Format("Mouse Click: X={0}, Y={1}", e.X, e.Y);
}
```

In this example, we see that the MouseEventArgs class provides public X and Y properties to provide the x and y coordinates associated with the MouseDown event. We'll look at a further example when we use CancelEventArgs to cancel an event in the WinPok application.

Note that the order in which we set a control's properties and add it to the form's Controls collection is unimportant. For example, the following two alternatives are both acceptable:

```
Button b = new Button();     // create button
b.Text = "Click Me";         // set text property
b.Width = 100;               // and width property
Controls.Add(b);             // finally, add to form
```

and:

```
Button b = new Button();     // create button
Controls.Add(b);             // add to form now
b.Text = "Click Me";         // then, set text property
b.Width = 100;               // and width property
```

In both cases, Windows Forms ensures that the underlying generated code is valid.

7.1.3 Anchoring and docking controls

Controls can be anchored to the edges of their containers. For example, the following code anchors a button to all four edges of the form:

```
Button b = new Button();
b.Anchor =  AnchorStyles.Top |
            AnchorStyles.Bottom |
            AnchorStyles.Left |
            AnchorStyles.Right;
```

The result is a button that stretches and shrinks in all four directions as the form is resized.

Likewise, a control can be docked to the edge of a container so that it remains in contact with that edge when the container is resized. The following example docks the button against the bottom edge of the form:

```
b.Dock =  DockStyle.Bottom;
```

7.1.4 Handling form events

You have two choices when deciding how to handle form events. You can use a delegate like we used in the button example. For example, we could handle a form's Resize event, as follows:

```
public class ResizeForm1 : Form {

  ...

  public ResizeForm1() {
    Resize += new EventHandler(resizeHandler);
  }

  private void resizeHandler(object sender, EventArgs e) {
    Text = String.Format(
            "Resize Handler Fired at {0:T}",
            DateTime.Now);
  }
}
```

Alternatively, since we derive our form from the Form class, we can override the virtual OnResize method to achieve the same result:

```
public class ResizeForm2 : Form {

  ...

  // override OnResize...
  protected override void OnResize(EventArgs e) {
    base.OnResize(e); // call any other registered delegates
    Text = String.Format(
            "OnResize Method Executed at {0:T}",
            DateTime.Now);
  }
}
```

Both techniques give identical results. In general, the Form class provides protected virtual methods corresponding to the different events: OnClick method for the Click event, OnActivated method for the Activated event, OnResize method for the Resize event, and so on. Using the provided methods is the preferred way to handle form events. It also saves coding. However, remember to call the corresponding base method, such as base.OnResize(e) in the above example, to ensure that any other registered delegates are invoked.

7.2 UNDERSTANDING THE WINDOWS FORMS PROGRAMMING MODEL

The Form class is the starting point for creating a variety of visible windows including tool, borderless, and floating windows, and modal dialog boxes. If you consult the SDK Help documentation, you'll see that the Form class derives from the hierarchy of classes shown in figure 7.3.

A form inherits additional functionality at each level of the inheritance tree. As you might expect, a Form is an object. It is also a MarshalByRefObject object which makes it a suitable candidate for remoting. Let's take a brief look at the other classes in the inheritance chain which contribute to a form's personality.

CHAPTER 7   CREATING THE WINDOWS FORMS USER INTERFACE

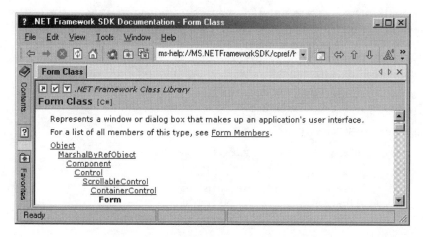

Figure 7.3   The Form class and its ancestors

7.2.1   The Component class

A `Form` is also a component. The `Component` class extends `MarshalByRefObject` by adding some new properties, methods, and events. These members support containment and cleanup and enable the sharing of components between applications. Components are invisible. (Controls, which we look at next, are essentially components with visual representation.) We show the most important, but not all, component members below:

- `Container`—A public instance property that returns a reference to an `IContainer` interface representing the `Container` that contains the component.

- `Site`—A public instance property that returns a reference to an `ISite` interface representing the `Site` object which binds the component to its container and enables communication between the two.

- `Dispose`—Disposes of the resources used by the component.

- `DesignMode`—A protected instance property that indicates whether the component is currently in design mode, such as when it is being used by the Visual Studio .NET designer.

The `System.Windows.Forms.Timer` and `System.Windows.Forms.ToolTip` classes are examples of Windows Forms components. The `Timer` class is used to raise timed events at defined intervals. It is optimized for use in a Windows Forms application and must be used in a window. The `ToolTip` class can be used to display brief help text when a user hovers over a control. However, neither is a visible form element and so both are implemented as components rather than as (visible) controls.

Listing 7.3 provides an example of a simple form which uses a `Timer` and a `ToolTip` to illustrate how components should be created, managed, and destroyed.

Listing 7.3   Coding with Windows Forms components

```csharp
// file    : timerform.cs
// compile : csc /t:winexe timerform.cs

using System;
using System.Windows.Forms;
using System.ComponentModel;

namespace MyForms {

  public class TimerForm : Form {

    public static void Main() {
      // create form and start Windows message loop...
      Application.Run(new TimerForm());
    }

    public TimerForm() {

      // set up form...
      Text = "TimerForm"; // title bar text
      Width = 400;           // form width
      Height = 100;          // form height
      CenterToScreen();      // display center screen

      // create container for components...
      components = new Container();

      // create timer and add to container...
      timer = new Timer(components);

      // set the clock...
      timer.Interval = 1000; // tick every second

      // register the tick handler...
      timer.Tick += new EventHandler(timerHandler);

      // start the clock...
      timer.Start();

      // create tooltip and add to container...
      tooltip = new ToolTip(components);

      // set tooltip target and text...
      tooltip.SetToolTip(this, "This is a Windows Form.");
    }

    private void timerHandler(object o, EventArgs e) {
      Text = String.Format("Time: {0:T}", DateTime.Now);  // tick
    }

    protected override void Dispose(bool disposing)  {
      if (disposing)
        if (components != null)
          components.Dispose(); // dispose of components
      base.Dispose(disposing);
    }
```

```
    private Timer timer;            // a component
    private ToolTip tooltip;        // also a component
    private Container components;    // contains components
  }
}
```

This example displays a ticking clock in the form's title bar. It also displays a ToolTip message when the mouse hovers over the form, as shown in figure 7.4.

Figure 7.4
Using the Timer and
ToolTip components

This example illustrates the typical approach to managing components in your code. The form contains a `Timer` component, a `ToolTip` component, and a `Container` called `components` to contain them. We create each component by using the form of the constructor that accepts a `Container` as an argument. For example, we create the timer, as follows:

```
timer = new Timer(components);
```

In general, a component is not subject to garbage collection even when it goes out of scope. Therefore, we typically add components to a container and override the form's `Dispose` method to dispose of the container and the components it contains. This ensures the release of any resources, used by your components, when the application is closed:

```
protected override void Dispose(bool disposing) {
  if (disposing)
    if (components != null)
      components.Dispose(); // dispose of components
  base.Dispose(disposing);
}
```

When you create a Windows Form using the Visual Studio .NET wizards, you'll automatically be provided with a container for your components and an overridden `Dispose` method.

7.2.2   The Control class

A control is a component that is visibly represented in a window and typically responds to user input in the form of keyboard events and mouse clicks. Being visible means that a control has a specified position and size. Examples include buttons, labels, check boxes, and list boxes. The `Control` class extends `Component` with more than 300 new properties, methods, and events. Some of the more commonly used members are shown in table 7.1.

Table 7.1   Control members

Member	Description
Anchor	A public instance property which specifies which edges of the control, if any, are anchored to the edges of its container
BackColor	A public instance property which specifies the background color of the control
Click	A public instance event which is fired when the control is clicked
DesignMode	A protected instance property which indicates whether the control is currently in design mode
Dispose()	Disposes of the resources used by the control
Dock	A public instance property which specifies which edge of its container, if any, the control is docked to
DoubleClick	A public instance event which is fired when the control is double-clicked
Enabled	A public instance property which specifies whether the control is enabled or disabled
Focus()	A public instance method which sets the input focus on the control
Font	A public instance property which specifies the control's font
ForeColor	A public instance property which specifies the foreground color of the control
GotFocus	A public instance event which is fired when the control receives the input focus
Height	A public instance property which specifies the height of the control in pixels
Hide()	A public instance method which sets the `Visible` property of the control to `false`
KeyDown	A public instance event which is fired when a key is pressed while the control has the input focus
KeyPress	A public instance event which is fired when a key is pressed and released while the control has the input focus
KeyUp	A public instance event which is fired when a pressed key is released while the control has the input focus
Left	A public instance property which specifies the x-coordinate of a control's left edge in pixels
Location	A public instance property which specifies the top-left corner of the control relative to the top-left corner of its container
LostFocus	A public instance event which is fired when the control loses the input focus
MouseDown	A public instance event which is fired when the mouse button is clicked on the control
MouseEnter	A public instance event which is fired when the mouse pointer enters the control
MouseHover	A public instance event which is fired when the mouse pointer hovers over the control
MouseLeave	A public instance event which is fired when the mouse pointer leaves the control
Show()	A public instance method which sets the `Visible` property of the control to `true`

continued on next page

Table 7.1 Control members *(continued)*

Member	Description
Size	A public instance property which specifies the width and height of the control
TabIndex	A public instance property which specifies the tab order of the control within its container
TabStop	A public instance property which specifies whether the user can give the input focus to the control using the TAB key
Text	A public instance property which specifies the text displayed on the control
Top	A public instance property which specifies the y-coordinate of a control's top edge in pixels
WndProc()	A protected instance method which can be overridden to process native Windows messages, (see example later in this chapter)

These are just a few of the many properties, methods, and events associated with controls, and inherited by forms. The good news is that you often need to use just a handful of these members to get the job done. For example, with a form, you may only need to set its `Location` and `Size` properties. For more complex controls, you may want to handle mouse activity, drag-drop events, keyboard entries, enabling, disabling, hiding, and showing the control, and so forth. The .NET SDK comes with extensive help documentation where you can find the full list of more than 300 properties, methods, and events associated with Windows Forms controls.

7.2.3 The ScrollableControl class

Returning to figure 7.3, we see that next in the inheritance hierarchy comes `ScrollableControl`. Unlike buttons and list boxes, a form is a scrollable control which means that it supports auto scrolling. The `ScrollableControl` class contains the public instance boolean `AutoScroll` property which determines whether the container will allow the user to scroll to controls placed outside its visible boundary. Listing 7.4 illustrates.

Listing 7.4 Coding a scrollable form

```
// file     : scrollform.cs
// compile : csc /t:winexe scrollform.cs

using System;
using System.Drawing;
using System.Windows.Forms;

namespace MyForms {

  public class ScrollForm : Form {

    public static void Main(string[] args) {

      ScrollForm f = new ScrollForm();
```

```
      f.AutoScroll = false;              // switch off AutoScroll
      f.Text = "AutoScroll Off";

      if (args.Length > 0)
        if (args[0].ToLower() == "/autoscroll") {
          f.AutoScroll = true;           // switch on AutoScroll
          f.Text = "AutoScroll On";
        }
      Application.Run(f);
    }

    public ScrollForm() {

      Width = 200;
      Height = 200;

      Button b = new Button();
      b.Location = new Point(10, 10);
      b.Size = new Size(300, 30);
      b.Text = "My Button";
      Controls.Add(b);
    }
  }
}
```

Figure 7.5
A scrollable form

In this example, we make the button deliberately too wide for the form. If we run the program with the /auto-scroll switch, the form automatically displays a horizontal scroll bar, as shown in figure 7.5.

7.2.4   The ContainerControl class

Finally, a form is a ContainerControl. This means that a form can act as a container for other controls. Because of this, a form can manage the input focus for contained controls by capturing the TAB key and moving the focus to the next control in the collection. It can retrieve and set its active control using the ContainerControl.ActiveControl property.

7.2.5   The Form class

As we've seen, a form inherits additional functionality at each level of the inheritance tree shown in figure 7.3. In addition, the Form class itself adds further form-specific members. These include properties, methods, and events that manage a main menu, support Multiple Document Interface (MDI) forms, position the form on the screen, set an icon for the form, and so forth. We'll use many of these members in the following sections.

Let's further explore Windows Forms by implementing a comprehensive GUI for our poker application. In doing so, we'll see a practical example of a moderately complex Windows Forms application.

7.3 WINPOK: THE WINDOWS FORMS-BASED POKER GAME

We return to our case study now and create a fully functional GUI for our poker game. This will be the first version that can honestly be called *video* poker. The GUI will approximately resemble a casino poker machine and allow the user to interact with the game using buttons, check boxes, and menus. We'll also use a set of 52 GIF images to display the cards.

7.3.1 The WinPok program structure

Listing 7.5 presents an outline of the structure of the WinPok application. The completed program will run to almost 600 lines of code, so we won't be able to show the full listing here. (Refer to appendix C for the full listing.) Luckily, we have our prebuilt *poker.dll* to provide the brain for the game. So our task is confined to creating the required code to build the Windows Forms GUI. In the process, you should get a good grounding in the techniques of Windows Forms-based programming.

Listing 7.5 The WinPok program outline

```
// file     : WinPok.cs
// compile : csc /r:poker.dll
//           /t:winexe
//           /win32icon:poker.ico
//           winpok.cs

namespace Poker {

  using System;
  using System.Windows.Forms;
  using System.Threading;
  using System.Drawing;
  using System.ComponentModel;
  using System.Runtime.InteropServices; // for API MessageBeep

  public class WinPokForm : Form {

    public static void Main() {
      // start the Windows message loop...
      Application.Run(new WinPokForm());
    }

    public WinPokForm() {
      initUI();    // create GUI controls
      newGame();   // init poker machine, user credits, etc.
    }

    private void initUI() {
```

```
    initForm();
    initMenu();
    initStartOverButton();
    initCredits();
    initMessage();
    initBet();
    initHoldCheckBoxes();
    initDealDrawButton();
    initPayoutTable();
    initMachineStats();
    initStatusBar();
    initCards();
}

...
...

// private form variables...
private Machine machine;                  // the poker machine
private int uiCredits;                     // amount of player credits
private int uiBet;                         // amount of player's bet
private Hand dealHand;                     // hand dealt
private Hand drawHand;                     // hand drawn
private Button dealDrawButton;             // click to deal/draw
private Button startOverButton;            // click to start over
private Label messageLabel;                // informational message
private Label creditsLabel;                // display credits remaining
private Label machineStatsLabel;           // display mechine stats
private TextBox betTextBox;                // input player bet

// start over menu item...
private MenuItem startOverMenuItem;

// display card images...
private PictureBox card1, card2, card3, card4, card5;

// display checkbox underneath each card...
private CheckBox hold1, hold2, hold3, hold4, hold5;

// status bar display...
private StatusBarPanel statusBarPanel;

[DllImportAttribute("user32.dll")]
public static extern int MessageBeep(int type); // error beep

  }
}
```

In listing 7.5, the important action is contained in the initUI routine where we call various methods to build the GUI. These methods, such as initForm and init-Menu, correspond to the areas of the WinPok form shown in figure 7.6. Building a complex GUI can involve a lot of code, so breaking up the task in this way makes it easier to keep track of where we are. In addition to the GUI-related code in listing 7.5, we'll have a private `newGame` method to start play, and `deal` and `draw` methods for interacting with the game. At the bottom of the listing we declare private fields to store references to controls which will be active during play. We don't bother to hold on to references to controls which remain static during play, such as the label which displays the (unchanging) payout table.

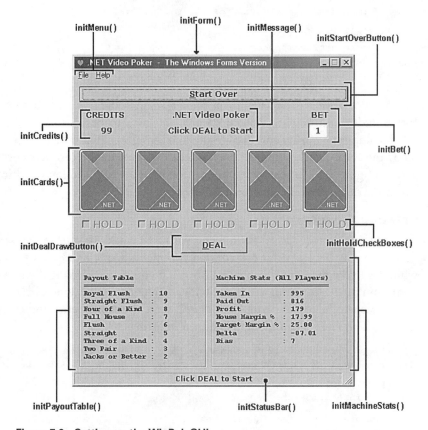

Figure 7.6   Setting up the WinPok GUI

Now that we've designed our form, let's lay out its different functional areas. We begin with the `initForm` method.

7.3.2   Setting up the form

The `initForm` method is shown in listing 7.6.

Listing 7.6   The initForm method

```
private void initForm() {
   // initialize the form...

   // set title bar...
   Text = ".NET Video Poker  -  The Windows Forms Version";
```

```
// set form height and width...
Height = 510;
Width= 445;

// center form and disallow resizing...
CenterToScreen();
MaximizeBox = false;
FormBorderStyle = FormBorderStyle.FixedDialog;

// set the form icon...
Icon = getIcon("poker");
}
```

In initForm we set the usual form properties including the title bar text and the form's width and height. We don't want the form to be resized, so we specify a fixed dialog-type border and disable the maximize box. The getIcon method call loads the form icon, *poker.ico*. You can see the icon in the top, left corner of the form in figure 7.6. To specify an application icon for the Windows desktop use the /win32icon:poker.ico compiler switch.

7.3.3 Creating the menu

We want our form to have a main menu with File and Help submenus, as seen in figure 7.6. The File menu will contain two menu items, Start Over and Quit, while the Help menu will contain an About menu item. Selecting the Start Over item from the File menu will be functionally identical to clicking the Start Over button seen at the top of figure 7.6. (They'll share the same event handler, as we'll see shortly.) The initMenu method is shown in listing 7.7.

> **Listing 7.7   The initMenu Method**

```
private void initMenu() {
  // initialize the menu...

  // create the form's main menu...
  Menu = new MainMenu();

  // create the File menu...
  MenuItem fileMenuItem = Menu.MenuItems.Add("&File");

  startOverMenuItem = new MenuItem(
    "&Start Over",
    new EventHandler(startOverHandler),
    Shortcut.CtrlS);
  fileMenuItem.MenuItems.Add(startOverMenuItem);

  MenuItem quitMenuItem = new MenuItem(
    "&Quit",
    new EventHandler(quitHandler),
    Shortcut.CtrlQ);
  fileMenuItem.MenuItems.Add(quitMenuItem);
```

```
    // create the Help menu...
    MenuItem helpMenuItem = Menu.MenuItems.Add("&Help");

    MenuItem aboutMenuItem = new MenuItem(
      "&About",
      new EventHandler(aboutHandler),
      Shortcut.CtrlA);
    helpMenuItem.MenuItems.Add(aboutMenuItem);
}
```

To attach a menu to a form, we need to create the menu and store its reference in the form's public `Menu` property, as we do at the start of the `initMenu` method. Next, we create the individual submenus, starting with `File`, and attach them to the main menu. Finally, to each submenu, we attach individual menu items which represent application commands such as `Start Over` and `Quit`. We use the 3-argument version of the `MenuItem` constructor:

```
MenuItem(string, EventHandler, Shortcut)
```

We provide the item text, the event handler associated with the command, and the shortcut key which invokes the command, as constructor arguments. The ampersand in the menu item text causes the following letter to be underlined when displayed. We create a new event handler and pass it as the second argument. For example, we specify that the `aboutHandler` method should be invoked when the `Help | About` menu item is selected:

```
new EventHandler(aboutHandler)
```

Since `aboutHandler` just displays a message box, we show its handler here:

```
    private void aboutHandler(object sender, EventArgs e) {
      // user selected "About" from the Help menu...
      string msg = ".NET Video Poker - Windows Forms Version\n";
      msg += "by Fergal Grimes\n";
      MessageBox.Show(
        msg,
        ".NET Video Poker",
        MessageBoxButtons.OK,
        MessageBoxIcon.Exclamation);
    }
```

Figure 7.7 Selecting Help | About from the menu

Being an event handler, our `aboutHandler` takes two arguments. The first is a reference to the object that sent the event, while the second is a reference to an `EventArgs` class potentially containing additional event-related data. We use neither in this example. Instead, we simply call `MessageBox.Show` passing the message, the message box title bar text, the buttons we need, and the icon to display, as arguments. This displays the message box in figure 7.7.

The `quitHandler` method closes the form and ends the application:

```
private void quitHandler(object sender, EventArgs e) {
   // user selected "Quit" from the File menu...
   Close(); // close this form
}
```

The `System.Windows.Forms` menu classes, `MainMenu`, `Menu`, and `MenuItem`, contain everything you need to create and manipulate menus including drop-down and pop-up menus. Our WinPok example is rather simple, but you can dynamically create and switch menus at run time, check, enable and disable individual menu items, and so forth. For more information, you should explore the Windows Forms samples in the .NET SDK. In the meantime, we move on to buttons.

7.3.4 Creating buttons

If you play a casino poker machine long enough, you'll eventually run out of money. In contrast, our version of the game will allow a player to start over by restoring the amount of credits on hand. To do this, the player clicks the `Start Over` button shown at the top of figure 7.6. So we need to set up this button and create an event handler to deal with button clicks. Listing 7.8 shows how we do this.

Listing 7.8   The initStartOverButton method

```
private void initStartOverButton() {
   startOverButton = new Button();
   startOverButton.Location = new Point(8, 8);
   startOverButton.Size = new Size(424, 24);
   startOverButton.Text = "&Start Over";
   startOverButton.Font =
      new Font("Verdana", 10f, FontStyle.Bold);
   startOverButton.Click +=
      new EventHandler(startOverHandler);
   Controls.Add(startOverButton);
}
```

Since a button is a visible GUI control, it inherits the properties of the `Control` class, which include `Location`, `Size`, `Text`, and `Font`, and also the control's `Click` event. Therefore, whether it is a button, a label, a text box, or a check box, you'll typically need to set these properties and any required event handlers, as we do here. The `Location` property specifies the upper-left corner of the control relative to the upper-left corner of its container. In this case, the container is the form, but we'll see an example of a `GroupBox` container in a moment. We place text on the button by setting its `Text` property and we set its font using the `Font` property. Then we register a new event handler for its `Click` event. We use the same event handler for both the `Start Over` menu item and `Start Over` button:

```
private void startOverHandler(object sender, EventArgs e) {
  // user selected "Start Over" from the File menu...
  newGame();
}
```

This calls the newGame method which restarts the game. This is the same method which is invoked from the WinPokForm constructor when the program is first launched, as shown in listing 7.5.

The initDealDrawButton method is almost identical, except that it registers the dealDrawHandler event handler which looks like:

```
private void dealDrawHandler(object sender, EventArgs e) {
  if (dealDrawButton.Text == "&DEAL")
    deal();
  else
    draw();
}
```

The dealDrawHandler just checks the button caption to see if it should call deal or draw.

7.3.5   Creating labels

In the top-left corner of figure 7.6, you'll find the credits display which consists of the static "CREDITS" label with a label underneath which provides a real-time display of the amount of player credits remaining. The player must bet to play. So each time the player clicks DEAL, the current bet is deducted from the remaining credits. When player credits are zero, the game is over. In listing 7.9 we set up the labels for the credits display.

Listing 7.9   The initCredits method

```
private void initCredits() {
  // display how many credits remaining...

  Label l = new Label();
  l.Location = new Point(8, 40);
  l.Text = "CREDITS";
  l.Size = new Size(88, 24);
  l.Font = new Font("Verdana", 10f, FontStyle.Bold);
  l.TextAlign = ContentAlignment.MiddleCenter;
  Controls.Add(l);

  creditsLabel = new Label();
  creditsLabel.Location = new Point(8, 64);
  creditsLabel.Size = new Size(88, 24);
  creditsLabel.Font = new Font("Verdana", 10f, FontStyle.Bold);
  creditsLabel.TextAlign = ContentAlignment.MiddleCenter;
  Controls.Add(creditsLabel);
}
```

For the "CREDITS" label, we set the Location, Text, Size, and Font, as usual. We also set the label's TextAlign property to System.Drawing.Content-Alignment.MiddleCenter to center the text in the middle of the label. The label underneath this will change text to reflect the number of credits as the game progresses. We set it up similarly, but we store a reference to it in the private creditsLabel.

Setting up the message labels in the top center of figure 7.6 is done by initMessage and is almost identical. We retain a reference to the dynamic message label in messageLabel and we use the following helper method to display messages:

```
private void showMessage(string s) {
  messageLabel.Text = s;
}
```

In the bottom left of figure 7.6, we display the poker machine's payout table. This gives the score for every winning hand and these values never change. The code to set up this table is shown in listing 7.10.

Listing 7.10   The initPayoutTable method

```
private void initPayoutTable() {

  // frame the payout table...
  GroupBox g = new GroupBox();
  g.Location = new Point(8, 272);
  g.Size = new Size(200, 168);
  Controls.Add(g);

  Label l = new Label();
  l.Location = new Point(5, 10);
  l.Text = Machine.PayoutTable; // payout text never changes
  l.Size = new Size(180, 150);
  l.Font =
    new Font(FontFamily.GenericMonospace, 8f, FontStyle.Bold);
  g.Controls.Add(l);
}
```

We create a GroupBox, to place a frame around the payout information, as you can see in figure 7.6. This acts as a container with its own Controls collection to which we add the label:

```
g.Controls.Add(l);
```

The payout table is implemented as a static property of the Machine class. Therefore, we don't have to create a new instance. Instead we can retrieve the payout table text, as follows:

```
l.Text = Machine.PayoutTable; // payout text never changes
```

Once again, the `initMachineStats` method is similar, so we don't show it here. One difference is that the machine statistics change as play progresses, so we'll have to update the label text throughout. We'll do that at the end of every hand.

7.3.6 Creating text boxes

The bet data, shown in the top right of figure 7.6, consists of a literal "BET" label with a text box underneath to display the amount of the player's current bet. The code to set this up is shown in listing 7.11.

Listing 7.11 The initBet method

```
private void initBet() {

    Label l = new Label();
    l.Text = "BET";
    l.Location = new Point(344, 40);
    l.Size = new Size(88, 24);
    l.Font = new Font("Verdana",10f, FontStyle.Bold);
    l.TextAlign = ContentAlignment.MiddleCenter;
    Controls.Add(l);

    betTextBox = new TextBox();
    betTextBox.Location = new Point(368, 64);
    betTextBox.MaxLength = 1;
    betTextBox.Font = new Font("Verdana",10f, FontStyle.Bold);
    betTextBox.Size = new Size(32, 22);
    betTextBox.TextAlign = HorizontalAlignment.Center;
    betTextBox.TabStop = false;
    betTextBox.TextChanged += new EventHandler(betChangedHandler);
    Controls.Add(betTextBox);
}
```

Setting up the label is straightforward. For the text box, `betTextBox`, we set the usual `Location`, `Font`, `Size`, and `TextAlign` properties. However, we also have two properties which we haven't seen before:

- `MaxLength`—The maximum number of characters allowed in the text box
- `TabStop`—Indicates whether the user can give the focus to this control using the TAB key

We also register a `TextChanged` handler, `betChangedHandler`, for this control. This handler will fire when the amount of the bet is changed. We'll use it to ensure that the user does not attempt to bet less than the minimum bet, more than the maximum bet, or more than the available credits:

```
private void betChangedHandler(object sender, EventArgs e) {

    int newBet;
    try {
```

```
        newBet = Int32.Parse(betTextBox.Text);
    }
    catch (Exception) {
        // use previous bet...
        beep(); // alert player
        showStatus("Error: Illegal bet!");
        newBet = uiBet;
    }
    betTextBox.Text = getBet(newBet).ToString();
}

private int getBet(int newBet) {
    Bet bet =
        new Bet(newBet,uiCredits, machine.MinBet, machine.MaxBet);
    if (bet.Amount != newBet) {
        beep(); // alert player
        string s =
            "Error: Minimum bet is " +
            machine.MinBet.ToString() +
            ".  Maximum bet is " +
            machine.MaxBet.ToString() + ".";
        showStatus(s);
    }
    return bet.Amount;
}
```

We first must check that we have a valid integer. If not, an exception is raised, we sound an audible beep, and we revert to the previous standing bet, uiBet. We're not done however, because the player may have insufficient credits to make the bet. Therefore, we call getBet to make any necessary adjustment to the amount of the bet. It does so by creating an instance of the Bet class, which we coded in chapter 4, and reading its Amount property to check for any adjustment.

Coding a method to create an audible beep provides us with an excuse to explore how to get our .NET programs to interact with the Win32 API. We'll get back to it when we finish setting up the GUI.

7.3.7 Creating check boxes

We've got five check boxes laid out left to right across the form. The player checks a box to indicate that the card above should be held when cards are drawn. Listing 7.12 sets up these check boxes.

> **Listing 7.12   The initHoldCheckBoxes method**

```
private void initHoldCheckBoxes() {
    // init hold CheckBoxes...

    hold1 = new CheckBox();
    hold1.Location = new Point(12, 208);

    hold2 = new CheckBox();
    hold2.Location = new Point(100, 208);
```

```
hold3 = new CheckBox();
hold3.Location = new Point(188, 208);

hold4 = new CheckBox();
hold4.Location = new Point(276, 208);

hold5 = new CheckBox();
hold5.Location = new Point(364, 208);

// set common HOLD checkbox attributes...
hold1.Text = hold2.Text = hold3.Text =
  hold4.Text = hold5.Text = "HOLD";
hold1.Font = hold2.Font = hold3.Font =
  hold4.Font = hold5.Font =
    new Font("Verdana", 11f, FontStyle.Bold);
hold1.Size = hold2.Size = hold3.Size =
  hold4.Size = hold5.Size = new Size(80, 24);
hold1.TextAlign = hold2.TextAlign = hold3.TextAlign =
  hold4.TextAlign = hold5.TextAlign =
    ContentAlignment.MiddleLeft;

// add the HOLD checkboxes to the UI...
Controls.Add(hold1);
Controls.Add(hold2);
Controls.Add(hold3);
Controls.Add(hold4);
Controls.Add(hold5);

}
```

We could use an array of check boxes but, for just 5 check boxes, it is hardly worth it. Instead, we lay out 5 individual check boxes and set their Location, Text, Font, Size, and TextAlign properties. Then we add each to the form's Controls collection. Note that we don't create any event handler to respond to checking, or unchecking, the boxes. Instead, when the user clicks DRAW, we'll look to see which boxes are checked and we'll hold the corresponding cards.

7.3.8   Displaying a status bar

At the bottom of figure 7.6, you'll see that the form has a status bar which displays "Click DEAL to Start." A status bar is a good place to display information about the application's status, or helpful hints as a user mouses over a control. We'll use it to display the score at the end of each hand. The code to set up the status bar is shown in listing 7.13.

Listing 7.13   The initStatusBar method

```
private void initStatusBar() {

  statusBarPanel = new StatusBarPanel();
  statusBarPanel.BorderStyle =
    StatusBarPanelBorderStyle.Sunken;
```

```
      statusBarPanel.AutoSize = StatusBarPanelAutoSize.Spring;
      statusBarPanel.Alignment = HorizontalAlignment.Center;

      StatusBar s = new StatusBar();
      s.ShowPanels = true;
      s.Font = new Font("Verdana", 8f, FontStyle.Bold);
      s.Panels.AddRange(new StatusBarPanel[]{statusBarPanel});
      Controls.Add(s);
   }
```

A status bar can contain one or more panels. To create a status bar, you create an array of panels and add them to the status bar. In this case, we create just one `StatusBarPanel` called `statusBarPanel` and set its `BorderStyle` to `StatusBarPanelBorderStyle.Sunken`. We also set its `AutoSize` property to `StatusBarPanelAutoSize.Spring` to enable it to share space with other panels, although we have just one here, and we set the `Alignment` property to center the panel in the status bar.

Next, we create the status bar, `s`, and add the panel to it. We set the status bar's `ShowPanels` property to `true` to enable panel display. Then we call `s.Panels.AddRange` and pass an array of panels to be displayed. In this case the array contains just one panel.

Note that we hold on to a reference to the status bar panel in the private `statusBarPanel` field. This will allow other methods to update the message displayed there. We'll use the following helper method to display status information:

```
      private void showStatus(string s) {
         statusBarPanel.Text = s;
      }
```

7.3.9 Creating picture boxes

All that remains is to set up the cards display. In listing 7.14 we show how to do this using picture boxes.

Listing 7.14   The initCards method

```
      private void initCards() {

         card1 = new PictureBox();
         card1.Location = new Point(8, 104);
         card1.Size = new Size(72, 96);
         Controls.Add(card1);

         card2 = new PictureBox();
         card2.Location = new Point(96, 104);
         card2.Size = new Size(72, 96);
         Controls.Add(card2);

         card3 = new PictureBox();
         card3.Location = new Point(184, 104);
```

CHAPTER 7   CREATING THE WINDOWS FORMS USER INTERFACE

```
      card3.Size = new Size(72, 96);
      Controls.Add(card3);

      card4 = new PictureBox();
      card4.Location = new Point(272, 104);
      card4.Size = new Size(72, 96);
      Controls.Add(card4);

      card5 = new PictureBox();
      card5.Location = new Point(360, 104);
      card5.Size = new Size(72, 96);
      Controls.Add(card5);
    }
```

You can download the card images, along with all of the code for this book, from http://www.manning.com/grimes. To display a hand of cards during play, we'll need to set the Image property for each picture box. The following helper function will do that for us:

```
    private void showCards(Hand h) {
      card1.Image = getImage(h.CardName(1)); pause();
      card2.Image = getImage(h.CardName(2)); pause();
      card3.Image = getImage(h.CardName(3)); pause();
      card4.Image = getImage(h.CardName(4)); pause();
      card5.Image = getImage(h.CardName(5)); pause();
    }
```

The getImage helper method simply retrieves a GIF file from disk and returns an Image reference:

```
    private Image getImage(string imgName) {
      string fileName = @"..\images\" + imgName + ".GIF";
      try {
        return Image.FromFile(fileName);
      } catch (Exception e) {
        MessageBox.Show(
          "Error loading card image file: " + e.Message,
          "Error!",
          MessageBoxButtons.OK, MessageBoxIcon.Error);
        return null;
      }
    }
```

If the image file is missing, an error message box will be displayed. If you dismiss it, you'll be able to continue playing, but you won't be able to see the cards!

We pause as each card is displayed to add suspense. This is implemented as:

```
    private void pause() {
      pause(200);
    }

    private void pause(int n) {
```

```
        Application.DoEvents();
        Thread.Sleep(n);
    }
```

The default pause is 200 milliseconds. Visual Basic programmers will be familiar with the DoEvents call which allows event processing to proceed before putting the thread to sleep.

To hide a hand of cards, we'll display a GIF image of the card back, *cb.gif*, in each picture box. We'll use the following two helper methods:

```
private void hideCards() {
    // display the backs of the cards...
    card1.Image = card2.Image = card3.Image =
        card4.Image = card5.Image = getImage("CB");
    Application.DoEvents();
}

private void hideCard(PictureBox card) {
    card.Image = getImage("CB");
}
```

7.3.10   Starting play

Now that we've looked at the code to set up the user interface and handle events, we take a look at how play begins. Recall that the form's constructor in listing 7.5 calls newGame immediately after the user interface is initialized. The newGame method is shown in listing 7.15.

Listing 7.15   Starting a new game

```
private void newGame() {
    // start (again) with full credits...
    initPokerMachine();
    hideCards();
    clearHoldCheckBoxes();
    disableHoldCheckBoxes();
    unfreezeBet();
    showMachineStatistics();
    showMoney();
    enableCommand("&DEAL");
    focusCommand();
    showMessage("Click DEAL to Start");
    showStatus("Click DEAL to Start");
}
```

The newGame method can also be called by startOverHandler as we saw earlier. The first thing newGame does is to initialize the poker machine:

```
private void initPokerMachine() {
    // initialize the poker machine...
    machine = Machine.Instance;
```

```
    uiBet = machine.MinBet;
    uiCredits = machine.StartCredits;
}
```

Next, it hides (displays the backs of) the playing cards. Then it clears and disables the HOLD check boxes. This involves setting the Checked and Enabled properties:

```
private void clearHoldCheckBoxes() {
  hold1.Checked = hold2.Checked = hold3.Checked =
    hold4.Checked = hold5.Checked = false;
}

private void disableHoldCheckBoxes() {
  hold1.Enabled = hold2.Enabled = hold3.Enabled =
    hold4.Enabled = hold5.Enabled = false;
}
```

The player must bet at the start of each hand, before cards are dealt. Therefore new-Game enables betting by calling unfreezeBet:

```
private void unfreezeBet() {
  betTextBox.ReadOnly = false;
}
```

Setting the ReadOnly property to false allows the player to change the text in the bet check box. A corresponding freezeBet method disables betting.

Next, the newGame method calls showMachineStatistics to display the current profit and performance statistics for the poker machine:

```
private void showMachineStatistics() {
  machineStatsLabel.Text = machine.Stats;
}
```

These statistics come from SQL Server and reflect the historical performance of the machine, in addition to the current and any concurrent games. In contrast, show-Money shows the game from the player's perspective:

```
private void showMoney() {
  showCredits();
  showBet();
}

private void showCredits() {
  creditsLabel.Text = uiCredits.ToString();
}

private void showBet() {
  betTextBox.Text = uiBet.ToString();
}
```

Next, the newGame method calls enableCommand("&DEAL") to enable the DEAL command. The caption of this button will flip from "DEAL" to "DRAW" as cards are dealt and drawn. It will also be disabled and enabled depending on the state of the game:

```
private void enableCommand(string s) {
  dealDrawButton.Text = s;
  dealDrawButton.Enabled = true;
  startOverButton.Enabled = true;
}

private void disableCommand(string s) {
  dealDrawButton.Enabled = false;
  dealDrawButton.Text = s;
  if (s.Equals("Game Over")) {
    startOverButton.Enabled = true;
    startOverMenuItem.Enabled = true;
  }
  else {
    startOverButton.Enabled = false;
    startOverMenuItem.Enabled = false;
  }
}
```

Both the Start Over and DEAL/DRAW buttons will generally be disabled while new cards are being displayed, and both then immediately enabled. The DEAL/DRAW button will be given a "DEAL" or "DRAW" caption, as appropriate. However, in the special case where the game is over, the DEAL/DRAW button is disabled and the Start Over button enabled to allow a new game to be started.

The focusCommand method simply places the Windows focus on the DEAL/DRAW button:

```
private void focusCommand() {
  dealDrawButton.Focus();
}
```

That completes application initialization. Note that we broke the task into two discrete sub-tasks:

- initUI—Adds controls to the form and sets static properties such as unchanging label text and menu items
- newGame—Sets dynamic controls to default values and initialize player variables

This partitioning enables us to call newGame to restart play without unnecessarily re-executing code to set up the GUI again. All that remains is to code the deal and draw methods.

7.3.11   Dealing cards

When the user clicks DEAL, dealDrawHandler calls the deal method. Figure 7.8 shows how the game looks when cards have been dealt. Just as we did in our ConPok program, we use the poker machine's Deal and Draw methods to handle the dealing and drawing of cards. Listing 7.16 presents the deal method.

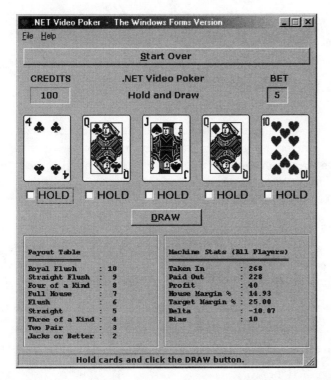

Figure 7.8
Getting ready to draw cards

Listing 7.16   Dealing cards

```
private void deal() {

   disableCommand("Dealing...");
   setBet();
   freezeBet();
   hideCards();

   // deal a hand...
   dealHand = machine.Deal();
   showCards(dealHand);

   // clear and enable the HOLD checkboxes...
   clearHoldCheckBoxes();
   enableHoldCheckBoxes();

   // tell player what to do...
   showMessage("Hold and Draw");
   showStatus("Hold cards and click the DRAW button.");
   enableCommand("&DRAW");
}

private void setBet() {
   int newBet = Int32.Parse(betTextBox.Text);
```

```
Bet bet =
  new Bet(newBet,uiCredits, machine.MinBet, machine.MaxBet);
uiBet = bet.Amount;
uiCredits = bet.Credits;
showMoney();
}
```

The setBet method is similar to getBet. However, since the player has clicked DEAL, we commit the bet by adjusting the player's bet amount and credits on hand. Then we freeze the bet so it cannot be altered during the hand, deal the hand, display it, clear and enable the HOLD check boxes, update the message and status areas, and enable the DRAW command, as seen in figure 7.8.

7.3.12 Drawing cards

Drawing cards is a bit more involved. Before we draw, we have to examine the HOLD check boxes to see which cards to hold. Then we draw cards, calculate winnings if any, update the user interface, and check if the game is over. Listing 7.17 illustrates.

Listing 7.17 Drawing cards

```
private void draw() {

    disableHoldCheckBoxes();
    disableCommand("Drawing...");

    // hold cards...
    string holdString = "";
    if (hold1.Checked) holdString += "1";
    if (hold2.Checked) holdString += "2";
    if (hold3.Checked) holdString += "3";
    if (hold4.Checked) holdString += "4";
    if (hold5.Checked) holdString += "5";

    drawHand = machine.Draw(dealHand, holdString, uiBet);

    // hide cards which have not been held...
    if (!hold1.Checked) hideCard(card1);
    if (!hold2.Checked) hideCard(card2);
    if (!hold3.Checked) hideCard(card3);
    if (!hold4.Checked) hideCard(card4);
    if (!hold5.Checked) hideCard(card5);
    pause(); // let the player see the backs of the cards

    showCards(drawHand);

    // update UI...
    int won = drawHand.Score * uiBet;
    uiCredits += won;
    showMoney();
    showMachineStatistics();
    showMessage(drawHand.Title);
```

```
      showStatus(drawHand.Title + "  -  Scores " + drawHand.Score);
      checkGameOver();
    }

    private void checkGameOver() {
      // check if player has enough money to go on...
      if (machine.MinBet > uiCredits) {
        disableCommand("Game Over");
        showStatus("Game over!");
        freezeBet();
        beep(); // alert player
      } else {
        enableCommand("&DEAL");
        focusCommand();
        unfreezeBet();
      }
    }
  }
```

The game is over when the player does not have enough credits to meet the minimum machine bet.

7.3.13   Accessing the Win32 API

You may have noticed the following declaration at the bottom of listing 7.5:

```
[DllImportAttribute("user32.dll")]
public static extern int MessageBeep(int type); // error beep
```

The `System.Runtime.InteropServices.DllImportAttribute` class is used to import an external DLL for use within a .NET program. We import *user32.dll* to gain access to the `MessageBeep` function which can be used to play sounds which are normally associated with Windows events such as a critical stop or an exclamation. Then we use the following method to sound the default beep when the user enters an illegal bet:

```
private void beep() {
  MessageBeep(0);
}
```

This approach is often better than displaying an annoying message box. We simply sound a beep, focus on the associated text box, and highlight the erroneous text. More importantly, this simple example illustrates how to make Win32 API calls.

The .NET SDK samples include many examples of the use of `DllImport` to make Win32 API calls to get the system time, display Win32 message boxes, get and set the current directory, get the disk drive type, search paths, load type libraries, create processes, get window text, get file attributes, and many more useful tasks.

7.3.14   Ending the application

Execution of our Windows Forms application can terminate in one of several ways:

- The user may select Quit from the menu
- The user may close the application window (the Windows form)
- Windows may send a message to the application to close, such as when the system is closing down, or when the user selects End Process from the Windows Task Manager

In the first case, quitHandler explicitly calls the base Close method to close the form, as we saw earlier. In all cases, you can override the OnClosing method to handle the Closing event, as we do below to confirm that the player wants to quit:

```
protected override void OnClosing(CancelEventArgs e) {
    base.OnClosing(e);
    // make sure the player really wants to quit...
    DialogResult r = MessageBox.Show(
        "Quit?",
        "Closing",
        MessageBoxButtons.YesNo, MessageBoxIcon.Question);
    if (r != DialogResult.Yes) e.Cancel = true;
}
```

The OnClosing method accepts a System.ComponentModel.CancelEventArgs reference as an argument. This class, which is derived from EventArgs, contains a public instance Cancel property which you can set to true to cancel the event. In this case, we use a message box to confirm that the user wants to quit. If the answer is not yes, we cancel the Closing event.

That completes our WinPok program. While a Windows Forms GUI takes some time to set up, the user interface is more usable and typically worth the extra effort. For example, the WinPok version of our poker machine is clearly more user-friendly than its ConPok cousin. Refer to appendix C for the complete WinPok listing.

7.4 CREATING WINDOWS FORMS APPLICATIONS USING VISUAL STUDIO .NET

Now let's explore the easy way to build Windows Forms applications. We'll use Visual Studio .NET to create a bare-bones GUI for the poker game using the drag-and-drop forms designer. To keep it short, we won't bother with credits, betting, or machine statistics. Instead, we'll just display the cards and a DEAL/DRAW button.

7.4.1 Creating a Visual Studio .NET project

Launch Visual Studio .NET and select File | New | Project from the main menu. You should be presented with a dialog box which lists the available project templates. Select Visual C# Projects in the left pane, and select Windows Application in the right. Call the project *VsWinPok*. See figure 7.9.

Click OK to create the project. You should see a screen similar to that shown in figure 7.10.

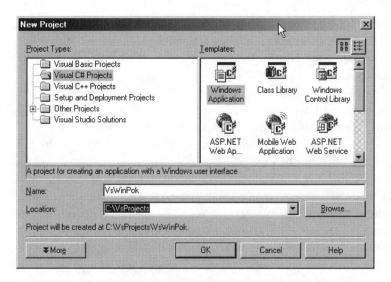

Figure 7.9   Creating a Visual Studio .NET project

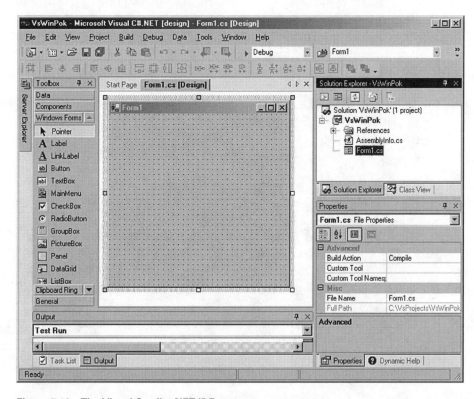

Figure 7.10   The Visual Studio .NET IDE

7.4.2 Designing a form

Figure 7.10 shows the default IDE layout which you can customize to your own preferences. It shows the Forms Designer window in the center. To its left is the toolbox containing controls which you can drag onto the form. The Solution Explorer, top right, lists the files and references in the project, while the properties of the currently selected control are shown in the Properties window at bottom right. By default, the new form is called `Form1`. You can change this by clicking the form to select it and changing its `Name` in the Properties window. We'll just accept the default control names as we work through the example.

To build our simplified poker GUI, we just need 5 cards, 5 hold check boxes, and a DEAL/DRAW button. In the toolbox, click the `PictureBox` control. Then click the form. This should place a `PictureBox` on the form. Repeat this procedure four more times to create 5 `PictureBox` controls to display the cards. Lay them out left-to-right across the form. For each `PictureBox`, select its `Image` property from the properties windows, open the File Dialog box and select *cb.gif* to display the back of a playing card in the `PictureBox`.

Next, select the `CheckBox` from the toolbox and drop it on the form. From the Properties window, change its `Text` to HOLD. Repeat this procedure to place a HOLD check box under each card. Finally, select a `Button` control from the toolbox and place it at the bottom of the form. Using the Properties window, change its text to DEAL. By now, the forms designer window should be similar to that shown in Figure 7.11.

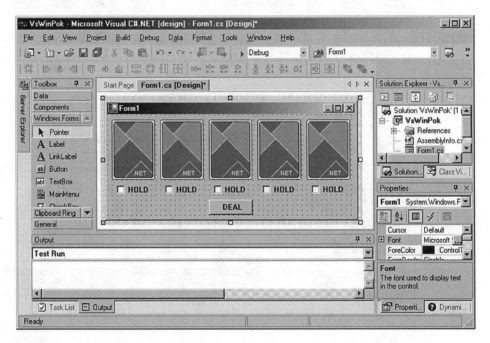

Figure 7.11   Designing the poker GUI

CHAPTER 7   CREATING THE WINDOWS FORMS USER INTERFACE

7.4.3　Adding code to the form

Figure 7.12
The Solution Explorer

Now it is time to attach the logic to the GUI. First, we need to add the *poker.dll* assembly to the project. To do this, right-click `References` in the Solution Explorer window, and select `Add Reference`. Click `Browse` to open the file dialog, select *poker.dll* from wherever it resides, and click OK. The Solution Explorer window should now look like figure 7.12.

To add the DEAL logic, double-click the DEAL button on the form. This drops you into the code editor at the `button1_Click` method. Now add the code for this method. See figure 7.13.

```
        this.Name = "Form1";
        this.Text = "Form1";
        this.ResumeLayout(false);

    }
    #endregion

    /// <summary>
    /// The main entry point for the application.
    /// </summary>
    [STAThread]
    static void Main()
    {
        Application.Run(new Form1());
    }

    private void button1_Click(object sender, System.EventArgs e)
    {

    }
}
}
```

Figure 7.13　Inserting code

At this point, you can begin coding the game's logic. For example, as we saw in WinPok, you need to check if the game should DEAL or DRAW, as follows:

```
private void button1_Click(object sender, System.EventArgs e)
   if (button1.Text == "DEAL")
     deal();
```

```
      else
        draw();
    }
```

Next, insert the code for the `deal()` and `draw()` methods. Remember to insert member variables for the poker machine and the hands. Since we won't support betting, you can use the `SimpleMachine` version of the poker machine:

```
private SimpleMachine machine;    // the poker machine
private Hand dealHand;            // hand dealt
private Hand drawHand;            // hand drawn
```

Completing this version of the game is left as an exercise, as it is mostly a matter of cutting and pasting code from `WinPok`. When you're done, hit F5 to compile and run the program.

As you can see, Visual Studio makes developing a Windows Forms GUI a snap. The Forms Designer provides a simple drag-drop interface for creating forms and laying out controls. The Solution Explorer enables you to easily add and remove project references, while the Properties window enables you to point-and-click to select control properties.

7.5 OVERRIDING WNDPROC

Before we leave Windows Forms, readers who have programmed in C with the original Windows SDK, may be wondering if Windows Forms provides access to underlying Windows messages. The answer is yes. For example, you may be familiar with C/SDK idiom for processing Windows messages:

```
LRESULT CALLBACK WndProc (HWND hwnd,
                          UINT msg,
                          WPARAM wParam,
                          LPARAM lParam) {
  ...

  switch (msg) {

    case WM_NCLBUTTONDOWN:
      ...

    case WM_NCLBUTTONUP:
      ...

    case WM_NCLBUTTONDBLCLK:
      ...
  }

  ...
}
```

Typically `WndProc` contained a long `switch` statement to identify and process individual messages. Of course, with Windows Forms, this type of low-level processing is typically unnecessary. However, for certain tasks, such as painting the nonclient areas (title bar and border) of a Window for example, it can be useful.

Let's look at a simple example of this technique. Listing 7.18 is a short program which overrides `WndProc` to process mouse messages associated with the nonclient area of the form.

```
// file    : wndprocform.cs
// compile : csc /t:winexe wndprocform.cs

using System;
using System.Windows.Forms;

namespace CustForms {

  public class WndProcForm : Form {

    public static void Main() {
      Application.Run(new WndProcForm());
    }

    public WndProcForm() {
      Height = 100;
      CenterToScreen();
      Text = "Title Bar Inactive - Alt-F4 to Close";
    }

    protected override void WndProc(ref Message m) {
      if (m.Msg >= WM_NCLBUTTONDOWN &&
          m.Msg <= WM_NCMBUTTONDBLCLK)
        return; // disable non-client clicks
      base.WndProc(ref m); // allow other messages to proceed
    }

    private int WM_NCLBUTTONDOWN   = 0x00A1;
    private int WM_NCMBUTTONDBLCLK = 0x00A9;
  }
}
```

In this simple example, `WndProc` checks for nonclient area mouse messages, in the range `0x00A1` to `0x00A9` hexadecimal, and disables them by returning immediately. Otherwise, the routine calls `base.WndProc(ref m)` to allow the base class `WndProc` to process them in the ordinary way.

When you execute this program (figure 7.14) you get a window which cannot be resized, moved, or closed using mouse clicks. You'll have to press ALT+F4 to close it, or use the Windows Task Manager.

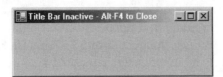

Figure 7.14
Disabling nonclient mouse messages

For more involved processing, the `System.Windows.Forms.Message` structure contains members similar to the traditional arguments passed to a C/SDK WndProc:

- `HWnd`—The window handle of the message
- `Msg`—The message number
- `WParam`—Extra message-specific parameters such as flags
- `LParam`—More message-specific parameter data

To make sense of the `Message` structure you'll need a knowledge of traditional Windows C/SDK programming. Also, remember that since the `Form` class is part of the language-neutral .NET Framework, this type of low-level interaction with the operating system is now possible using other .NET languages. This is a major improvement. On the other hand, beware that any future non-Windows implementation of Windows Forms may not support such techniques.

7.6 SUMMARY

That completes our look at Windows Forms. We started with some simple forms and explored components and controls. We looked at anchoring and docking controls and handling control events. We also developed a full-scale GUI for our poker game and saw how to make Win32 API calls. We explored Visual Studio .NET and used the Forms Designer to quickly create a simple GUI for our poker machine. We finished by exploring `WndProc`.

Next, in our final chapter, we explore ASP.NET.

CHAPTER 8

Creating the Web Forms user interface

In this, the final chapter, we explore ASP.NET, Microsoft's successor to the popular ASP platform for Web-based applications. In order to get the most out of this chapter, you should be familiar with HTML and Web development, including posting forms and processing them using a tool such as CGI, or ASP.

Since ASP.NET subsumes ASP, we'll start with a look at legacy ASP development and progress to discuss the new features added by ASP.NET. We'll develop an ASP.NET version of the poker game that hosts the *poker.dll* assembly and presents an attractive Web-based version of the game. In doing so, we'll acquaint ourselves with the new server-side controls, which make developing a Web application as intuitive as developing a regular desktop application. We'll close with a final version of video poker developed using the Mobile Internet Toolkit to run on a handheld device.

241

8.1 COMPARING ASP.NET TO ASP

We begin by examining an ASP application and comparing it to its ASP.NET equivalent. ASP applications will still run under ASP.NET and an ASP application can be converted to ASP.NET by simply changing its file extension from *.asp* to *.aspx*. So let's take a look at the similarities and differences.

8.1.1 A simple ASP application

There's a good chance that you have already dabbled with ASP. With a simple programming model and just a handful of objects, such as `Request` and `Response`, ASP unleashed a new wave of Windows-based Web development. Its use of VBScript for back-end scripting meant that Visual Basic programmers migrated easily to the platform. Listing 8.1 shows how to code an ASP page.

Listing 8.1   Hello from ASP

```
<!-- hello.asp -->
<script language="VBScript" runat="server">

function buildForm()

  firstName = Trim(Request.Form("firstName"))
  s = ""

  if firstName = "" then ' need a name...
    s = s & "What's Your First Name? "
    s = s & "<input type='text' name='firstName' />"
    s = s & "<input type='submit' />"
  else ' we know the user's name...
    s = s & "Hello, " & firstName & "!"
  end if
  buildForm = s
end function
</script>

<html><head><title>Hello ASP App</title></head>
  <body>
    <h1>Hello ASP Application</h1>
    <form action='hello.asp' method='POST'>
      <%=buildForm()%>
    </form>
  </body>
</html>
```

A typical ASP page is usually a mixture of back-end scripting and client-side HTML/JavaScript. In this example, the scripting is contained within the `<script>` tags at the start of the page. The HTML follows directly below it. This page displays a simple form that asks for the user's first name, as seen in figure 8.1.

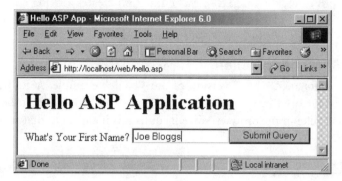

Figure 8.1
A simple form

When the user clicks the SUBMIT button, the form is submitted and the application responds by displaying a greeting, as shown in figure 8.2. Therefore, this ASP application is really two separate Web pages. The script block just contains a single VBScript function that checks if the form has been filled in by the user. If not, the input form is displayed. Otherwise, the greeting is displayed.

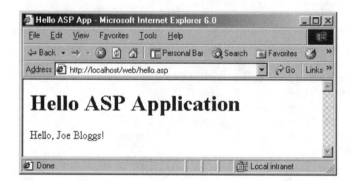

Figure 8.2
Response to the sub-mitted form

If you examine the HTML in listing 8.1, you'll see the following line sandwiched between the <form> tags:

```
<%=buildForm()%>
```

The delimiters, <% and %>, are used to mark the beginning and end of a scripting block. In this case, this causes the VBScript buildForm() function to be evaluated and the result inserted into the form. In turn, the buildForm() function checks if the user's first name has been entered:

```
firstName = Trim(Request.Form("firstName"))
```

The Request object is one of the built-in ASP objects, and Request.Form is a collection of the field values in the submitted form keyed by their name attribute. In this case, we're interested in the value of the text input field called firstName. If the form has not yet been displayed, this string will be blank. If the form has already been displayed, but the user submitted it without entering a name, the string will also be blank. In both cases, the buildForm() function creates a string containing the input form elements and returns it. On the other hand, if the name is not blank, buildForm() builds and returns a greeting string.

8.1.2 A simple ASP.NET application

Listing 8.2 presents an ASP.NET version of our "Hello" example. ASP.NET applications are typically stored in files with an *.aspx* extension. We won't bother to show you what it looks like in the browser, since its output is identical to that shown in figures 8.1 and 8.2.

Listing 8.2   Hello from ASP.NET

```
<!-- hello.aspx -->

<%@ Page Language="C#"%>
<%@ Import Namespace="System.Web.UI"%>

<script runat="server">

private string buildForm() {

  string firstName = this.Request.Form["firstName"];
  if (firstName == null) firstName = "";

  string s = "";
  if (firstName.Trim() == "") { // need a name...
    s += "What's Your First Name? ";
    s += "<input type='text' name='firstName' />";
    s += "<input type='submit' />";
  } else { // we know the user's name...
    s +=  "Hello, " + this.Request.Form["firstName"] + "!";
  }
  return s;
}
</script>

<html><head><title>Hello ASP.NET App</title></head>
  <body>
    <h1>Hello ASP.NET Application</h1>
    <form action='hello.aspx' method='POST'>
      <%=buildForm()%>
    </form>
  </body>
</html>
```

As you can see, the ASP.NET version of this simple application is very similar. (As I mentioned, you can turn an ASP page into an ASP.NET page by simply changing its file extension from *.asp* to *.aspx*.) However, there are two important differences to note:

1 This time, the page logic is coded in C#. ASP.NET is a first-class citizen of the .NET world and ASP.NET applications can be coded in C# or any other .NET language. Code is fully compiled when the page is requested and is cached for reuse. In other words, server-side VBScript is obsolete.

2 Note the `<%@ Import Namespace="..."%>` directive at the top of the file. This is similar to C#'s `using` statement. It allows you to import .NET namespaces and use the full power of the .NET Framework in your ASP.NET applications.

These two features alone make ASP.NET potentially much more powerful than its predecessor. However, there's more.

8.2 THE SYSTEM.WEB.UI.PAGE CLASS

You probably noticed the following line of code in listing 8.2:

```
string firstName = this.Request.Form["firstName"];
```

You may be wondering just exactly what `this` refers to in the context of an ASP.NET page. Our page is, in fact, an instance of the `System.Web.UI.Page` class, thus giving us an object-oriented model of an ASP.NET page in keeping with the rest of the .NET Framework.

8.2.1 The Page.Request and Page.Response properties

The ubiquitous `Request` and `Response` objects of legacy ASP are now properties of the `Page` class. Listing 8.3 illustrates.

Listing 8.3   Using the Page.Request and Page.Response properties

```
<!-- dumpprops.aspx -->

<%@ Page Language="C#" Debug="true"%>

<script runat="server">

private void dumpProps() {

  // get Request and Response objects...
  HttpRequest req = this.Request;
  HttpResponse resp = this.Response;

  // and use them...
  resp.Write("Request.FilePath: " +
    req.FilePath + "<br/>");
  resp.Write("Request.PhysicalApplicationPath: " +
    req.PhysicalApplicationPath + "<br/>");
  resp.Write("Request.HttpMethod: " +
    req.HttpMethod + "<br/>");
  resp.Write("Request.UserAgent: " +
    req.UserAgent + "<br/>");
  resp.Write("Request.UserHostAddress: " +
```

```
        req.UserHostAddress + "<br/>");
}
</script>

<html><head><title>Dump Page Properties</title></head>
  <body>
    <h1>Page Properties</h1>
    <% dumpProps(); %>
  </body>
</html>
```

Here we grab references to the Request and Response objects, as follows:

```
HttpRequest req = this.Request;
HttpResponse resp = this.Response;
```

We use them to dump some of the Request properties to the browser, as seen in figure 8.3.

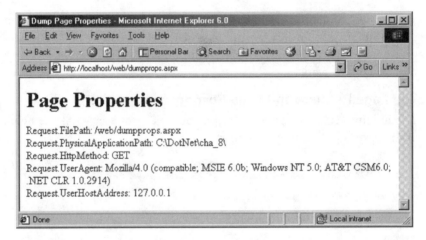

Figure 8.3   Displaying Request properties

8.2.2   The Page lifecycle

When an HTTP request is received, ASP.NET responds by creating and returning the requested page. This process causes several page events to occur and the Page class contains protected instance methods, inherited from the System.Web.UI.Control, which you can override to handle these events:

- OnInit—Override to handle the Init event and perform any necessary initialization required to create and set up the page instance. At this stage in the page's lifecycle, viewstate (which we'll discuss shortly) has not yet been populated.

- OnLoad—Override to handle the Load event and perform any actions common to each HTTP request for the page. For example, this would be a good

CHAPTER 8   CREATING THE WEB FORMS USER INTERFACE

place to set up a database query whose results will be used in building the page. At this stage, the page's viewstate has been populated.

- OnPreRender—Override to handle the PreRender event and perform any necessary steps before the page is rendered.

- OnUnload—Override to handle the Unload event and perform cleanup, such as closing database connections.

Listing 8.4 illustrates the discussion with a short application that displays the page events in the order they occur.

Listing 8.4   Handling page events

```
<!-- pageevents.aspx -->

<%@ Page Language="C#" Debug="true" %>

<script runat="server">

protected override void OnInit(EventArgs e) { base.OnInit(e); p("Init"); }
protected override void OnLoad(EventArgs e) { base.OnLoad(e); p("Load"); }
protected override void OnPreRender(EventArgs e)
  {base.OnPreRender(e); p("PreRender");}

private void p(string s) {
  Message.InnerHtml += s + "<br>";
}
</script>

<html><head><title>Hello Web Page</title></head>
<body>
<h1>Page Events...</h1>
<form action='pageevents.aspx' method='POST'>
  <span id="Message" runat="server" />
  <p>
    <input type="submit" />
  </p>
</form>
</body>
</html>
```

In this example, we override the page's Init, Load, and PreRender events and display a message in the browser. Note that we don't handle the Unload event since it occurs after the page has been rendered. If you run this example, you should see the output shown in figure 8.4.

You may be wondering about the runat="server" attribute of the <span> tag. This enables the page element to be processed by server-side code, as we'll see next.

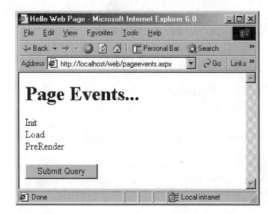

Figure 8.4
Displaying page events

8.3 WORKING WITH WEB FORMS AND SERVER CONTROLS

ASP.NET introduces some new terms to the ASP developer's vocabulary: *Web Forms* and *server controls*. A Web Form is a form with a `runat="server"` attribute that causes it to be processed on the server. A server control is a control which also contains a `runat="server"` attribute. It too is processed on the server and generates HTML/JavaScript to be rendered in the browser. To the developer, server controls appear similar to the Windows Forms controls we saw in the previous chapter. Indeed, using Visual Studio .NET, you can design Web Forms using the built-in drag-and-drop forms designer. Server controls expose properties, methods, and events as do Windows Forms controls.

8.3.1 The anatomy of the Web Form

Listing 8.5 presents a new version of our "Hello" application that uses a Web Form and server controls.

Listing 8.5   The Hello Web Form

```
<!-- helloform.aspx -->

<%@ Page Language="C#" Debug="true" %>

<script runat="server">

  // greet the user...
  private void greetHandler(object sender, EventArgs e) {

    firstNameTextBox.Text = firstNameTextBox.Text.Trim();
    if (firstNameTextBox.Text == "") {
      // no name, so no greeting...
      greetingLabel.Text = "";
    } else {
      // greet the user...
```

```
      greetingLabel.Text =
        "Hello, " + firstNameTextBox.Text + "!";
    }
  }
</script>

<html><head><title>Hello Web Form</title></head>

<body>
  <h1>Hello Web Form</h1>
  <form action='helloform.aspx' method='POST' runat='server'>

  <asp:label text="What's Your First Name?" runat="server"/>
  <asp:textbox id="firstNameTextBox" runat="server"/>
  <asp:button
    id="greetButton"
    text="Greet"
    OnClick="greetHandler"
    runat="server"/>
  <p>
  <asp:label id="greetingLabel" runat="server"/>
  </p>

  </form>
</body>
</html>
```

Note the form declaration, `<form ... runat="server"/>` that identifies this example as a Web Form. Also, instead of using HTML tags for the labels, text box, and button, we use markup of the form:

```
<asp:control-type ... runat="server"/>
```

These are server controls. They expose properties, methods, and events that can be programmed by server-side code. When they are sent to the browser, they are translated into HTML for display. For example, if you select View | Source from your browser menu, you should see the generated HTML shown in listing 8.6.

Listing 8.6   Viewing the HelloForm HTML source

```
<!-- helloform.aspx -->

<html><head><title>Hello Web Form</title></head>
  <body>
    <h1>Hello Web Form</h1>
    <form
      name="ctrl0"
      method="POST"
      action="helloform.aspx"
      id="ctrl0">
      <input
        type="hidden"
```

```
      name="__VIEWSTATE" value="dDwt  ...   j47Pg==" />
    <span>What's Your First Name?</span>
    <input
      name="firstNameTextBox"
      type="text"
      id="firstNameTextBox" />
    <input
      type="submit"
      name="greetButton"
      value="Greet"
      id="greetButton" />
    <p>
      <span id="greetingLabel"></span>
    </p>
  </form>
  </body>
</html>
```

ASP.NET generates plain HTML that is easily digested by down-level browsers. In fact, using ASP.NET server controls is a good way to produce pages that are compatible across the different browsers.

If you launch your browser and open the application, you should see the page shown in figure 8.5.

Figure 8.5
Displaying the Hello Web Form

This is identical to the previous examples. Now, enter your name and click the Greet button to be presented with the page shown in figure 8.6.

This time, we've done things a little differently. When we display the greeting, we also display the form again above it. Note that the text in the text box ("Joe") is preserved across the server roundtrip. By default, server controls are "sticky," meaning that they preserve their values across HTTP requests. This is achieved by preserving control properties in a hidden form variable called __VIEWSTATE. You can confirm this by viewing the HTML source in the browser. See listing 8.6. The __VIEWSTATE field looks something like:

```
<input type="hidden" name="__VIEWSTATE" value="dDwt  ...   j47Pg==" />
```

Figure 8.6
Greeting the user

The value of __VIEWSTATE is a base-64 encoded string containing the viewable state of the controls. If you decode the field using the Base64Service presented in chapter 5, you'll find the text property of the text box in there somewhere:

```
encoded  : dDwt  ...  j47Pg==
decoded  : ...  Hello, Joe!  ...
```

A control's *viewstate* is the sum of its property values, and it makes it easy to preserve the contents of a text box, the checked state of a check box, the currently selected item in a list box, and so forth, across HTTP requests.

Returning to listing 8.5, note the code:

```
<asp:button
  id="greetButton"
  text="Greet"
  OnClick="greetHandler"
  runat="server"/>
```

The OnClick attribute associates a server-side button click handler with the button's click event. Therefore, while the button is clicked in the client, the associated event is fired, and handled, on the server, causing an HTTP roundtrip to occur.

The event handler has an identical signature to its Windows Forms equivalent:

```
private void greetHandler(object sender, EventArgs e) {

  ...

}
```

Instead of specifying an OnClick attribute, you can, if you prefer, assign an event handler by overriding the OnLoad method and using the delegate approach seen in our Windows Forms examples:

```
protected override void OnLoad(EventArgs e) {
  base.OnLoad(e);
  // use delegate...
  greetButton.Click += new EventHandler(greetHandler);
}
```

8.3.2 The System.Web.UI.WebControls and System.Web.UI.HtmlControls namespaces

Server controls consist of *HtmlControls* and *WebControls*. Those controls that we have seen in our examples so far, `<asp:label>`, `<asp:textbox>`, `<asp:button>`, and so forth, are examples of Web (server) controls. Web controls are abstract, strongly typed objects, which do not necessarily reflect HTML syntax. For example, using a simple `<asp:calendar>` control in your page can automatically generate almost 150 lines of HTML for display in the browser. This can be a major time saver when developing complex pages. There are about 30 Web controls in the `System.Web.UI.WebControls` namespace so we won't list them all here. Table 8.1 lists a few that are worth knowing about. We'll take a closer look at some of these controls in the course of this chapter.

Table 8.1   The System.Web.UI.WebControls namespace

WebControl	Use
Button	Provides a command button. Use its `OnClick` attribute to specify a click event handler, or wire up an event handler in the page's `OnLoad` method.
Calendar	Displays a calendar that allows the user to select a date.
CheckBox	Can be used to allow the user to enter boolean (`true`/`false`) data. If selected, its `Checked` property is `true`. The `CheckBox` control can trigger postback to the server if its `AutoPostBack` property is `true`.
CheckBoxList	Provides a multiple-selection checked list with an `Items` collection containing the members in the list. To determine if an item is checked, you can test its boolean `Selected` property.
DataGrid	Provides a convenient way to generate a tabular display of data from a data source. The data can optionally be selected, sorted, paged, and so forth. By default, field names are displayed in the grid's column headers and values displayed as text labels.
DataList	Displays data in a list according to a template.
DropDownList	Provides a single-selection drop-down list.
Label	Displays text in a specific location on the page. Use its `Text` property to set the text to be displayed.
ListBox	Provides a single- or multiple-selection list.
Panel	Provides a container for other controls.
RadioButton	Can be used to allow the user to enter boolean (`true`/`false`) data. If selected, its `Checked` property is `true`. Only one radio button in a group can be checked. A radio button's group can be assigned using its `GroupName` property.
RadioButton-List	Provides a single-selection checked list with an `Items` collection containing the members in the list. To determine which item is selected, you can test the boolean `Selected` property of the items.
Table, Table-Row, TableCell	The `Table` control can be used to programmatically build a table by adding `TableRow` controls to the `Rows` collection of the table, `TableCell` controls to the `Cells` collection of any row, and controls to the `Controls` collection of any cell.
TextBox	Allows the user to enter text. Set its `TextMode` to `MultiLine` to enable multiple lines of text, or to `Password` to hide password characters.

Unlike WebControls, HtmlControls such as `HtmlAnchor` and `HtmlTable`, typically have a one-to-one correspondence with an equivalent HTML tag. However, they offer a convenient model that allows you to manipulate them programmatically on the server side. The SDK documentation provides a complete list and, since they map so closely to the HTML elements they represent, we won't list them here. Instead, we'll explore an example of using the `HtmlTable` control to build a table later in this chapter. But first, we explore examples which use the `Calendar` and `DataGrid` Web server controls.

8.3.3 Using the Calendar Web control

Listing 8.7 provides an example that uses the `Calendar` Web control to allow the user to select a date.

Listing 8.7   Using the Calendar Web control

```
<!-- calform.aspx -->

<%@ Page Language="C#" Debug="true" %>

<script runat=server>

  private void dateHandler(object sender, EventArgs e) {
    myMessage.Text =
      "You selected " + myCalendar.SelectedDate.ToShortDateString();
  }
</script>

<html><head><title>Calendar ASP.NET App</title></head>
  <body>
    <h1>Calendar ASP.NET Application</h1>
    <form runat="server">
      <asp:calendar
        id="myCalendar"
        onSelectionChanged="dateHandler"
        Font-Name="Verdana"
        Font-Size="8pt"
        Font-Bold="true"
        BorderColor="black"
        BackColor="Gainsboro"
        runat="server" />
      <p>
        <asp:Label
          id="myMessage"
          Font-Name="Verdana"
          Font-Size="8pt"
          Font-Bold="true"
          runat="server" />
      </p>
    </form>
  </body>
</html>
```

By now, you're probably getting the hang of server controls, so this example doesn't need much explanation. We use the `onSelectionChanged` property of the control to specify a server-side handler to execute when the user selects a date. This causes a postback roundtrip to display the selected date in the message label. If you examine the generated HTML source in the browser, you'll see that this is achieved by using links for the dates combined with autogenerated JavaScript:

```
<a href="javascript:__doPostBack( ... )"> ... </a>
```

In fact, using this simple calendar control automatically generates almost 150 lines of combined HTML and JavaScript, thus saving valuable time and effort.

Browsing the application, and selecting a date, produces the page shown in figure 8.7.

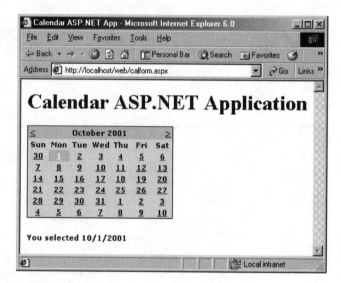

**Figure 8.7
Browsing the calendar
application**

8.3.4 Using the DataGrid Web control

Listing 8.8 provides an example that uses the `DataGrid` Web control. This example uses the *games* table in the *poker* database as the data source for a simple report.

Listing 8.8   Using the DataGrid Web control

```
<!-- dataform.aspx -->

<%@ Page Language="C#" %>
<%@ Import Namespace="System.Data" %>
<%@ Import Namespace="System.Data.SqlClient" %>

<script runat="server">

protected override void OnLoad(EventArgs e) {

  base.OnLoad(e);
```

```
    SqlConnection con =
      new SqlConnection(
        @"server=(local)\NetSDK;database=poker;trusted_connection=yes");

    SqlDataAdapter com =
      new SqlDataAdapter("select * from games", con);

    DataSet ds = new DataSet();
    com.Fill(ds, "games");

    gamesGrid.DataSource=ds.Tables["games"].DefaultView;
    gamesGrid.DataBind();
}
</script>

<html><head><title>DataGrid ASP.NET App</title></head>
  <body>
    <h1>DataGrid ASP.NET Application</h1>
    <form runat="server">
      <asp:dataGrid
        id="gamesGrid"
        BackColor="Gainsboro"
        BorderColor="black"
        CellPadding="10"
        CellSpacing="0"
        Font-Name="Verdana"
        Font-Size="8pt"
        Font-Bold="true"
        HeaderStyle-BackColor="lightGreen"
        EnableViewState="false"
        runat="server" />
    </form>
  </body>
</html>
```

We use the `<asp:dataGrid ... />` tag to place the `DataGrid` on the form. Then, in the page's `OnLoad` method, we load the *games* table from the *poker* database into `gamesGrid`. We do so by setting its `DataSource` property and calling the `DataBind` method. The result is a page such as that shown in figure 8.8.

The `DataGrid` supports paging so that you can page forward and back through the data source. Use the `PageSize` property to specify the number of rows to be displayed on a page, and then set `AllowPaging` to `true` to display `Previous` and `Next` buttons on the page.

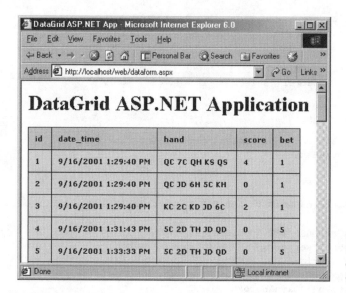

Figure 8.8
Using the DataGrid Web control to display poker games

8.3.5 Using the HtmlTable control

The HtmlTable control is an HTML control that maps directly to the HTML table. You can use it to programmatically build an HTML table for display in the browser, as shown in listing 8.9. This example allows the user to highlight a cell in the table, causing a roundtrip to the server where the table is rebuilt and the selected cell highlighted.

Listing 8.9 Building an HTML table using the HtmlTable control

```
<!-- tableform.aspx -->

<%@ Page Language="C#" Debug="true" %>
<%@ Import Namespace="System"%>
<%@ Import Namespace="System.Web.UI"%>

<script runat="server">

protected override void OnLoad(EventArgs e) {

  base.OnLoad(e);

  int cellNum = 0;
  if (IsPostBack) {
    try {
      cellNum = Int32.Parse(cellTextBox.Text);
    } catch (Exception) {
      cellNum = 0; // don't highlight any cell
    }
  }

  int rows = 3, cols = 3, num = 0;
  for (int i = 0; i < rows; i++) {
    HtmlTableRow htmlRow = new HtmlTableRow();
```

```
    for (int j = 0; j < cols; j++) {
      num++;
      HtmlTableCell htmlCell = new HtmlTableCell();
      htmlCell.Controls.Add(new LiteralControl(num.ToString()));
      if (num == cellNum)
        htmlCell.BgColor="Yellow";
      htmlRow.Cells.Add(htmlCell);
    }
    myTable.Rows.Add(htmlRow);
  }
}
</script>

<html><head><title>HtmlTable Example</title></head>
<body>
  <h1>HtmlTable Example</h1>

  <form runat="server">

    <table
      id="myTable"
      border="1"
      cellPadding="10"
      cellSpacing="1"
      runat="server" />

    <p>
      Cell#
      <asp:textbox
        id="cellTextBox"
        columns="1"
        maxLength="1"
        runat="server"/>
      <br>
      <input
        type="submit"
        value="Highlight Cell"
        runat="server">
    </p>

  </form>
</body>
</html>
```

Note the test:

```
if (IsPostBack) {

    ...

}
```

When a user first requests a Web form, its page's `IsPostBack` property will be false. This indicates that the form is being loaded for the first time, so the form will not yet contain any viewstate information. In this example, we test the `IsPostBack` property before attempting to retrieve the cell number to highlight. Then we attempt to parse the integer from the text box, create the table, and highlight the cell.

The `HtmlTableCell` object has its own controls collection to which we add a new literal control containing the string representation of the cell number. ASP.NET compiles any HTML elements and text, which do not require server-side processing, into instances of the `LiteralControl` class.

Running this example produces the page shown in figure 8.9.

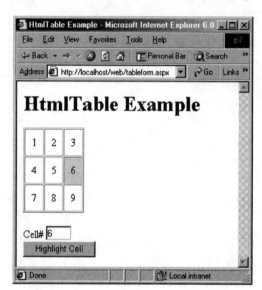

Figure 8.9
The table generated by the
HtmlTable control

8.4 CREATING USER CONTROLS

A *user control* allows you to capture one or more commonly used UI elements into a single reusable control. You can reuse your Web Forms by turning them into user controls. Doing so involves making a few modifications to the form, after which it is no longer usable as a stand-alone Web Form. User controls provide a convenient way to build Web Forms by assembling customized reusable components.

The first step in converting a Web Form to a user control is to save the form as a new file with an *.ascx* extension. Since a user control will be embedded in a Web Form, you also need to remove any `<html>`, `<head>`, `<title>`, `<body>`, or `<form>` tags. Typically, it will contain just a script block followed by some Web server, or HTML, controls. Listing 8.10 presents *usercolor.ascx*, a user control to allow a user to select colors.

Listing 8.10 A user control to pick colors

```
<!-- usercolor.ascx -->

<script language="C#" runat="server">

  public string Color {
```

CHAPTER 8 CREATING THE WEB FORMS USER INTERFACE

```
      get {
        if (colorTextBox.Text == "") return "white";
        return colorTextBox.Text;
      }
  }

  public bool Visible {
    get {
      return colorPanel.Visible;
    }
    set {
      colorPanel.Visible = value;
    }
  }
}
</script>

<asp:panel id="colorPanel" visible="false" runat="server">
  <asp:label
    Font-Name="Verdana"
    Font-Size="7pt"
    text="Color : "
    runat="server"/>
  <asp:textbox
    Font-Name="Verdana"
    Font-Size="7pt"
    columns="10"
    id="colorTextBox"
    runat="server"/>
</asp:panel>
```

This example contains just a label control and a text box control for the user to enter the name of a color. Both are contained within a panel control. In the script block, we define two public properties: Color returns the entered color, while Visible allows the caller to set the visibility of this user control. Placing the two controls on the same panel allows us to conveniently hide them both by setting the panel's Visible property. Also, notice that our user control does not participate in any page processing, such as handling page events, or setting page properties. Instead, we implement a nice clean interface to the control by implementing public properties.

To place this control on a Web Form, we first need to declare it at the top of our form, as follows:

```
<%@ Register
  TagPrefix="userColors"
  TagName="userColor"
  Src="usercolor.ascx" %>
```

We set the TagPrefix and TagName properties to enable us to refer to the control as <userColors:userColor> when we use it on the form. We also specify the location of the source code, *usercolor.ascx*. Once declared, we can place the control on the form using regular Web Forms syntax:

```
<userColors:userColor id="userColorControl" runat="server"/>
```

Listing 8.11 illustrates with a Web Form, *colorform.aspx*, which uses the control.

Listing 8.11   Using the UserColor control

```
<!-- colorform.aspx -->

<%@ Page Language="C#" Debug="true" %>
<%@ Register
  TagPrefix="userColors"
  TagName="userColor"
  Src="usercolor.ascx" %>

<script runat="server">
  protected override void OnLoad(EventArgs e) {
    base.OnLoad(e);
    body.Attributes["bgcolor"]  = userColorControl.Color;
    userColorControl.Visible = !userColorControl.Visible;
  }
</script>


<html><head><title>The UserColor Control</title></head>
  <body id="body" runat="server">
    <h1>The UserColor Control</h1>
    <form runat='server'>
      <userColors:userColor id="userColorControl" runat="server"/>
      <p>
        This form uses the UserColor user control.
        When you submit the form the selected color
        will be used to set the page's background color.
      </p>
      <asp:button
        text="Submit"
        Font-Name="Verdana"
        Font-Size="7pt"
        BorderColor="black"
        type="submit"
        runat="server"/>
    </form>
  </body>
</html>
```

In the OnLoad method, the application sets the background color of the form to the control's Color property. Also, to demonstrate showing and hiding the control, it flips the control's Visible property on each roundtrip. See figure 8.10.

If you've found yourself constantly reinventing the wheel when developing ASP applications in the past, then user controls are for you. With a well-stocked library of

Figure 8.10
Reusing the UserColor user control

user controls, common functionality can more easily be shared across projects, and productivity can be substantially enhanced.

8.5   *VALIDATING USER INPUT*

The Web Forms infrastructure provides a selection of validation controls that you can use to validate user input, and display error messages to the user. Common validation scenarios are supported including requiring that a field contains data, ensuring that an entry is within a specified range, matching an entry against a pattern, and so forth. You can attach one or more validation controls to an input control.

The built-in validation controls include:

- `RequiredFieldValidator`—Requires an entry in a field
- `CompareValidator`—Compares an entry with a value or a property of another control
- `RangeValidator`—Requires an entry to be between specified lower and upper bounds
- `RegularExpressionValidator`—Requires an entry to match a pattern specified by a regular expression
- `CustomValidator`—Requires an entry to pass a validation test that you code yourself
- `ValidationSummary`—Displays a summary of validation errors for all the validation controls on a page

Listing 8.12 presents a simple Web Form that asks for a user's age. It uses the `RequiredFieldValidator`, `RegularExpressionValidator`, and `Range-Validator` controls to validate the user's input.

Listing 8.12   Validating a user's age

```
<!-- ageform.aspx -->
<%@ Page Language="C#" Debug="true" %>

<script runat="server">
  private void ageHandler(object sender, EventArgs e) {
    if (IsValid)
      ageLabel.Text = "You are " + ageTextBox.Text + " years old.";
    else
      ageLabel.Text = "Please Enter Your Age.";
  }
</script>

<html><head><title>Validating a User's Age</title></head><body>
  <form runat='server'>

    <h1>Validating a User's Age</h1>
    <asp:label text="Age : " runat="server"/>
    <asp:textbox
      id="ageTextBox"
      columns="3"
      maxLength = "3"
      runat="server"/>
    <asp:button
      id="submitButton"
      text="Submit"
      onClick="ageHandler"
      runat="server"/>
    <p>
      <asp:label
        id="ageLabel"
        text="Please Enter Your Age."
        runat="server"/>
    </p>

    <!-- require an entry...  -->
    <asp:requiredFieldValidator
      controlToValidate="ageTextBox"
      errorMessage="Age required"
      enableClientScript="true"
      display="static"
      runat=server />

    <br/>

    <!-- must be an integer...  -->
    <asp:regularExpressionValidator
      controlToValidate="ageTextBox"
      errorMessage="Age must be an integer"
      enableClientScript="true"
      display="static"
      validationExpression="^\d{1,3}$"
      runat="server" />

    <br/>
```

```
<!-- must be aged between 1 and 120 years...  -->
<asp:rangeValidator
  controlToValidate="ageTextBox"
  errorMessage="Age must be between 1 and 120 years"
  enableClientScript="true"
  display="static"
  type="Integer"
  minimumValue="1"
  maximumValue="120"
  runat="server" />

<hr/>

</form>
</body></html>
```

In this example, we have redundancy for illustration purposes. We use the `RequiredFieldValidator` to ensure that the user makes an entry in the `age-TextBox`, while the `RegularExpressionValidator` requires the entry to consist of 1 to 3 digits:

```
validationExpression="^\d{1,3}$"
```

Finally, we use a `RangeValidator` to ensure that the user be between 1 and 120 years of age:

```
type="Integer"
minimumValue="1"
maximumValue="120"
```

Note that the following properties are common to all three controls:

- `controlToValidate`—Specifies the control to be validated. That's `age-TextBox` in this example.

- `errorMessage`—The error text to be displayed if validation fails.

- `enableClientScript`—If you set this property to `true`, the control will attempt to generate client-side JavaScript to perform the validation, if the browser supports it. This saves a roundtrip to the server.

- `display`—Validation controls are invisible by default. They are displayed only if an error occurs, in which case they may cause other page elements to move on the page. Specify `static` to create space for the error display whether it is visible or not.

Note the test in the `ageHandler`:

```
if (IsValid)
  ...
else
  ...
```

If a validation control triggers an error, it sets the page's IsValid property to false. If there are multiple validation controls on the form, the IsValid property provides a convenient way to check for any input errors.

If you run this example, and submit the form without making an entry in the age field, you should see the result shown in figure 8.11.

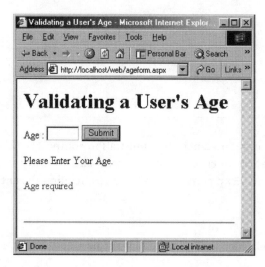

Figure 8.11
Using RequiredFieldValidator control

Entering an age outside of the permissible range results in the error message shown in figure 8.12.

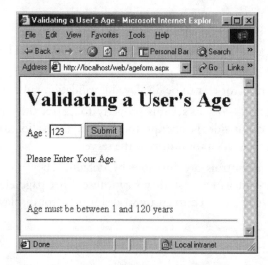

Figure 8.12
Using the RangeValidator control

Note that the ValidationSummary control provides a means of displaying error messages in summary form in a single location, such as the top or bottom of a form:

CHAPTER 8 CREATING THE WEB FORMS USER INTERFACE

```
<!-- summarize errors...  -->
<asp:validationSummary
  displayMode="BulletList"
  HeaderText="Error Summary:"
  runat="server"/>
```

8.6 CONFIGURING AND CUSTOMIZING ASP.NET APPLICATIONS

In chapter 5, we took a brief look at the *Web.config* file when we configured `RemoteEncoder.Base64Service` and deployed it on IIS. ASP.NET provides a hierarchical configuration system that allows an administrator to define configuration data at the application, site, or machine level. This file is called *Web.config* and, to configure an application, it is typically placed in the application root directory. Its format is the same as the *<appname>.exe.config* file used with desktop .NET applications. Since it is a regular text file, it can be copied together with the application files to a new sever, thus obviating the need for duplicating registry configuration settings, and the like.

ASP.NET supports separate configuration files in application subdirectories. Each applies its settings to the directory in which it is located and any virtual directories beneath. Settings in child directories can override or modify settings inherited from the parent directory.

The ASP.NET configuration system is part of .NET's machinewide configuration infrastructure. Therefore, the configuration settings for http://server/app/dir/page.aspx are computed by applying the settings in the following files, in the following order:

1 *C:\WINNT\Microsoft.NET\Framework\<version>\CONFIG\machine.config*: The base configuration settings for the machine

2 *C:\inetpub\wwwroot\web.config*: The base configuration settings for the root Web site

3 *C:\app\web.config*: Application-specific settings

4 *C:\app\dir\web.config*: Subdirectory-specific settings

While the structure of the XML-based *Web.config* file is the same as the configuration files we explored in chapter 5, the number and variety of possible configuration settings is a bit intimidating. Scenarios covered include the installation of custom ISAPI-like HTTP handlers, implementing custom security and logging, specifying session timeout, supporting alternate locales, configuring application tracing and debugging, and so forth. However, the good news is that the default settings may be sufficient for your application's needs, in which case you don't need a *Web.config* file at all.

You can also store application parameters in the *Web.config* file and retrieve them using the technique used in the `Bank` class in chapter 4. (However, you might want to use the *global.asax* file for application parameters, as we'll see in a moment.)

ASP.NET caches configuration files and reloads them in the event of a change. Therefore, you don't need to stop and restart the server for configuration settings to take effect. Also, by default, ASP.NET prevents access to configuration files by unauthorized users of your application.

We'll look at some examples of ASP.NET application configuration and customization in the sections that follow. This will include the development, installation, and use of a custom HTTP module, configuring tracing and debugging, and managing application and session state.

8.6.1 Creating a custom HTTP module

HTTP requests can be processed by one or more HTTP modules to implement authentication, logging, error handling, or some specialized custom handling as required by the application. You can create your own custom module to handle HTTP requests and install it by including it in the `httpModules` section of the *Web.config* file. Listing 8.13 presents a simple example.

> **Listing 8.13   A custom HTTP module to count HTTP requests**

```
// file    : custhttpmodules.cs
// compile : csc /t:library custhttpmodules.cs

using System;
using System.Web;
using System.Web.SessionState;

namespace CustHttpModules {

  public class RequestCounterModule : IHttpModule {

    public void Init(HttpApplication ha) {
      ha.AcquireRequestState += new EventHandler(gotState);
    }

    public void Dispose() {
      // perform any necessary cleanup here
    }

    private void gotState(object sender, EventArgs e) {

      HttpApplication ha = (HttpApplication)sender;
      HttpSessionState s = ha.Session;

      if (s["numRequests"] == null) {
        s["numRequests"] = 1;
      } else {
        int numRequests = (int)s["numRequests"];
        s["numRequests"] = ++numRequests;
      }
    }
  }
}
```

The purpose of this module is to count HTTP requests for the current session. To code the custom `HttpModule` we need to create a class that implements the `IHttpModule` interface and provides `Init` and `Dispose` methods. The `Init` method takes an `HttpApplication` object as an argument. This object exposes several events, such as `BeginRequest`, `AcquireRequestState`, and `EndRequest`, which are fired in the process of handling the HTTP request. In this example, we add an event handler for the `AcquireRequestState` event. This event is fired at the point in processing where session state has been established, enabling us to store the request count in `Session["numRequests"]`. If, instead, we override `BeginRequest`, we won't be able to read and write session data.

In order to install the module, we need to add an entry to the `<httpModules>` section of the *Web.config* file, as shown in listing 8.14.

Listing 8.14 Installing an HTTP module

```
<configuration>
 <system.web>
  <httpModules>
   <add
    name="Request Counter Module"
    type="CustHttpModules.RequestCounterModule,custhttpmodules" />
  </httpModules>
 </system.web>
</configuration>
```

In order for ASP.NET to find our module, we must compile it and place it in the *bin* subdirectory of the application directory. Once the module has been installed, our ASP.NET application will have access to the number of HTTP requests received during the current session. Listing 8.15 presents a simple *.aspx* page which uses the counter.

Listing 8.15 Using the HTTP request counter

```
<!-- dumpreqs.aspx -->

<%@ Page Language="C#" Debug="true"%>

<script runat="server">
  private void dumpReqs() {
    string s = "Number of Requests: " + Session["numRequests"];
    Response.Write(s);
  }
</script>

<html><head><title>HTTP Request Count</title></head>
  <body>
    <h1>HTTP Request Count</h1>
    <% dumpReqs(); %>
  </body>
</html>
```

If you run the application and refresh the page in your browser a few times, you should see an incrementing count of HTTP requests.

Installing a custom HTTP module provides an elegant way to preprocess requests before they reach your ASP.NET pages. You can use this approach to implement your own custom authentication or logging, or to set defaults or load user preferences, or any number of useful tasks that might better be performed before your ASP.NET pages are invoked.

8.6.2   Creating a custom HTTP handler

The HTTP handler is similar to an HTTP module, in that it provides custom processing of incoming HTTP requests. However, the HTTP handler is designed to process the request completely, and return a result to the browser. Therefore, if the Web Forms infrastructure is not essential to the handling of the HTTP request, you can implement an HTTP handler instead. Listing 8.16 provides a simple example.

Listing 8.16   A custom HTTP handler

```
// file    : custhttphandlers.cs
// compile : csc /t:library custhttphandlers.cs

using System.Web;

namespace CustomHttpHandlers {

  public class HelloHandler : IHttpHandler {

    public void ProcessRequest(HttpContext hc) {
      hc.Response.Write("Hello, World!");
    }

    public bool IsReusable {
      get {
        return true;
      }
    }
  }
}
```

Installing an `HttpHandler` intercepts requests before they are processed by the page framework. This example returns a plain text greeting to the browser and can be installed using the following configuration file entries shown in listing 8.17.

Listing 8.17   Installing a custom HTTP handler

```
<httpHandlers>
  <add
    verb="*"
    path="hellohandler.aspx"
```

```
       type="CustomHttpHandlers.HelloHandler, custhttphandlers" />
</httpHandlers>
```

The configuration entry specifies that all requests for *hellohandler.aspx* should be routed to our `HelloHandler` handler. To run this example, remember to place the compiled handler DLL in the application's *bin* subdirectory.

8.7 TRACING ASP.NET APPLICATIONS

ASP.NET provides a new tracing feature to aid the developer in testing applications and isolating problems. This enables you to trace through the execution of your application and write trace data to the browser. You can also leave your trace statements in the application and simply switch them off in production. Tracing can be enabled at two levels:

- Page-level tracing
- Application-level tracing

To enable page-level tracing, you need to switch it on in the `Page` directive at the start of the ASP.NET file:

```
<%@ Page Language="C#" Trace="true"%>
```

Doing so appends trace information to the output sent to the browser. You can also insert your own trace information into the output using `Trace.Write` and `Trace.Warn` statements. Listing 8.18 is a reworking of the *helloform.aspx* application seen earlier. This version enables tracing and inserts some custom output into the trace.

Listing 8.18 Tracing an ASP.NET application

```
<!-- traceform.aspx -->

<%@ Page Language="C#" Trace="True" %>

<script runat="server">

  // greet the user...
  private void greetHandler(object sender, EventArgs e) {

    Trace.Warn("*** Entering greetHandler ***");

    firstNameTextBox.Text = firstNameTextBox.Text.Trim();

    Trace.Warn("*** First Name = '" +
      firstNameTextBox.Text + "' ***");

    if (firstNameTextBox.Text == "") {
      // no name, so no greeting...
      greetingLabel.Text = "";
      Trace.Warn("*** No greeting ***");
```

```
    } else {
      // greet the user...
      greetingLabel.Text =
        "Hello, " + firstNameTextBox.Text + "!";
    }
    Trace.Warn("*** Greeting = '" + greetingLabel.Text + "' ***");
  }
</script>

<html><head><title>Hello Web Form</title></head>

<body>
  <h1>Hello Web Form</h1>
  <form action='helloform.aspx' method='POST' runat='server'>

  <asp:label text="What's Your First Name?" runat="server"/>
  <asp:textbox id="firstNameTextBox" runat="server"/>
  <asp:button
    id="greetButton"
    text="Greet"
    OnClick="greetHandler"
    runat="server"/>
  <p>
  <asp:label id="greetingLabel" runat="server"/>
  </p>

  </form>
</body>
</html>
```

Note the use of `Trace.Warn` to write out trace data. Executing this application, entering your name, and submitting the form produces the output shown in figure 8.13.

As you can see there is a lot of information in the trace including events processed and their duration. If you scroll downward, you'll also see information about controls and the size in bytes of their viewstate data, any session objects and their values, cookies if any, HTTP headers, and server variables. Typically more useful, however, is the custom trace information that we created ourselves. This is included in the *Trace Information* section.

When the application is debugged, we can simply leave our trace statements in place, and switch off tracing at the top of the file:

```
<%@ Page Language="C#" Trace="false"%>
```

You can also turn on tracing at the application level using a configuration file entry:

```
<configuration>
  <system.web>
    <trace
      enabled="true"
```

```
        localOnly="true"
        pageOutput="false"
        requestLimit="10"
        traceMode="SortByTime"
    />
  </system.web>
</configuration>
```

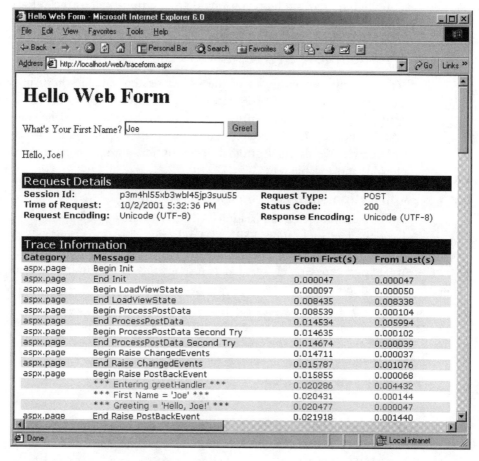

Figure 8.13   Displaying trace information

Switching on application-level tracing switches on tracing for every page in the application. You can control application-level tracing using the following attributes:

- enabled—Set to true to switch on tracing
- localOnly—Set to true to enable tracing on *localhost* only
- pageOutput—Set to true to append trace information to the end of each page

- requestLimit—The maximum number of trace requests to store on the server, (the default is 10)
- traceMode—Set to SortByTime or SortByCategory

Note that, if pageOutput is false, the trace data can be viewed by browsing the trace.axd file in the browser. For example, to access trace information for the *hello* application on the localhost, you would go to http://localhost/hello/trace.axd.

8.8 MANAGING APPLICATION AND SESSION STATE

We've already seen examples of the use of session variables both in our ASP.NET applications and XML Web services. We've also explored how Web Forms implement a viewstate mechanism to store the state of a form and its controls between server roundtrips. In addition, ASP.NET provides an application state store which we explore next. We also look at the different options for managing state information in a flexible and scalable way.

8.8.1 Application state and the Global.Asax file

Unlike session objects, application objects are shared by all sessions and live for the duration of an application. ASP.NET application objects are typically created and initialized in the *global.asax* file. Listing 8.19 provides an example in which we code an Application_Start method to extract the allowed minimum and maximum bets from the *poker* database.

> **Listing 8.19 Creating application-based objects in the Global.Asax file**

```
<%@ Import Namespace="System.Data" %>
<%@ Import Namespace="System.Data.SqlClient" %>

<script language="C#" runat="server">

  // global.asax methods...

private void Application_Start(object sender, EventArgs e) {

  SqlConnection con =
    new SqlConnection(
    @"server=(local)\NetSDK;database=poker;trusted_connection=yes");

  string sql;
  SqlDataAdapter com;
  DataSet ds = new DataSet();

  sql = "SELECT value From Integers WHERE name = 'MaxBet'";
  com = new SqlDataAdapter(sql, con);
  com.Fill(ds, "MaxBet");
  Application["MaxBet"] = ds.Tables["MaxBet"].Rows[0][0];

  sql = "SELECT value From Integers WHERE name = 'MinBet'";
```

```
   com = new SqlDataAdapter(sql, con);
   com.Fill(ds, "MinBet");
   Application["MinBet"] = ds.Tables["MinBet"].Rows[0][0];
  }
</script>
```

The `Application_Start` method is executed when the application starts. Typically, this is when our site receives its first visitor causing the first HTTP request to be generated. Listing 8.20 shows how we can retrieve application objects in an ASP.NET page.

Listing 8.20 Accessing application-based objects

```
<!-- dumpbets.aspx -->
<%@ Page Language="C#" Debug="true"%>

<script runat="server">
  private void dumpBets() {
    string s = "Minimum Bet: " + Application["MinBet"] + "<br/>";
    s += "Maximum Bet: " + Application["MaxBet"];
    Response.Write(s);
  }
</script>

<html><head><title>Application State</title></head>
  <body>
    <h1>Application State</h1>
    <% dumpBets(); %>
  </body>
</html>
```

Here we access `Application["MaxBet"]` and write it to the response stream. The advantage of using application-based objects is that, once the first application request occurs, all subsequent requests have immediate access to the application object. In this example, that means that the SQL statements are executed just once. Therefore, the application store is a good place to store data that doesn't change, or changes only infrequently, during the application's lifetime. (The poker machine parameters are good candidates, while the machine statistics are not.)

Since application objects can be concurrently accessed by different sessions, changing application data requires locking the application object and this results in a performance penalty as several threads compete for the same resource. Therefore, if you must change an application object, you'll need to use the following approach in your pages:

```
Application.Lock();
Application["someVar"] = someVal;
Application.UnLock();
```

8.8.2 Managing session state

We looked at session-based storage in chapter 6 when we explored Web services. `Session` is a public instance property of both `System.Web.UI.Page` and `System.Web.Services.WebService`. Typically, we store and retrieve session-based data, as follows:

```
int numRequests = (int)Session["numRequests"];

...

Session["numRequests"] = ++numRequests;
```

In ASP.NET terms, a session begins when a user first visits our application and ends when the session expires. Expiration occurs when there has been no activity for a period of time, unless we provide an explicit mechanism, such as a logout feature, which allows us to end the session with `Session.Abandon`. The expiration time, and other session parameters, can be set in the configuration file, as follows:

```
<configuration>
  <system.web>
    <sessionState
      mode="InProc"
      cookieless="true"
      timeout="20"
      stateConnectionString=" ... "
      sqlConnectionString=" ... " />
  </system.web>
</configuration>
```

The meanings of these attributes are:

- `mode`—Specify `Off` to switch off sessions, `InProc` to store session state data locally in the same process that processes the request, `StateServer` to store remotely, or `SqlServer` to store in SQL Server. If you specify `StateServer`, ASP.NET will store session data in an external process, which can be on another machine. In that case, you'll also need to set the `stateConnectionString` attribute.
- `cookieless`—Specify `true` for sessions without cookies, `false` otherwise. If you set to `true`, ASP.NET tracks a session by adding a session identifier to the URL.
- `timeout`—Specify the number of minutes a session must be idle before it is abandoned.
- `stateConnectionString`—If mode is `StateServer`, specify the server name and port for the remote server, such as `127.0.0.1:42424`. By default, the state service listens on port 42424.
- `sqlConnectionString`—If mode is `SqlServer`, specify the SQL Server connection string here.

Perhaps the most important attribute is mode, which enables you to separate session state management from the application and place it in a separate process, or on a different machine, or even in SQL Server. This insulates state data from application crashes or IIS restarts. It also allows an application to be partitioned across multiple processes or multiple machines. Each process can communicate separately with the state service.

8.9 CREATING WEB FORMS USING VISUAL STUDIO .NET

So far, we've done things the hard way and hand-coded all our ASP.NET examples. While this is the best way to learn, you'll eventually want to take advantage of some of the powerful features of Visual Studio .NET to ease the burden and reduce the tedium. So let's see what Visual Studio .NET can do for us. We'll create a base 64 encoding form similar to the remote service we developed in chapter 5.

8.9.1 Creating a Web application using Visual Studio .NET

Launch Visual Studio .NET, select File | New | Project... from the menu. Then, in the left pane, select Visual C# Projects, and, in the right pane, select ASP.NET Web Application. Call your new project *Base64App* and click OK to create it. See figure 8.14.

If everything works properly, Visual Studio .NET should create a new Web Forms project, and the solution explorer should display the contents of the project. You'll notice that the project workspace looks very similar to that seen in the previous chapter when we created a Windows Forms project. If you launch Internet Services Manager,

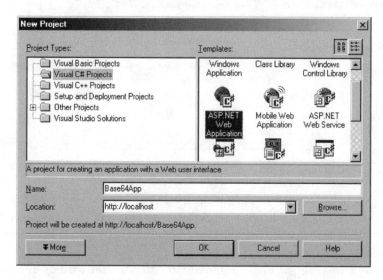

Figure 8.14   Creating a Web application using Visual Studio .NET

you'll find that Visual Studio .NET has created a new virtual directory on the server and placed the project files there. By default, the files will be placed in the physical *C:\inetpub\wwwroot\Base64App* directory.

So, as you can see, Visual Studio .NET automatically creates the project, generates the project files, and puts them in their proper places. Also, you'll note that we've got an *AssemblyInfo.cs* file, a *Global.asax* file, a DISCO file called *Base64App.vsdisco*, a *Web.config* file, and, of course, a new Web Form file, *WebForm1.aspx*, and finally a file called *WebForm1.aspx.cs*. Visual Studio .NET separates the Web Form itself, and the code behind the form, into the latter two files. If, for example, you examine the *.aspx* file, you'll see the following directive at the top:

```
<%@ Page
    language="c#"
    Codebehind="WebForm1.aspx.cs"
    AutoEventWireup="false"
    Inherits="Base64App.Base64Form" %>
```

Visual Studio .NET uses the value of the `Codebehind` attribute to locate the programming code associated with the page. We'll look more closely at the code-behind model in the next section.

8.9.2   Using the toolbox to design a Web Form

Visual Studio .NET supports a drag-and-drop approach to Web Forms design. Our base 64 encoding application is shown in figure 8.15.

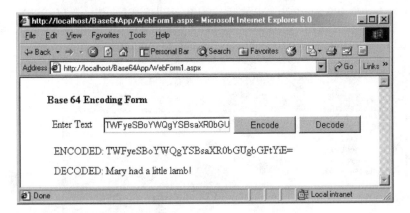

Figure 8.15   Using the Base 64 encoding application

To use the application, enter some plain text in the text box and click `Encode`. The encoded result is shown below the text entered. You can paste the encoded result back into the text box and click the `Decode` button, in which case the encoded text is decoded and also displayed at the bottom of the form.

We begin by dragging the appropriate controls from the toolbox to create the UI. See figure 8.16.

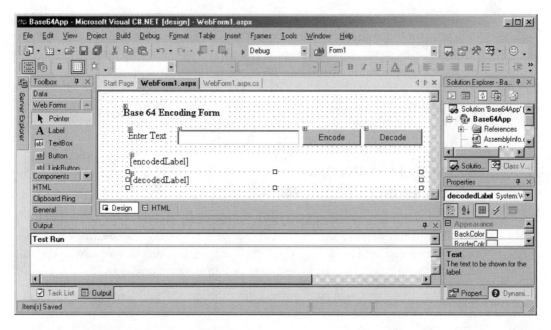

Figure 8.16 Designing the Base 64 user interface

At this point, double-click both the encodeButton and decodeButton and enter the code shown in figure 8.17.

```
        }
        #endregion

        private void encodeButton_Click(object sender, System.EventArgs e) {
            base64TextBox.Text = base64TextBox.Text;
            if (base64TextBox.Text == "") {
                encodedLabel.Text = "";
            } else {
                byte[] b = Encoding.ASCII.GetBytes(base64TextBox.Text);
                encodedLabel.Text = "ENCODED: " + Convert.ToBase64String(b);
            }
        }

        private void decodeButton_Click(object sender, System.EventArgs e) {
            base64TextBox.Text = base64TextBox.Text;
            if (base64TextBox.Text == "") {
                decodedLabel.Text = "";
            } else {
                byte[] b = Convert.FromBase64String(base64TextBox.Text);
                decodedLabel.Text = "DECODED: " + Encoding.ASCII.GetString(b);
            }
        }
    }
}
```

Figure 8.17 Coding the Encode and Decode button handlers

Finally, press F5 to execute the application. If you've followed each step, Visual Studio .NET should compile the application, and launch Internet Explorer so that you can browse the result, as seen in figure 8.15. Depending on your setup, you may get an error saying that the System.Text or some other namespace is missing, in which case you should edit the *WebForm1.aspx.cs* file and add the appropriate using statement.

That's all there is to it. In just a couple of minutes, we've used Visual Studio to create and deploy a fully functional ASP.NET application.

8.10 MANUALLY CREATING CODE-BEHIND WEB FORMS

You need to do things a little differently to manually create a code-behind application. To illustrate, let's create a code-behind version of the *helloform.aspx* application that we explored earlier. We place the presentation markup in *behindform.aspx* and the C# code in *behindform.cs*. Listing 8.21 presents *behindform.aspx*.

Listing 8.21   ASP.NET markup for code-behind Hello application

```
<!-- behindform.aspx -->

<%@ Page Language="C#" Inherits="BehindForm" Src="behindform.cs" %>

<html><head><title>Hello Web Form</title></head>

<body>
  <h1>Hello Web Form (Code-Behind Version)</h1>
  <form action='behindform.aspx' method='POST' runat='server'>

  <asp:label text="What's Your First Name?" runat="server"/>
  <asp:textbox id="firstNameTextBox" runat="server"/>
  <asp:button
    id="greetButton"
    text="Greet"
    OnClick="greetHandler"
    runat="server"/>
  <p>
  <asp:label id="greetingLabel" runat="server"/>
  </p>

  </form>
</body>
</html>
```

The important line is:

```
<%@ Page Language="C#" Inherits="BehindForm" Src="behindform.cs" %>
```

This tells us that the page is derived from the `BehindForm` class located in the file, *behindform.cs*. Note that we don't use a `CodeBehind` attribute. It is used by Visual Studio .NET to help locate the files involved, and is unnecessary here.

We've also deleted the script code from the file and moved it to `behindform.cs`, shown in listing 8.22.

Listing 8.22   C# code for code-behind Hello application

```
// file : behindform.cs

using System;
using System.Web.UI;
using System.Web.UI.WebControls;

public class BehindForm : Page {

  protected TextBox firstNameTextBox;
  protected Label greetingLabel;

  // greet the user...
  protected void greetHandler(object sender, EventArgs e) {

    firstNameTextBox.Text = firstNameTextBox.Text.Trim();
    if (firstNameTextBox.Text == "") {
      // no name, so no greeting...
      greetingLabel.Text = "";
    } else {
      // greet the user...
      greetingLabel.Text =
        "Hello, " + firstNameTextBox.Text + "!";
    }
  }
}
```

Since this is a regular C# class, we use the `using` statement to identify the namespaces used. Note that, the class derives from `Page` and declares protected members for the text box and label. The `greetHandler` method is also marked protected. Recall that the *.aspx* file itself defines a class that inherits from our code-behind class. Therefore, the page will inherit these members. If you place both files into a new virtual IIS directory and use your browser to test the application, you should get results identical to those we saw earlier.

8.11   *WEBPOK: THE WEB FORMS-BASED POKER MACHINE*

Now, we return to our case study and build a Web Forms-based user interface to the *poker.dll* assembly. We'll just code a simple version of the game that deals and draws cards, and scores hands. Figure 8.18 shows what the game looks like in the browser.

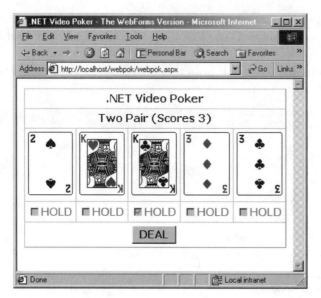

Figure 8.18
Playing WebPok

The user interface consists of a table, 5 rows long, and 5 columns wide, and is laid out as follows:

- *Row 1*—A static <asp:label> which reads ".NET Video Poker"
- *Row 2*—A dynamic <asp:label> to display game messages and the score
- *Row 3*—Five <asp:image> controls to display the cards
- *Row 4*—Five <asp:checkbox> controls to allow the user to hold cards
- *Row 5*—An <asp:button> control for dealing and drawing cards

We'll use the code-behind approach. Listing 8.23 presents *webpok.aspx* which contains the user interface markup.

Listing 8.23   The WebPok Web Form

```
<!-- WebPok.aspx -->
<%@ Page Language="C#" Inherits="Poker.WebPok" Src="WebPok.cs" %>

<html>
<head>
  <title>
    .NET Video Poker - The WebForms Version
  </title>
</head>
<body>
<center>
<form runat="server">

<asp:table
    border="1"
    cellSpacing="0"
```

CHAPTER 8   CREATING THE WEB FORMS USER INTERFACE

```
      cellPadding="5"
     runat="server">

    <asp:tablerow runat="server">
      <asp:tableCell
        columnSpan="5"
        horizontalAlign="center"
        runat="server">
        <asp:label
          text=".NET Video Poker"
          Font-Name="Verdana"
          Font-Size="12pt"
          Font-Bold="true"
          runat="server"/>
      </asp:tableCell>
    </asp:tablerow>

    <asp:tablerow runat="server">
      <asp:tableCell
        columnSpan="5"
        horizontalAlign="center"
        runat="server">
        <asp:label
          id="messageLabel"
          text="Click DEAL to Start"
          Font-Name="Verdana"
          Font-Size="12pt"
          Font-Bold="true"
          runat="server"/>
      </asp:tableCell>
    </asp:tablerow>

    <asp:tablerow runat="server">

      <asp:tableCell
        horizontalAlign="center"
        runat="server">
        <asp:image
          id="card1"
          ImageUrl="images/cb.gif"
          runat="server"/>
      </asp:tableCell>

      <asp:tableCell
        horizontalAlign="center"
        runat="server">
        <asp:image
          id="card2"
          ImageUrl="images/cb.gif"
          runat="server"/>
      </asp:tableCell>

      <asp:tableCell
        horizontalAlign="center"
```

```
        runat="server">
      <asp:image
        id="card3"
        ImageUrl="images/cb.gif"
        runat="server"/>
    </asp:tableCell>

    <asp:tableCell
      horizontalAlign="center"
      runat="server">
      <asp:image
        id="card4"
        ImageUrl="images/cb.gif"
        runat="server"/>
    </asp:tableCell>

    <asp:tableCell
      horizontalAlign="center"
      runat="server">
      <asp:image
        id="card5"
        ImageUrl="images/cb.gif"
        runat="server"/>
    </asp:tableCell>

</asp:tablerow>

<asp:tablerow runat="server">

    <asp:tableCell
      horizontalAlign="center"
      runat="server">
      <asp:checkBox
        id="hold1"
        text="HOLD"
        enabled="false"
        Font-Name="Verdana"
        Font-Size="12pt"
        Font-Bold="true"
        runat="server"/>
    </asp:tableCell>

    <asp:tableCell
      horizontalAlign="center"
      runat="server">
      <asp:checkBox
        id="hold2"
        text="HOLD"
        enabled="false"
        Font-Name="Verdana"
        Font-Size="12pt"
        Font-Bold="true"
        runat="server"/>
    </asp:tableCell>
```

```
<asp:tableCell
  horizontalAlign="center"
  runat="server">
  <asp:checkBox
    id="hold3"
    text="HOLD"
    enabled="false"
    Font-Name="Verdana"
    Font-Size="12pt"
    Font-Bold="true"
    runat="server"/>
</asp:tableCell>

<asp:tableCell
  horizontalAlign="center"
  runat="server">
  <asp:checkBox
    id="hold4"
    text="HOLD"
    enabled="false"
    Font-Name="Verdana"
    Font-Size="12pt"
    Font-Bold="true"
    runat="server"/>
</asp:tableCell>

<asp:tableCell
  horizontalAlign="center"
  runat="server">
  <asp:checkBox
    id="hold5"
    text="HOLD"
    enabled="false"
    Font-Name="Verdana"
    Font-Size="12pt"
    Font-Bold="true"
    runat="server"/>
</asp:tableCell>

</asp:tablerow>

<asp:tablerow runat="server">
  <asp:tableCell
    columnSpan="5"
    horizontalAlign="center"
    runat="server">
    <asp:button
      id="dealDrawButton"
      text="DEAL"
      Font-Name="Verdana"
      Font-Size="12pt"
      Font-Bold="true"
      OnClick="dealDrawHandler"
```

```
          runat="server"/>
      </asp:tableCell>
    </asp:tablerow>

</asp:table>

<asp:label id="handLabel" visible="false" runat="server"/>
</form>
<center>
</body>
</html>
```

As you can see, the markup is very simple. When the page is first loaded, we display
the backs of the cards and tell the user "Click DEAL to Start." Also, we have just one
event handler in the page, which deals and draws cards:

```
<asp:button
  id="dealDrawButton"
  ...
  OnClick="dealDrawHandler"
  .../>
```

The dealDrawHandler is contained in the code behind the form, shown in
listing 8.24.

Listing 8.24 The WebPok Web Form code

```
// file : WebPok.cs
// This is the codebehind logic for WebPok.aspx.

namespace Poker {

  using System;
  using System.Web.UI;
  using System.Web.UI.WebControls;

  public class WebPok : System.Web.UI.Page {

    protected void dealDrawHandler(object Source, EventArgs e) {
      Hand h;
      if (dealDrawButton.Text == "DEAL") {

        // deal...
        h = new SimpleMachine().Deal();
        handLabel.Text = h.Text;
        card1.ImageUrl="images/" + h.CardName(1) + ".gif";
        card2.ImageUrl="images/" + h.CardName(2) + ".gif";
        card3.ImageUrl="images/" + h.CardName(3) + ".gif";
        card4.ImageUrl="images/" + h.CardName(4) + ".gif";
        card5.ImageUrl="images/" + h.CardName(5) + ".gif";
        enableCheckBoxes(true);
        clearCheckBoxes();
        dealDrawButton.Text = "DRAW";
        messageLabel.Text = "Hold Cards and Click DRAW";
```

```
        return;
    }

    // draw...
    string holdCards = "";
    if (hold1.Checked) holdCards += "1";
    if (hold2.Checked) holdCards += "2";
    if (hold3.Checked) holdCards += "3";
    if (hold4.Checked) holdCards += "4";
    if (hold5.Checked) holdCards += "5";
    h = new SimpleMachine().Draw(handLabel.Text, holdCards);
    card1.ImageUrl="images/" + h.CardName(1) + ".gif";
    card2.ImageUrl="images/" + h.CardName(2) + ".gif";
    card3.ImageUrl="images/" + h.CardName(3) + ".gif";
    card4.ImageUrl="images/" + h.CardName(4) + ".gif";
    card5.ImageUrl="images/" + h.CardName(5) + ".gif";
    dealDrawButton.Text = "DEAL";
    enableCheckBoxes(false);
    messageLabel.Text = h.Title + " (Scores " + h.Score + ")";
}

private void enableCheckBoxes(bool flag) {
    hold1.Enabled = hold2.Enabled = hold3.Enabled =
      hold4.Enabled = hold5.Enabled = flag;
}

private void clearCheckBoxes() {
    hold1.Checked = hold2.Checked = hold3.Checked =
      hold4.Checked = hold5.Checked = false;
}

protected Button dealDrawButton;
protected Label handLabel,messageLabel;
protected Image card1, card2, card3, card4, card5;
protected CheckBox hold1, hold2, hold3, hold4, hold5;
    }
}
```

The WebPok class consists of the dealDrawHandler method and a couple of utility methods for clearing and enabling/disabling the check boxes. Since we don't allow betting, we use the Poker.SimpleMachine class which supports dealing and drawing only. The dealDrawHandler method checks the caption of the button. If it is DEAL, it deals cards. Otherwise cards are drawn.

8.12 MOBPOK: THE MOBILE INTERNET-BASED POKER MACHINE

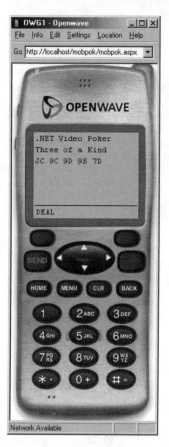

Figure 8.19 Playing MobPok

At the time of writing, Microsoft was providing the Mobile Internet Toolkit for .NET as a separate download. The toolkit consists of a set of classes in the `System.Web.Mobile` and `System.Web.UI.MobileControls` namespaces, deployed in the *System.Web.Mobile.dll* assembly. A mobile Web Form is a specialized type of ASP.NET Web Form containing mobile server controls. Like regular Web Forms, mobile Web Forms are stored as *.aspx* pages. The chief advantage of the mobile Web Forms infrastructure is that it can detect supported mobile devices and render a page to suit a device's capabilities.

We're going to develop a simple mobile interface to the poker game. Figure 8.19 shows the game in play using the *UP.Simulator* from Openwave Systems. (See http://developer.openwave.com.)

To hold cards, we'll use the approach used in `ConPok`, so that the user can hold cards by entering card numbers using the numeric phone keypad. Listing 8.25 presents the mobile markup for the UI.

Listing 8.25 The MobPok Web Form

```
<!-- MobPok.aspx -->

<%@ Page
  Language="C#"
  Inherits="Poker.MobPok"
  Src="MobPok.cs" %>

<%@ Register TagPrefix="mobile"
  Namespace="System.Web.UI.MobileControls"
  Assembly="System.Web.Mobile" %>

<mobile:Form runat="server">
<mobile:label runat="server" text=".NET Video Poker"/>
<mobile:label runat="server" id="messageLabel" text="Click DEAL"/>
```

```
<mobile:label runat="server" id="handLabel"/>
<mobile:textbox
  runat="server"
  id="holdTextBox"
  numeric="true"
  maxLength="5"
  size="5"
  visible="false"/>
<mobile:command
  runat="server"
  id="dealDrawCommand"
  text="DEAL"
  OnClick="dealDrawHandler"/>
</mobile:form>
```

As you can see, the markup is very simple. We start by registering the mobile tag prefix to tell ASP.NET the names of the namespace and assembly where the mobile controls reside. Then, we use just three labels, a text box, and a command button to present the user interface. The code behind the page is shown in Listing 8.26.

Listing 8.26   The MobPok Web Form code

```
// file : MobPok.cs
// This is the codebehind logic for MobPok.aspx.

namespace Poker {

  using System;
  using System.Web.UI.MobileControls;

  public class MobPok : System.Web.UI.MobileControls.MobilePage {

    protected void dealDrawHandler(object Source, EventArgs e) {
      Hand h;
      if (dealDrawCommand.Text == "DEAL") {

        // deal...
        h = new SimpleMachine().Deal();
        handLabel.Text = h.Text;
        dealDrawCommand.Text = "DRAW";
        holdTextBox.Visible = true;
        holdTextBox.Text = " ";
        messageLabel.Text = "Hold and Draw";
        return;
      }

      // draw...
      string holdCards = holdTextBox.Text;
      h = new SimpleMachine().Draw(handLabel.Text, holdCards);
      handLabel.Text = h.Text;
      dealDrawCommand.Text = "DEAL";
      holdTextBox.Visible = false;
```

```
            messageLabel.Text = h.Title;
        }

        protected Label handLabel,messageLabel;
        protected TextBox holdTextBox;
        protected Command dealDrawCommand;
    }
}
```

8.13 SUMMARY

In this chapter, we explored ASP.NET and the Web Forms programming model. We compared ASP.NET to ASP and examined the System.Web.UI.Page class. We looked at Web Forms and server controls, built a reusable user control of our own, and saw how to validate user input.

We learned about configuring ASP.NET applications, tracing execution, and the management of session and application state. We took a brief look at Visual Studio .NET and the code-behind programming model, and we also saw how to manually create code-behind applications. Finally, we developed two new versions of the poker game using regular Web Forms and the Mobile Internet Toolkit.

If you are new to the platform, I hope this book has helped you to understand how all the pieces of .NET hang together. For Windows developers, it is no longer enough to be a VB virtuoso, a C++ connoisseur, an MFC master, a Win32 wizard, or an ASP authority. Instead, the key to making the most of .NET is a grasp of the underlying concepts, familiarity with the Framework, and effective programming skills in the language of your choice.

Please visit http://www.manning.com/grimes where you can share your comments or criticism and download updated examples.

APPENDIX A

Introduction to C#

C# is the latest in an evolutionary line of C-based programming languages which includes C, C++, and Java. It was used by Microsoft to develop much of the code for the .NET Framework and is considered by many to be the language of choice for .NET development. This appendix provides an introduction to the C# language.

Since C# was created with .NET in mind, many features of this language reflect underlying features of the .NET platform. One example is the boxing mechanism, which we explore in detail in chapter 2. It can be difficult to separate C# from .NET when discussing such features. In general, I have tried to cover .NET-specific topics in the main body of this book, while exploring the C# language in this appendix. However, neither can be discussed in isolation. Therefore, you'll find the following related material in the main body of the book:

- Compiling and executing a first C# program—See chapter 1
- An overview of important namespaces—See chapter 1
- C# types—See chapter 2
- Value versus reference types—See chapter 2
- Boxing and unboxing—See chapter 2
- The object type (System.Object)—See chapter 2
- Finalizing and disposing objects—See chapter 2
- Assemblies—See chapter 2
- Reflection—See chapter 2

In addition, you'll find almost 100 C# sample programs throughout the text, together with a complete case study. These support a *learn-by-example* approach to supplement the material in this appendix.

This appendix does not provide complete coverage of the C# language. To do so would require a further book. Instead, the intention is to introduce the important features of the language and equip the reader with the information necessary to understand the main text. At the end of this appendix, I have provided a list of resources where you can find further C# tutorials and reference material.

A.1 C# LANGUAGE OVERVIEW

The C# language is an evolution of C and C++, and also has much in common with the Java programming language. Therefore, readers familiar with one or more of these languages will immediately feel comfortable with many features of the C# language, including C# statements, expressions, and operators. C# introduces several modern improvements over C++ in the areas of type safety, versioning, events, and garbage collection. C# also provides full access to operating system and COM APIs, and supports an unsafe mode, which enables the use of C-style pointers to manipulate memory. Therefore, C# offers a simpler and safer programming language without sacrificing much of the power and flexibility of C++.

A.1.1 Structure of a C# program

A C# program consists of one or more files, each of which can contain one or more namespaces, which in turn contain types. Examples of types include classes, structs, interfaces, enumerations, and delegates. Listing A.1 illustrates the structure of a C# program.

Listing A.1 The structure of a C# program

```
namespace N1 {

  class C1 {
    // ...
  }

  struct S1 {
    // ...
  }

  interface I1 {
    // ...
  }

  delegate int D1();

  enum E1 {
    // ...
  }
}
```

```
namespace N2 {

  class C2 {

    public static void Main(string[] args) {
      // execution starts here
    }
  }
}
```

If no namespace is declared, then a default global namespace is assumed. Note that an executable C# program must include a class containing a `Main` function member, or *method*, which represents the program entry point where execution begins. Any command-line arguments are passed as parameters to the `Main` method in the form of a zero-based array of strings.

To access and use a type, you can use its fully qualified name, which includes its containing namespace name and type name. For example, the following example invokes the `WriteLine` method of the `Console` class, which is contained in the `System` namespace:

```
System.Console.WriteLine(...);
```

Alternatively, you can use the `using` statement to reference the namespace. Thereafter, you can omit the namespace name when referring to the type:

```
using System;
...
Console.WriteLine(...);
```

Finally, note the comments in listing A.1. C# uses C-style comments. Therefore, // marks the beginning of a comment which runs to the end of the current line. Multi-line comments can be enclosed between /* and */.

Refer to chapter 1 for more about coding, compiling, and executing a simple C# program.

A.2 IDENTIFIERS, VARIABLES, AND CONSTANTS

The rules for creating C# identifiers to name program elements are straightforward. We take a look at identifiers and at the declaration of variables and constants next.

A.2.1 Identifiers

Identifiers are used to give names to program elements such as variables, constants, and methods. An identifier must start with a letter or underscore and consist of Unicode characters. Typically, an identifier will consist of letters, underscores, and decimal digits. C# identifiers are case sensitive.

You cannot use a C# keyword as an identifier. However, you may prefix an identifier with the @ character to distinguish it from a keyword:

```
object @this;  // prevent clash with "this" keyword
```

Although C# identifiers are case sensitive, you should generally not distinguish public members by case alone. Apart from encouraging confusion, the cross language nature of .NET means that your types may be reused by a case insensitive language such as Visual Basic.

A.2.2 Variables

A C# variable represents a location in memory where an instance of some type is stored. The C# type system is really just a layer on top of .NET's *language-independent type system*, which we explore in detail in chapter 2. In particular, we explore the differences between value and reference types, so we won't repeat that discussion here. Briefly, value types are the simple types such as `int`, `long`, and `char`, which are common to most programming languages. You can also create your own value types. Objects, strings, and arrays are examples of reference types.

Value types can be directly declared and initialized:

```
bool bln = true;
byte byt1 = 22;
char ch1 = 'x', ch2 = '\u0066';
decimal dec1 = 1.23M;
double dbl1 = 1.23, dbl2 = 1.23D;
short sh = 22;
int i = 22;
long lng1 = 22, lng2 = 22L;
sbyte sb = 22;
float f = 1.23F;
ushort us1 = 22;
uint ui1 = 22, ui2 = 22U;
ulong ul1 = 22, ul2 = 22U, ul3 = 22L, ul4 = 2UL;
```

Note that you can explicitly specify the type of a literal value by appending a suffix such as U for unsigned, or L for long. You can also specify a character value using a Unicode escape sequence. For example, `'\u0061'` is the letter a.

Normally, reference types are created using the new keyword:

```
object o = new System.Object();
```

However, although the string type is a reference type, it can be directly initialized:

```
string s = "Hello!";
```

C# supports C-style escape sequences in strings:

```
string s1 = "Hello\n"; // ends with newline character
string s2 = "Hello\tthere!"; // contains embedded tab character
```

Escape sequences begin with a \ (backslash) character. Therefore, if your string otherwise contains a \, you'll need to double it:

```
string s3 = "C:\\WINNT";
```

C# also provides the verbatim string for this purpose. To create a verbatim string literal, include the @ character before the opening quote:

```
string s4 = @"C:\WINNT";
```

This causes any escape sequences within the string to be ignored.

In C# both the `string` and `char` types use 2-byte Unicode characters.

There are no global variables in C#. Therefore, all variables are either member variables of a class or struct, or they are local variables created within the scope of a method.

A.2.3 Constants

C# provides the `const` modifier which can be used in front of a declaration to create program constants:

```
const int min = 1;
const int max = 100;
const int range = max - min;
```

Constants are typically initialized with a literal value. They can also be given the value of an expression, as we do with the `range` constant above, provided that the compiler can evaluate the expression at compile time. Therefore, the following would generate a compiler error because the value of the expression assigned to i cannot be known until run time:

```
System.Random r = new System.Random();
const int i = r.Next(1, 7); // error - compiler cannot evaluate
```

A.3 ARRAYS

Arrays in C# are zero-based and, for the most part, work like they do in other common programming languages. The array type is a reference type:

```
string[] a;
```

This declares an array of strings, a, but does not allocate space for any elements. The array name serves as a reference to the array. This is similar to C/C++ where the array name is a pointer to the first array element. Note that the type of a, in this example, is `string[]`. In other words, unlike C-style arrays, the square brackets are part of the type declaration.

To create an array and allocate space for array elements use:

```
string[] a = new string[100];
```

This defines an array of strings, a, and allocates space for 100 string elements. The index of the first element is zero while the last index is 99.

Arrays can be directly initialized:

```
string[] a1 = {"cat", "dog", "mouse", "horse"};
int[] a2 = {1, 2, 3};
```

The first line creates an array with four string elements and initializes their values with the strings in curly braces. The second line creates and initializes a three-element array of integers.

We can have multi-dimensional arrays:

```
string[,] ar = {
                {"cat", "rabbit"},
                {"dog", "fox"},
                {"mouse", "horse"}
               };
```

This declares a two-dimensional (3 x 2) array and initializes it. (C/C++ programmers will find C#'s multi-dimensional array syntax a little different.) We can also have arrays of arrays:

```
int[][] matrix;
```

Array elements must be of the same type. However, we can declare an array of type `object` and put anything in it:

```
object[] ar = {3, "cat", 2.45};
```

This may not be particularly useful since you may need to cast to the correct type when accessing an element:

```
string animal = (string)ar[1];
```

A.4   EXPRESSIONS AND OPERATORS

A C# expression consists of a sequence of operators and their operands. If you are a C or C++ programmer you'll be pleased to find that most C# operators look familiar and retain their original C-like meanings. In this section, we explore the full list of C# operators.

A.4.1   Arithmetic operators

C# provides all the usual arithmetic operators for addition, subtraction, multiplication, division, and so forth, as seen in table A.1.

Table A.1   C# arithmetic operators

Operator	Description	Examples
+	Unary Plus	+a
–	Unary Minus	–a
++	Increment	++a or a++
––	Decrement	––a or a––
+	Addition	a + b

continued on next page

Table A.1   C# arithmetic operators *(continued)*

Operator	Description	Examples
–	Subtraction	a – b
*	Multiplication	a * b
/	Division	a / b
%	Remainder	a % b

For non-C programmers, the increment (++) and decrement (--) operators may be new. Each comes in pre and post forms. Where a pre-increment operator appears inside an expression, the increment operation takes place before the expression is evaluated. With a post-increment operator, the expression is evaluated first. The same rules apply to both forms of the decrement operator. Table A.2 shows some examples.

Table A.2   Using the increment operators

i Before	Assignment Expression	j After	i After
3	j = ++i;	4	4
3	j = i++;	3	4
3	j = --i;	2	2
3	j = i--;	3	2

A.4.2   Relational operators

The C# relational operators are the same as those found in C and C++.

Table A.3   C# relational operators

Operator	Description	Example
==	Equality	a == b
!=	Inequality	a != b
<	Less Than	a < b
<=	Less Than or Equal To	a <= b
>	Greater Than	a > b
>=	Greater Than or Equal To	a >= b

Visual Basic programmers should note that C# uses a double equals, ==, to test for equality and a single equals, =, for assignment. Also, inequality is denoted by != instead of <>.

A.4.3 Logical operators

The logical operators also owe their heritage to C/C++.

Table A.4 C# logical operators

Operator	Description	Example
!	Negation	!a
&	Bitwise And	a & b
|	Bitwise Or	a | b
^	Exclusive Or (XOR)	a ^ b
~	Bitwise Complement	~ a
&&	Logical And	a && b
||	Logical Or	a || b

A.4.4 Bit-shifting operators

The << and >> operators perform left and right bitwise shifts on integral arguments:

```
int i1 = 32;
int i2 = i1 << 2; // i2 == 128
int i3 = i1 >> 3; // i3 == 4
```

A.4.5 Assignment in C#

Table A.5 presents the C# assignment operators. Like C/C++, C# provides compound assignment operators of the form a op= b. In general, a op= b, where op is an arithmetic operator, is just a convenient shorthand for a = a op b.

Table A.5 C# assignment operators

Operator	Expression	Expression Value (a==3 and b==7)
=	a = b	7
+=	a += b	10
-=	a -= b	-4
*=	a *= b	21
/=	a /= b	0
%=	a %= b	3
&=	a &= b	3
|=	a |= b	7
>>=	a >>= b	0
<<=	a <<= b	384

A.4.6 Miscellaneous operators

C# also includes the conditional, ?, operator found in C/C++:

```
min = a < b ? a : b;
```

This is just shorthand for the `if-else` statement:

```
if (a < b)
  min = a;
else
  min = b;
```

In addition to operators already described, C# includes the following miscellaneous operators:

- *. (Dot)*—For member access as in `args.Length`
- *() (Cast)*—For type conversion
- *[] (Indexing)*—For indexing arrays, pointers, properties, and attributes
- *new*—For creating new objects
- *typeof*—For obtaining the runtime type of an object
- *is*—For comparing the runtime type of two objects
- *sizeof*—For obtaining the size of a type in bytes
- *checked, unchecked*— For checking arithmetic overflow at runtime
- ** (Pointer Indirection)*—For obtaining the variable to which a pointer points
- *-> (Pointer Member Access)*—`p->m` is the same as `(*p).m`
- *& (Address Of)*—Returns the address of its operand

A.4.7   A note about operator precedence and associativity

Operator precedence determines the order in which individual operators are evaluated. For example, `a+b*c` is evaluated as `a+(b*c)` because the `*` operator has higher precedence than the `+` operator.

When an operand occurs between two operators with the same precedence, the associativity of the operators controls the order in which the operations are performed. Except for the assignment operators, all binary operators are left-associative, meaning that operations are performed from left to right. The assignment operators and the conditional operator are right-associative.

For the most part, operator precedence and associativity in C# follow the C/C++ tradition. (You'll find a complete list in the .NET SDK and Visual Studio .NET documentation.) Since few programmers can remember the rules anyway, it is best to use parentheses to explicitly convey your intentions. For example, `a+b*c` first multiplies b by c and then adds the result to a, but `(a+b)*c` first adds a to b and then multiplies the result by c.

A.5 C# STATEMENTS

C# statements can span more than one line, and are terminated by a semicolon. In addition, statements can be grouped into statement blocks, where a block is a sequence of statements enclosed in curly braces ({ and }). You can use a statement block wherever a single statement is valid:

```
int i, j;

// a single statement...
i = 1;

// a statement block...
{
  j = 2;
  i = i + j;
}
```

A.5.1 if

The `if` statement is used to branch based on some condition:

```
if (i < 5)
  System.Console.WriteLine("i < 5");
```

This example displays a message if `i` is less than 5. An `if` statement can include an `else` clause which will be executed if the test condition is false:

```
if (i < 5)
  System.Console.WriteLine("i < 5");
else
  System.Console.WriteLine("i >= 5");
```

Note that, where there are two or more statements governed by the `if` or `else` condition, the statements must be enclosed in curly braces to form a statement block:

```
if (i < 5) {
  System.Console.WriteLine("i < 5");
  System.Console.WriteLine("i is smaller");
} else {
  System.Console.WriteLine("i >= 5");
  System.Console.WriteLine("i is not smaller");
}
```

This is a case of the general rule, mentioned earlier, that you can use a statement block wherever a single statement is valid.

A.5.2 do

The `do` statement is used for repetition:

```
int i = 1;
do
  System.Console.WriteLine(i++);
while(i <= 5);
```

This example displays the digits 1 to 5. Since the loop condition is tested at the bottom of the loop, a `do` loop is always executed at least once.

A.5.3 while

The `while` statement is also used for repetition:

```
int i = 1;
while(i <= 5)
   System.Console.WriteLine(i++);
```

This example also displays the digits 1 to 5. In this case, the loop condition is tested at the top of the loop.

A.5.4 for

The `for` statement is also used for repetition and will be familiar to C/C++ programmers. Unlike `while` and `do`, it is typically used when the number of iterations is known at the start of the loop:

```
for (int i = 1; i <= 5; i++)
   System.Console.WriteLine(i);
```

This example also displays the digits 1 to 5. The `for` loop contains three expressions separated by semicolons and enclosed in parentheses. The first is the initializing expression which is executed once before looping begins. In this case, it declares an integer, `i`, and initializes it to 1. The second expression contains the looping condition. In this example, it checks if `i` is less than or equal to 5. The loop terminates when this condition becomes false. The third expression is known as the iterator expression and is evaluated after each iteration. In this case, it increments the variable, `i`.

Note that you can code an infinite loop by omitting the loop expressions:

```
for (;;) {
    // infinite loop
    ...
}
```

You can also insert multiple expressions in place of the initializing and iterator expressions:

```
for (int i=1, j=2; i <= 5; i++, j+=2) {
    System.Console.WriteLine("i=" + i + ", j=" + j);
}
```

This example initializes the integers `i` and `j` and also updates them at the end of each iteration.

A.5.5 continue

The `continue` statement is used within a loop to skip the remainder of the current iteration and begin the next:

```
for (int i = 1; i <= 5; i++) {
  if (i == 3)
    continue;
  System.Console.WriteLine(i);
}
```

This loop displays the digits 1, 2, 4, and 5. The digit 3 is skipped.

A.5.6 break

The break statement is used to break out of a loop:

```
for (int i = 1; i <= 5; i++) {
  if (i == 3)
    break;
  System.Console.WriteLine(i);
}
```

This example displays the digits 1 and 2. The remaining loop iterations are skipped.

A.5.7 switch

The switch statement is slightly different from its C/C++ counterpart:

```
uint i = 2;
switch(i) {
  case 0:
    goto case 2;
  case 1:
    goto case 2;
  case 2:
    System.Console.WriteLine("i < 3");
    break;
  case 3:
    System.Console.WriteLine("i == 3");
    break;
  default:
    System.Console.WriteLine("i > 3");
    break;
}
```

This example displays the message: i < 3. The switch statement evaluates the expression in parentheses and uses the result to select from among several cases. In this example, the result is 2 and the statement following case 2 is executed. Note that the break statements are required since C#, unlike C/C++, does not allow fall through from one case to the next. Instead, C# provides the goto case (as seen in the example) and goto default, to allow multiple cases to execute the same statement block. Omitting the break statements causes a compiler error.

The default case, which is executed when no other case matches, is not required, although it is good practice to include it.

A.5.8   foreach

The foreach statement provides a convenient way to iterate over an array or collection:

```
int[] arr = {2, 4, 6, 8};
foreach (int i in arr)
  System.Console.WriteLine(i);
```

This example displays the integers 2, 4, 6, and 8.

A.5.9   return

The return statement terminates execution of the current method and returns control to the caller. It can optionally return a value to the caller. The following example illustrates:

```
class Add {

  public static void Main() {
    System.Console.WriteLine("2+3=" + add(2, 3));
  }

  private static int add(int i, int j) {
    return i + j;
  }
}
```

This short program contains a method called add which accepts two integer arguments, adds them, and returns the result.

A.5.10   goto

The goto statement transfers control to a statement marked with a label:

```
using System;
public class SomeClass {
  public static void Main (string[] args) {
    if (args.Length == 0) {
      Console.WriteLine("No args provided... aborting!");
      goto end;
    }
    Console.WriteLine("First arg is " + args[0]);
    end: return;
  }
}
```

This example uses goto to jump to the end of the program if no arguments are provided on the command line. The target of the goto is the return statement prefixed with an end label. We can choose any name for a label, as long as it is not a C# keyword.

A.5.11 throw

The throw statement throws an exception. It is typically used to signal an error or abnormal condition:

```
if (val > max)
    throw new Exception("value exceeds maximum");
```

We'll look more closely at exceptions later in this appendix.

A.6 CLASSES AND STRUCTS

While early versions of C++ were implemented by bolting a preprocessor onto the C compiler, C# is designed from the ground up to be a modern, object-oriented language. The fundamental building block of a C# application is the *class*.

A.6.1 Programming with classes

Listing A.2 presents a short program in which we use a class to define a new type called Person.

Listing A.2   The Person class

```
using System;

class Person {

  // fields...
  string firstName, lastName;
  int age;

  // constructor method...
  public Person(string firstName, string lastName, int age) {
    this.firstName = firstName;
    this.lastName = lastName;
    this.age = age;
  }

  // method...
  public void DisplayName() {
    Console.WriteLine(firstName + " " + lastName);
  }

  // property...
  public int Age {
    get { return age; }        // get age
    set { age = value; }       // set age field
  }

  // property...
  public string LastName {
    get { return lastName; } // get lastName
  }
}
```

```
class Test {

  public static void Main() {

    // create an instance of the Person class...
    // this causes the Person constructor to execute...
    Person p = new Person("Joe", "Bloggs", 33);

    // call the DisplayName method...
    p.DisplayName(); // displays "Joe Bloggs"

    // display the age property...
    Console.WriteLine("Age is " + p.Age); // displays "Age is 33"

    // display the LastName property...
    Console.WriteLine("Last name is " + p.LastName);

    // set the age property...
    p.Age = 34;

    // display the updated age property...
    Console.WriteLine("Age is " + p.Age); // displays "Age is 34"
  }
}
```

We define a class using the `class` keyword followed by the name of the class and then the class body contained in curly braces. In this example, the `Person` class body contains fields, methods, and properties. These are collectively known as *class members*. Fields, also called data members, are regular variables. Methods, also known as function members, contain executable code.

The `Test` class in listing A.2 is used to execute the program and create an instance of the `Person` class:

```
Person p = new Person("Joe", "Bloggs", 33);
```

This creates a reference `p` to an instance of the `Person` class. Creating a class instance causes a special method, known as a constructor, to be executed. A constructor method always has the same name as the class itself and no return type. It is executed automatically when an instance of the class is created at run time. In this case, the constructor takes three arguments representing the first name, last name, and age of the person. These values are used by the constructor to initialize the fields in the class instance, as in:

```
this.firstName = firstName;
```

The `this` keyword is used within a method to reference the current class instance.

The `DisplayName` method is used here to display the `firstName` and `lastName` fields. The method is called using the `ref.MethodName(...)` syntax:

```
p.DisplayName();
```

In C#, the dot operator is typically used for member access. C# also supports C-style pointers and pointer member access (p->m) when operating in an unsafe context, denoted by the use of the `unsafe` modifier in a type or member declaration.

Note that all methods, except the constructor, must declare a return type. If a method does not return a value, then it should declare a `void` return type, as `DisplayName` does in listing A.2.

It is generally considered poor programming practice to allow calling code to reach into a class instance and change field values. Instead, C# provides properties for this purpose:

```
public int Age {
   get { return age;  }      // get age
   set { age = value; }      // set age field
}
```

A property may have a `get` and/or `set` accessor associated with it. In this example, the `get` accessor returns the value of the age field. The `set` accessor is used to set the value of the age field. Within a `set` accessor block, C# automatically provides a variable called `value` which holds the new value to which the property can be set, as follows:

```
p.Age = 34;
```

Note that the methods and properties of the `Person` class are marked with the access modifier `public`. (We look at the full list of access modifiers later in this appendix.) This makes them publicly accessible to calling code through a reference to the class instance, as in `p.Age`. Members which omit an access modifier, such as the fields in the `Person` class, are private by default. This means that they are inaccessible outside the class. Therefore the following attempt to access the `firstName` field will generate a compiler error:

```
Console.WriteLine("First name is " + p.firstName); // error!
```

The recommended naming convention is that private member names should begin with a lowercase letter while other member names should begin with an uppercase letter. However, this is not a rule.

A class can include *static* members which can be accessed without first creating an instance of the class. For example, the following snippet defines a static `MinimumAge` field in the `Person` class:

```
class Person {

  public static int MinimumAge = 18;

  ...

}
```

We can access the static `MinimumAge` field directly using the class name, as follows:

```
int age = Person.MinimumAge;
```

Since C# does not provide global variables, static fields are often used to store global values.

Finally, classes can be nested:

```
class C1 {
  int i, j;
  string s;

  void m() {
    // ...
  }

  class c2 {
    // ...
  }
}
```

The class is at the heart of object-oriented programming in C#. We'll return to this topic when we consider inheritance.

A.6.2   Programming with structs

C# provides the ability to create a *lightweight* class using a `struct`. Structs are value types and are created on the stack at run time. (Refer to chapter 2 for a complete discussion of value and reference types.) This removes the overhead of using references and obviates the need for garbage collection. The following example uses a `struct` to create a type that stores the *x* and *y* coordinates of a point:

```
struct Point {
  public int X, Y;

  public Point(int x, int y) {
    X = x;
    Y = y;
  }
}
```

Although a struct can contain methods, typically structs are used for types that contain just a few data members. Like classes, structs can also be nested. However, unlike a class, a `struct` may not inherit from another class or struct, nor may it serve as a base class for inheritance purposes.

A.7   *INHERITANCE*

C# allows us to design a class by using inheritance to embrace and extend an existing class. Unlike C++, which supports multiple inheritance, C# supports only single inheritance. However, like Java, C# also supports implementation inheritance using interfaces which provide some of the advantages of multiple inheritance. We'll explore interfaces later in this appendix.

Many application domains contain hierarchies that are naturally modeled by inheritance. Object-oriented GUI libraries often use this technique. For example, depending on the implementation, a check box may be a special type of button, and a button is a control, and a control is a type of component, and a component is an object. In such cases we might implement this as an inheritance hierarchy. The check box would extend the button class by adding a `checked` property, and so forth. A class that inherits from another is sometimes referred to as a *derived* class.

A.7.1 Simple inheritance

Let's return to our `Person` class. Listing A.3 provides a new implementation of the `Person` class, together with a class called `Man` which derives from `Person`.

Listing A.3   Simple inheritance

```
using System;

class Person {

  protected string firstName, lastName;

  // constructor method...
  public Person(string firstName, string lastName) {
    this.firstName = firstName;
    this.lastName = lastName;
  }

  // method...
  public void Greet() {
    Console.WriteLine("Hello " + firstName + " " + lastName + "!");
  }
}

// Man derives from Person class...
class Man : Person {

  // create a Man by calling base Person constructor...
  public Man(string fName, string lName) : base(fName, lName) {}

  // replace base Greet method with a new implementation...
  public new void Greet() {
    Console.WriteLine("Hello Mr. " + lastName + "!");
  }
}

class Test {

  public static void Main() {

    Person p = new Person("Joe", "Bloggs");
    p.Greet(); // displays "Hello Joe Bloggs!"

    Man m = new Man("Joe", "Bloggs");
    m.Greet(); // displays "Hello Mr. Bloggs!"
  }
}
```

Inheritance is used to model an *is-a* relationship. (A man is a person). In this example, we've changed the accessibility of the `firstName` and `lastName` fields of the `Person` class to `protected`, thus making them accessible to any derived class. We specify that `Man` derives from `Person`, as follows:

```
// Man derives from Person class...
class Man : Person {
  ...
}
```

The only difference between the `Man` and `Person` classes is the greeting displayed. Therefore, we leverage the base `Person` class constructor to build an instance of `Man`, as follows:

```
// create a Man by calling base Person constructor...
public Man(string fName, string lName) : base(fName, lName) {}
```

The `base` keyword is used to refer to the parent object. In this example, the body of the `Man` constructor is empty. Instead the `Person` constructor is called to construct the object.

In the derived `Man` class, we reimplement the `Greet` method using the new keyword to make clear to the compiler that we are not inadvertently hiding the parent's `Greet` method.

A.7.2 Using virtual methods

One of the advantages of inheritance is the ability to use a base class reference to refer to an instance of a derived class. This allows us to write code without caring whether the reference is to a parent or derived class, as follows:

```
Person p = new Man("Joe", "Bloggs");
p.Greet(); // problem? calls base class Greet method
```

Here, we create a reference p to a `Person` object, but store in it a reference to a `Man` object. This is fine, but calling `p.Greet()` calls the base class `Greet` method, which is probably not what we intended. The solution lies in virtual methods. See listing A.4.

Listing A.4 Overriding the Greet method

```
using System;

class Person {

  protected string firstName, lastName;

  // constructor method...
  public Person(string firstName, string lastName) {
    this.firstName = firstName;
    this.lastName = lastName;
  }

  // Greet method is now marked virtual...
  public virtual void Greet() {
    Console.WriteLine("Hello " + firstName + " " + lastName + "!");
```

```
      }
   }

   // Man derives from Person class...
   class Man : Person {

      // create a Man by calling base Person constructor...
      public Man(string fName, string lName) : base(fName, lName) {}

      // override base Greet method with a new implementation...
      public override void Greet() {
         Console.WriteLine("Hello Mr. " + lastName + "!");
      }
   }

   class Test {

      public static void Main() {

         Person p1 = new Person("Joe", "Bloggs");
         p1.Greet(); // displays "Hello Joe Bloggs!"

         Person p2 = new Man("John", "Doe");
         p2.Greet(); // displays "Hello Mr. Doe!"

      }
   }
```

Placing the virtual modifier in front of the base class's method definition causes the compiler to generate code to look up a data structure, known as a virtual dispatch table, at run time to find the correct method. A corresponding override modifier is required in front of the derived class's method in order for virtual dispatching to locate the correct method. So virtual dispatching allows an object to assume different forms, Man or Person in this example, as necessary. This is sometimes referred to as polymorphism.

A.7.3   Abstract classes

Let's assume that we are interested in modeling men and women, but not persons per se. In other words, while both are persons, we don't want to allow the creation of Person objects directly. Instead, we only allow the creation of Man and Woman objects directly. However, we want both to inherit from, and share the implementation of, the Person class. We can do this using an abstract Person class, as seen in listing A.5.

Listing A.5   Using an abstract Person class

```
using System;

abstract class Person {

   protected string firstName, lastName;

   // constructor method...
   public Person(string firstName, string lastName) {
```

```
      this.firstName = firstName;
      this.lastName = lastName;
   }

   // force derived classes to implement the Greet method by...
   // marking it abstract...
   abstract public void Greet();
}

class Man : Person {

   public Man(string fName, string lName) : base(fName, lName) {}

   public override void Greet() {
      Console.WriteLine("Hello Mr. " + lastName + "!");
   }
}

class Woman : Person {

   public Woman(string fName, string lName) : base(fName, lName) {}

   public override void Greet() {
      Console.WriteLine("Hello Ms. " + lastName + "!");
   }
}

class Test {

   public static void Main() {

      Man m = new Man("Joe", "Bloggs");
      m.Greet(); // displays "Hello Mr. Bloggs!"

      Woman w = new Woman("Jane", "Doe");
      w.Greet(); // displays "Hello Ms. Doe!"
   }
}
```

We use the abstract modifier in front of the Person class definition to prevent
the class being instantiated. Attempting to instantiate the Person class causes a
compiler error. We also declare the Greet method to be abstract, thus requiring all
derived classes to override this method. In other words, the Person class specifies a
template, or contract, for classes which derive from it.

A.7.4   Sealed classes

You can disable further inheritance by marking a class sealed:

```
// prevent derivation...
sealed class Person {

   ...

}
```

Any attempt to use a sealed class as a base class for inheritance purposes will result in a compiler error. Use the `sealed` modifier to prevent unintended derivation.

A.8   MORE ABOUT METHODS

As we've seen, a method may accept parameters and return a result. The following example takes two integer parameters and returns an integer result containing the sum of the two:

```
int Add(int x, int y) {
  return x + y;
}
```

The combination of the method name, and the number and type of its parameters, is known as the method's signature. The signature of a method does not include its return type.

A.8.1   Using ref and out parameters

Value types, such as the integer parameters in the previous example, are passed by value to a method. In other words, the method receives a copy of the value type. Therefore, the following example leaves i unchanged following the call to `Increment`:

```
void Increment(int i) {
  i++;
}

...

int i = 0;
Increment(i); // i unaffected
```

In contrast, a reference type passed as a parameter contains the original object reference and can be used to directly modify the object.

C# provides `ref` and `out` parameters to enable value types to be passed by reference. Use the `ref` keyword to specify that an initialized value should be passed by reference:

```
void Increment(ref int i) {
  i++;
}

...

int i = 0; // initialized
Increment(ref i); // now i==1
```

Note that the `ref` keyword must be used both in the call and in the method signature. Also, i must first be initialized before being passed as a parameter to `Increment`. The `ref` keyword is used to allow the modification, by a method, of an existing initialized variable. If, instead, the method assigns the initial value to the variable, you should use the `out` keyword:

```
void Init(out int i) {
  i=1;
}

...

int i; // uninitialized
Init(out i); // now i==1
```

A.8.2   Passing a variable-length parameter list

C# provides the `params` keyword to facilitate the passing of a variable-length parameter list to a method. The following example illustrates the passing of an array of integers:

```
class Adder {

  int Add(params int[] ints) {
    int sum = 0;
    foreach (int i in ints)
      sum += i;
    return sum;
  }

  public static void Main() {
    Adder a = new Adder();
    int sum = a.Add(1, 2, 3, 4, 5);
    System.Console.WriteLine(sum); // displays "15"
  }
}
```

In this case, we pass an array of integers. However, the parameters in the list may not all be the same type, in which case we need to use an array of objects:

```
void ProcessParameters(params object[] objs) {
  ...
}
```

When objects are used, value types are automatically boxed. Boxing and unboxing are discussed in chapter 2.

A.8.3   Overloading methods

C# supports method overloading, which allows a class, struct, or interface to declare multiple methods with the same name, provided the signatures of the methods are all different. Constructor methods can be overloaded too:

```
class Person {

  string firstName, midName, lastName;

  public Person(string firstName, string lastName) {
    this.firstName = firstName;
    this.lastName = lastName;
  }

  public Person(string firstName, string midName, string lastName) {
```

```
      this.firstName = firstName;
      this.midName = midName;
      this.lastName = lastName;
   }
}
```

In this example, we overload the constructor method so that we can create Person objects with or without a middle name:

```
Person p1 = new Person("Joe", "Bloggs");
Person p2 = new Person("John", "Joe", "Bloggs");
```

A.9   ACCESS MODIFIERS

Access modifiers control the visibility of class members. We have seen examples of the use of public and protected modifiers already. The full list follows:

- private—Only code within the same containing class has access to a private member. In other words, a private member is not part of the class's public interface. This is the default access level if none is specified.
- public—A public member is visible to all users of the class. It is part of the class's public interface.
- protected—Code within the same containing class and any derived classes can access a protected member.
- internal—An internal member can be accessed only by code within the same assembly. (We look at assemblies in detail in chapter 2.)
- protected internal—Permits both protected and internal access.

The visibility of a member can never exceed that of its containing class. So, for example, if a class has internal visibility the visibility of its public members is downgraded to internal.

A.10   EXCEPTIONS

Using exceptions is the recommended way to handle unexpected errors in C#. In fact, support for exceptions is provided in the underlying .NET runtime. Let's revisit our Person class to explore an example. Listing A.6 illustrates.

Listing A.6   Using exceptions

```
using System;

class Person {

   string firstName, lastName;
   int age;

   public Person(string firstName, string lastName, int age) {

      this.firstName = firstName;
      this.lastName = lastName;
```

```
      if (age < 18)
        throw new Exception("ERROR: Person is underage.");
      this.age = age;
    }
}

class Test {

  public static void Main() {
    try {
      Person p = new Person("Joe", "Bloggs", 16);
    }
    catch (Exception e) {
      // displays "ERROR: Person is underage." ...
      Console.WriteLine(e.Message);
    }
  }
}
```

In this case, we require persons to be at least 18 years of age. If not, the constructor throws an exception:

```
if (age < 18)
   throw new Exception("ERROR: Person is underage.");
```

To catch an exception, the code that throws it must be enclosed in a try ... catch block. Otherwise, the program will terminate:

```
try {
  Person p = new Person("Joe", "Bloggs", 16);
}
catch (Exception e) {
   // displays "ERROR: Person is underage." ...
  Console.WriteLine(e.Message);
}
```

When the exception is thrown, the catch code is executed. In this example, it just displays the Message property of the exception, which was specified when the exception was thrown.

You can also include a finally block which will always execute, whether an exception occurs, or not:

```
try {
  ...
}
catch {
  ...
}
finally {
  ...
}
```

If, for example, you obtain resources in the `try` block, you may want to include a `finally` block to ensure those resources are released regardless of whether an exception occurs. You can have multiple `catch` blocks to catch different exceptions. Examples of built-in exceptions include `ArgumentException` and `FileNotFoundException`, and you can create your own custom exception classes. If an exception is not caught, it bubbles upwards to the next innermost matching `catch` block or, if none exists, the program terminates.

A.11 ENUMS

C# provides the enum keyword, which you can use to define an ordered set of integral types known as an enumeration:

```
enum Suit {
  Clubs=1, Diamonds, Hearts, Spades
}

class Enums {
  public static void Main() {
    Suit s = Suit.Clubs;
    System.Console.WriteLine(s); // displays "Clubs"
  }
}
```

By default, enum elements are given a zero-based index. In this example, we override the default and set the index of the first element to one. Using an enum is preferable to using integer constants when the values represented belong to an ordered set.

A.12 DELEGATES AND EVENTS

A delegate is a type-safe reference to a method. Its purpose is similar to that of a function pointer in C++. Delegates are typically used to implement event handlers and callbacks. We look at both delegates and events in this section.

A.12.1 Using delegates

When you declare a delegate, you specify its signature. Thereafter, the delegate can store references to methods that match that signature. So a delegate is equivalent to a type-safe function pointer. Listing A.7 provides an example of using a delegate to indirectly call a method.

Listing A.7 Using delegates

```
using System;

public delegate void Callback(string name);

public class DelgHello {

  public static void Main(string[] args) {

    string name = "Stranger";
```

```
        if (args.Length > 0) name = args[0];

        // create reference to sayHello method...
        Callback cb = new Callback(sayHello);
        // use delegate to call sayHello method...
        cb(name);
    }

    private static void sayHello(string name) {
        Console.WriteLine("Hello, {0}!", name);
    }
}
```

In this case, we declare a delegate, `Callback`, which takes a string as its only parameter. In the `Main` routine, we create an instance of the delegate passing the name of the `sayHello` method. The delegate now references the `sayHello` method. In the next line, we use the delegate reference to indirectly call `sayHello`.

Clearly, in this example, we could have called the `sayHello` method directly. A delegate is best used when a program needs to dynamically set the method to be called at run time, such as when setting an event handler.

A.12.2 Handling events

Support for events is at the heart of every modern GUI-based operating environment. Events occur when applications are launched, when buttons are clicked, when keys are pressed, when network responses arrive, when windows are resized, and so forth. Many events can be safely ignored but others need to be captured and handled in some way.

An event is typically handled using an event handler delegate. You can create your own custom event handler delegate or use one provided by the Framework. The standard `System.EventHandler` delegate looks like:

```
public delegate void EventHandler(
    object sender,
    EventArgs e
);
```

Listing A.8 presents a program which uses the `System.Timers.Timer` class and the `System.Timers.ElapsedEventHandler` delegate to implement a ticking clock.

Listing A.8 Handling events

```
using System;
using System.Threading;
using System.Timers;

public class Clock {

    public Clock(int interval) {
```

```
      this.interval = interval;
      System.Timers.Timer timer = new System.Timers.Timer();
      ElapsedEventHandler tickHandler = new ElapsedEventHandler(Tick);
      timer.Elapsed += tickHandler;
      timer.Interval = interval * 1000; // milliseconds
      timer.Enabled = true;
    }

    public void Tick(object source, ElapsedEventArgs e) {
      Console.WriteLine("{0}: {1} second tick", source, interval);
    }

    private int interval;
  }

public class MyClock {

  public static void Main() {
    Clock c1 = new Clock(7); // tick every 7 secs
    Clock c2 = new Clock(11); // tick every 11 secs
    Console.WriteLine("clocks ticking... press Ctrl-c to end");
    while (true) Thread.Sleep(500); // sleep and loop forever
  }
}
```

The Clock class constructor creates a System.Timers.Timer object and registers an event handler for the Timer.Elapsed event:

```
ElapsedEventHandler tickHandler = new ElapsedEventHandler(Tick);
timer.Elapsed += tickHandler;
```

Note the use of the += operator to add an instance of the delegate to the event. You
can add multiple event handler delegates, if appropriate. This is because the
ElapsedEventHandler is a type of delegate known as a multicast delegate.

   Adding the delegate instance causes the Clock.Tick method to be executed after
the timer interval elapses. Once the delegate is added, we set the interval and enable
the timer.

A.13 INTERFACES

C# supports an interface type, which provides a means of specifying a contract similar
to the contract imposed by an abstract class on derived classes. Any class or struct that
implements an interface must adhere to its contract. However, while C# does not
support multiple inheritance, a C# class or struct can implement multiple interfaces.
Interfaces can contain methods, properties, and events, but not fields. The following
example illustrates:

```
interface IGreet {
  void Greet();
}
```

```
class Person : IGreet {

  protected string firstName, lastName;

  // constructor method...
  public Person(string firstName, string lastName) {
    this.firstName = firstName;
    this.lastName = lastName;
  }

  public void Greet() {
    Console.WriteLine("Hello " + firstName + " " + lastName + "!");
  }
}
```

Here, we declare the `IGreet` interface containing a single method called `Greet`. Then we code a new version of the `Person` class which implements the interface:

```
class Person : IGreet {
  ...
}
```

Note that we use the same syntax when implementing an interface, as we do when deriving from a class. Once we declare that we are implementing the interface, the compiler will complain if the `Person` class does not implement the `Greet` method.

Interfaces are used heavily throughout the .NET Framework classes. Examples include `IComparable` which a type can implement to support type-specific comparison, and `IEnumerable` which supports iteration over collection types. You'll find numerous examples of the use of interfaces in the SDK and Visual Studio .NET samples.

The `as` operator is often used with interfaces. For example, if multiple types implement a particular interface, we can reference them through their common interface type:

```
Person p = new Person("Joe", "Bloggs");
IGreet greeter = p as IGreet; // convert to interface type
greeter.Greet();
```

A.14 PREPROCESSOR DIRECTIVES

C# compilation does not include a separate preprocessing stage, so there are no C-style preprocessor macros. However, C# does retain many familiar preprocessor-type directives:

- `#define`—Defines a symbol (for use with `#if`)
- `#undef`—Undefines a symbol (for use with `#if`)
- `#if-#elif-#else-#endif`—Tests a symbol and evaluates code accordingly
- `#warning`—Generates a warning from a location in the code
- `#error`—Generates an error from a location in the code
- `#line`—Modifies the compiler's line number

- #region—Used with Visual Studio .NET to mark the beginning of a code region
- #endregion—Used with Visual Studio .NET to mark the end of a code region

The #define and #if directives are often used to compile extra code into the program for debugging purposes. The following example illustrates:

```
class PreProc {

  public static void Main() {

    System.Console.Write("Hello. What's your name? ");
    string nm = System.Console.ReadLine();

    #if DEBUG
      System.Console.WriteLine("user entered " + nm);
    #endif

    if (nm.Equals(""))
      nm = "Stranger";

    System.Console.WriteLine("Hello, " + nm + "!");
  }
}
```

If the DEBUG symbol is defined, the line of code between #if and #endif is compiled into the program, otherwise it is omitted. This is different from a regular if statement which is evaluated at run time. We could include #define DEBUG directly in the program, but a better approach is to define this at compile-time, as follows:

```
csc /define:DEBUG preproc.cs
```

To remove the extra debug code, we simply compile the release version without the /define:DEBUG option.

A.15 ATTRIBUTES

C# provides a mechanism to specify extra declarative information for various program entities through the use of attributes. This information can be retrieved and used at run time. There are many built-in attributes provided in the .NET Framework, and we make use of many throughout this book. Examples are the AssemblyVersion attribute for specifying the version of an assembly, the Serializable attribute to declare that a type is serializable, RunInstallerAttribute to denote an installable type, and the WebService and WebMethod attributes for Web services.

Attributes can be applied to almost all application elements including assemblies, types, methods, parameters. The information declared is stored with the compiled code. At run time it can be extracted using a technique called reflection. (We examine reflection in Chapter 2.)

The following example illustrates the use of the `Conditional` attribute to achieve the same effect as the `#if` directive:

```
using System;
using System.Diagnostics;

class Go {

  public static void Main() {

    Console.Write("Hello. What's your name? ");
    string nm = Console.ReadLine();

    debug("user entered " + nm);

    if (nm.Equals(""))
      nm = "Stranger";

    Console.WriteLine("Hello, " + nm + "!");
  }
  [Conditional("DEBUG")]
  private static void debug(string msg) {
    Console.WriteLine("DEBUG: " + msg);
  }
}
```

In this case, we include a `debug` method which is prefixed with the conditional attribute, `[Conditional("DEBUG")]`. This causes the `debug` method, and any calls to it, to be compiled into the program only if `DEBUG` is defined.

You can create custom attribute classes to support the insertion and use of specialized declarative information in your own applications.

A.16 THREADING

Using multiple threads in a program creates the effect of several tasks executing at the same time. C# supports the use of threads and provides several types to support the creation of multi-threaded applications. Listing A.9 provides another example of a ticking clock. This example uses a separate thread for the clock.

Listing A.9 Using threads

```
using System;
using System.Threading;

public class ThreadClock {

  public static void Main() {

    // create thread start delegate...
    ThreadStart clockThread = new ThreadStart(startClock);
    // create thread...
    Thread t = new Thread(clockThread);
    Console.WriteLine("starting new thread...");
    // start the thread...
    t.Start();
```

```
    // wait for thread to finish...
    t.Join();
    Console.WriteLine("thread stopped.");
  }

  private static void startClock() {
    Console.WriteLine("running on new thread...");
    for (int i = 0; i < 5; i++) {
      Thread.Sleep(1000); // tick every second
      Console.WriteLine("Tick!");
    }
  }
}
```

Note the use of the delegate, ThreadStart, to provide a reference to the method to be run by the thread. To start the thread, we call its Start method, while a call to its Join method causes the program to wait for the thread to complete.

A.17 FURTHER RESOURCES

In this appendix, we explored the C# programming language. In addition to the material presented here, you'll find supplementary discussion and many more sample programs throughout the book, as well as a complete case study. You'll also find a complete C# reference and several tutorials in the help documentation provided with both Visual Studio .NET and the .NET SDK, as seen in figure A.1.

You'll also find many helpful tutorials and samples at the Microsoft sites: http://msdn.microsoft.com/net, and at http://www.gotdotnet.com.

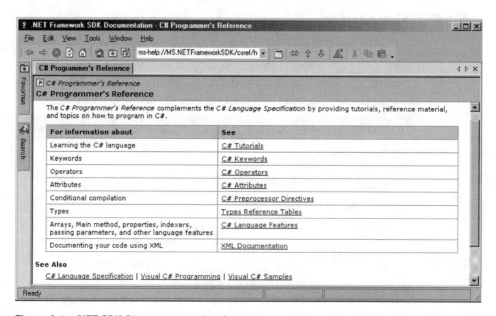

Figure A.1   .NET SDK C# programmer's reference

The poker engine listings

All the different versions of the video poker machine case study use a common game "engine" implemented as the assembly, *poker.dll*. This appendix contains the source code for the engine classes, together with a makefile to build the assembly.

B.1   THE MAKEFILE

Run nmake from the command line to run the makefile.

```
poker.dll:  bank.cs \
            bet.cs \
            card.cs \
            hand.cs \
            machine.cs \
            msglog.cs \
            simplemachine.cs
    csc /t:library /out:poker.dll \
            bank.cs \
            bet.cs \
            card.cs \
            hand.cs \
            machine.cs \
            msglog.cs \
            simplemachine.cs
```

B.2   THE BANK CLASS

The Bank class is discussed in chapter 4, *Working with ADO.NET and databases*.

```
namespace Poker {

  using System;
  using System.Configuration;
  using System.IO;
  using System.Data;
  using System.Data.SqlClient;

  public class Bank {

    public Bank() {
      setConnectString();
      TargetMargin = GetParm("TargetMargin", 25);
      refresh();
    }

    public readonly int TargetMargin;

    public int TakenIn { get { return takenIn; } }
    public int PaidOut { get { return paidOut; } }
    public int Profit  { get { return profit;  } }

    public double HouseMargin { get {
      if (takenIn == 0) return TargetMargin;
      return (double) profit * 100.0 / takenIn;
    } }

    public double Delta { get {
      return HouseMargin - TargetMargin;
    } }

    public int Bias { get {
      if (Delta >= 0.0) return 0;
      int bias = (int) Math.Round(Math.Abs(Delta));
      if (bias > 10) return 10;
      return bias;
    } }

    public string Status { get {
      return status;
    } }

    public string Text { get {
        return "\n" +
        status + "\n" +
        "===========================\n" +
        "Taken In        : " + takenIn + "\n" +
        "Paid Out        : " + paidOut + "\n" +
        "Profit          : " + profit + "\n" +
        "House Margin %  : " +
          String.Format("{0:00.00}", HouseMargin) + "\n" +
        "Target Margin % : " +
```

```
          String.Format("{0:00.00}", TargetMargin) + "\n" +
    "Delta          : " +
          String.Format("{0:00.00}", Delta) + "\n" +
    "Bias           : " + Bias + "\n";
} }

public override string ToString() {
  return Text;
}

public void SaveGame(string hand, int score, int bet) {

  if (connectString == "") return;

  SqlConnection conn = null;
  try {
    conn = new SqlConnection(connectString);
  } catch (Exception e) {
    new MsgLog(String.Format( "Bank.SaveGame(): {0} - {1}",
                              "Cannot create SqlConnection",
                              e.Message));
    return;
  }

  string sql =
    "INSERT INTO games(hand, score, bet) VALUES " +
    "('" + hand + "'," + score + "," + bet + ")";
  SqlCommand comm = null;
  try {
    comm = new SqlCommand(sql, conn);
  } catch (Exception e) {
    new MsgLog(String.Format( "Bank.SaveGame(): {0} - {1}",
                              "Cannot create SqlCommand",
                              e.Message));
    return;
  }

  try {
    conn.Open();
  } catch (Exception e) {
    new MsgLog(String.Format( "Bank.SaveGame(): {0} - {1}",
                              "Cannot open SqlConnection",
                              e.Message));
    return;
  }

  try {
    comm.ExecuteNonQuery();
  } catch (Exception e) {
    new MsgLog(String.Format( "Bank.SaveGame(): {0} - {1}",
                              "Cannot execute SqlCommand",
                              e.Message));
    return;
  } finally {
```

```
      if (conn.State == ConnectionState.Open) conn.Close();
    }

    refresh();
  }

  public int GetParm(string parmName, int defaultValue) {

    int parmValue = defaultValue;

    if (connectString == "") return parmValue;

    string sql =
      "SELECT value FROM integers WHERE name='" + parmName + "'";
    DataSet ds = new DataSet("PokerParm");
    SqlDataAdapter sda = new SqlDataAdapter(sql, connectString);

    try {
      sda.Fill(ds, "result");
      parmValue = (int) ds.Tables["result"].Rows[0][0];
    } catch (Exception e) {
      connectString = "";
      new MsgLog(
        String.Format("Bank.GetParm(): {0}", e.Message));
    }
    return parmValue;
  }

  private void setConnectString() {
    connectString = ConfigurationSettings.AppSettings["dsn"];
    if (connectString == null) connectString = "";
    if (connectString == "")
      connectString =
       @"server=(local)\NetSDK;" +
       @"database=poker;trusted_connection=yes";
  }

  private void refresh() {

    if (connectString == "") return;

    string sql =
      "SELECT " +
        "SUM(bet) AS taken_in, " +
        "SUM(score * bet) AS paid_out, " +
        "SUM(bet) - SUM(score * bet) as profit " +
      "FROM games";

    SqlDataAdapter sda = null;
    try {
      sda = new SqlDataAdapter(sql, connectString);
      DataSet ds = new DataSet("PokerProfit");
      sda.Fill(ds, "stats");
      DataRow dr = ds.Tables[0].Rows[0];
      takenIn = (int) dr[0];
      paidOut = (int) dr[1];
```

```
        profit   = (int) dr[2];
        status = "Machine Stats (All Players)";
      } catch (Exception e) {
        new MsgLog(
           String.Format("Bank.refresh(): {0}", e.Message));
      }
    }

    // private static Bank bank = null;
    private string connectString = "";
    private string status = "Machine Stats Unavailable";
    private int     takenIn = 0;
    private int     paidOut = 0;
    private int     profit = 0;
  }
}
```

B.3   THE BET CLASS

The Bet class is discussed in chapter 4, *Working with ADO.NET and databases.*

```
using System;
namespace Poker {
  public class Bet {
    public Bet(int bet, int credits, int minBet, int maxBet) {
      if (credits < minBet) {
        Message =
           "You don't have enough credits to bet...  Game over!";
        Amount = 0;
        return;
      }
      if (bet < minBet) {
        Message = String.Format(
           "You must bet the minimum... betting {0}.", minBet);
        Amount = minBet;
        Credits = credits - Amount;
        return;
      }
      maxBet = credits < maxBet ? credits : maxBet;
      if (bet > maxBet) {
        Message = String.Format(
           "You can only bet {0}... betting {0}.", maxBet);
        Amount = maxBet;
        Credits = credits - Amount;
        return;
      }
      Message = "";
      Amount = bet;
      Credits = credits - Amount;
    }
    public readonly int Amount;
    public readonly int Credits;
```

```
      public readonly string Message;
  }
}
```

B.4   THE CARD CLASS

The Card class is discussed in chapter 3, *Case study: a video poker machine.*

```csharp
using System.Reflection;
[assembly:AssemblyVersion("1.0.0.0")]

namespace Poker {

  using System;

  internal class Card {

    public Card() : this(new Random()) {}

    public Card(Random r) {
      Number = r.Next(2, 15);
      Suit = r.Next(1, 5);
      Name = numberArray[Number - 2] + suitArray[Suit - 1];
    }

    public Card(string name) {
      string n = name.Substring(0, 1);
      string s = name.Substring(1, 1);
      Number = numberString.IndexOf(n) + 2;
      Suit = suitString.IndexOf(s) + 1;
      Name = name;
    }

    public readonly int Number;
    public readonly int Suit;
    public readonly string Name;

    public override string ToString() {
      return Name;
    }

    public override bool Equals(object o) {
      try {
        Card c = (Card)o;
        return c.Number == Number && c.Suit == Suit;
      } catch (Exception) {
        return false;
      }
    }

    public override int GetHashCode() {
      return (Suit<<4) + Number;
    }

    // private fields...
    private static string[] numberArray
      = {"2","3","4","5","6","7","8","9","T","J","Q","K","A"};
```

```
      private static string[] suitArray = {"C","D","H","S"};
      private static string numberString = "23456789TJQKA";
      private static string suitString = "CDHS";
    }
  }
```

B.5   THE HAND CLASS

The Hand class is discussed in chapter 3, *Case study: a video poker machine.*

```
namespace Poker {

  using System;

  public class Hand {

    public Hand() {
      Random r = new Random();
      for (int i = 0; i < 5; i++) {
        while (true) {
          cards[i] = new Card(r);
          if (containsCard(cards[i], cards, i)) continue;
          break;
        }
      }
    }

    public Hand(string handText) {
      cardsFromString(handText);
    }

    public Hand(string handText, string holdString) {
      cardsFromString(handText);
      holdCards(holdString);
      draw();
    }

    public Hand(Hand hand, string holdString) {
      this.cards = hand.cards;
      holdCards(holdString);
      draw();
    }

    public int Score { get {
      if (score < 0) calcScore();
      return score;
    } }

    public string Title { get {
      return titles[Score];
    } }

    public string CardName(int cardNum) {
      return cards[cardNum - 1].Name;
    }
```

```
public string Text { get {
  return  CardName(1) + " " +
          CardName(2) + " " +
          CardName(3) + " " +
          CardName(4) + " " +
          CardName(5);
} }

public override string ToString() {
  return Text;
}

private void cardsFromString(string handText) {
  char[] delims = {' '};
  string[] cardStrings = handText.Split(delims);
  for (int i = 0; i < cardStrings.Length; i++)
    cards[i] = new Card(cardStrings[i]);
}

private void holdCards(string holdString) {
  for (int i = 0; i < 6; i++) {
    int cardNum = i + 1;
    if (holdString.IndexOf(cardNum.ToString()) >= 0)
      isHold[cardNum - 1] = true;
  }
}

private void draw() {

  // remember which cards player has seen...
  Card[] seen = new Card[10];
  for (int i = 0; i < 5; i++) {
    seen[i] = cards[i];
  }

  int numSeen = 5;
  Random r = new Random();
  for (int i = 0; i < 5; i++) {
    if (!isHold[i]) {
      while (true) {
        cards[i] = new Card(r);
        if (containsCard(cards[i], seen, numSeen)) continue;
        break;
      }
      seen[numSeen++] = cards[i];
    }
  }
}

private bool containsCard(Card c, Card[] cs, int count) {
  for (int i = 0; i < count; i++)
    if (c.Equals(cs[i]))
      return true;
  return false;
}
```

```
private void calcScore() {
  // are cards all of the same suit?
  bool isFlush = true;
  int s = cards[0].Suit;
  for (int i = 1; i < 5; i++) {
    if (s != cards[i].Suit) {
      isFlush = false;
      break;
    }
  }

  // sort card values...
  int[] sortedValues = new int[5];
  for (int i = 0; i < 5; i++)
    sortedValues[i] = cards[i].Number;
  Array.Sort(sortedValues);

  // do we have a straight?
  bool isStraight = true;
  for (int i = 0; i < 4; i++) {
    if (sortedValues[i] + 1 != sortedValues[i+1]) {
      isStraight = false;
      break;
    }
  }
  // is it a straight to the ace?
  bool isTopStraight = (isStraight && sortedValues[4] == 14);

  // maybe it is a straight from the ace (i.e. A, 2, 3, 4, 5)
  if (! isStraight)
    if (sortedValues[0] == 2 &&
      sortedValues[1] == 3 &&
      sortedValues[2] == 4 &&
      sortedValues[3] == 5 &&
      sortedValues[4] == 14) // ace on top
    isStraight = true;


  // now calculate score...

  // royal flush...
  if (isTopStraight && isFlush) {
    score = 10;
    return;
  }

  // straight flush...
  if (isStraight && isFlush) {
    score = 9;
    return;
  }

  // four of a kind...
  if (sortedValues[0] == sortedValues[1] &&
      sortedValues[1] == sortedValues[2] &&
```

```
            sortedValues[2] == sortedValues[3]) {
    score = 8;
    return;
  }
  if (sortedValues[1] == sortedValues[2] &&
      sortedValues[2] == sortedValues[3] &&
      sortedValues[3] == sortedValues[4]) {
    score = 8;
    return;
  }

  // full house...
  if (sortedValues[0] == sortedValues[1] &&
      sortedValues[1] == sortedValues[2] &&
      sortedValues[3] == sortedValues[4]) {
    score = 7;
    return;
  }
  if (sortedValues[0] == sortedValues[1] &&
      sortedValues[2] == sortedValues[3] &&
      sortedValues[3] == sortedValues[4]) {
    score = 7;
    return;
  }

  // flush...
  if (isFlush) {
    score = 6;
    return;
  }

  // straight...
  if (isStraight) {
    score = 5;
    return;
  }

  // three of a kind...
  if (sortedValues[0] == sortedValues[1] &&
      sortedValues[1] == sortedValues[2]) {
    score = 4;
    return;
  }
  if (sortedValues[1] == sortedValues[2] &&
      sortedValues[2] == sortedValues[3]) {
    score = 4;
    return;
  }
  if (sortedValues[2] == sortedValues[3] &&
      sortedValues[3] == sortedValues[4]) {
    score = 4;
    return;
  }
```

```
    // two pair...
    if (sortedValues[0] == sortedValues[1] &&
        sortedValues[2] == sortedValues[3]) {
      score = 3;
      return;
    }
    if (sortedValues[0] == sortedValues[1] &&
        sortedValues[3] == sortedValues[4]) {
      score = 3;
      return;
    }
    if (sortedValues[1] == sortedValues[2] &&
        sortedValues[3] == sortedValues[4]) {
      score = 3;
      return;
    }

    // jacks or better...
    if (sortedValues[0] > 10 &&
      sortedValues[0] == sortedValues[1]) {
      score = 2;
      return;
    }
    if (sortedValues[1] > 10 &&
      sortedValues[1] == sortedValues[2]) {
      score = 2;
      return;
    }
    if (sortedValues[2] > 10 &&
      sortedValues[2] == sortedValues[3]) {
      score = 2;
      return;
    }
    if (sortedValues[3] > 10 &&
      sortedValues[3] == sortedValues[4]) {
      score = 2;
      return;
    }
    score = 0;
    return;
  }
private Card[] cards = new Card[5];
private bool[] isHold = {false, false, false, false, false};

private static string[] titles = {
  "No Score",
  "",
  "Jacks or Better",
  "Two Pair",
  "Three of a Kind",
  "Straight",
  "Flush",
```

```
            "Full House",
            "Four of a Kind",
            "Straight Flush",
            "Royal Flush",
        };

        private int score = -1;
    }
}
```

B.6   THE MACHINE CLASS

The Machine class is discussed in chapter 4, *Working with ADO.NET and databases.*

```
namespace Poker {

  using System;

  public class Machine {

      public readonly int MinBet;
      public readonly int MaxBet;
      public readonly int StartCredits;
      public readonly int Bias;

      // private constructor...
      private Machine() {
        bank = new Bank();
        MinBet = bank.GetParm("MinBet", 1);
        MaxBet = bank.GetParm("MaxBet", 5);
        StartCredits = bank.GetParm("StartCredits", 100);
        Bias = bank.Bias;
      }

      public static Machine Instance {
        get {
          // allow just one instance...
          if (machine == null) machine = new Machine();
          return machine;
        }
      }

      public Hand Deal() {
        Hand hand = new Hand();
        int bias = Bias;
        while (hand.Score > 0 && bias-- > 0)
          hand = new Hand();
        return hand;
      }

      public Hand Draw(Hand oldHand, string holdCards, int bet) {
        int bias = Bias;
        Hand newHand = new Hand(oldHand, holdCards);
        while (newHand.Score > 0 && bias-- > 0)
          newHand = new Hand(oldHand, holdCards);
```

```
      bank.SaveGame(newHand.ToString(), newHand.Score, bet);
      return newHand;
    }

    public Hand Draw(string handString, string holdCards, int bet) {
      return Draw(new Hand(handString), holdCards, bet);
    }

    public string Stats { get {
      return bank.Text;
    } }

    public static string PayoutTable { get {
        return "\n" +
        "Payout Table\n" +
        "===========\n" +
        "Royal Flush    : 10\n" +
        "Straight Flush :  9\n" +
        "Four of a Kind :  8\n" +
        "Full House     :  7\n" +
        "Flush          :  6\n" +
        "Straight       :  5\n" +
        "Three of a Kind :  4\n" +
        "Two Pair       :  3\n" +
        "Jacks or Better :  2\n";
    } }

    private static Machine machine = null;
    private Bank bank = null;
  }
}
```

B.7   THE MSGLOG CLASS

The MsgLog class is discussed in chapter 4, *Working with ADO.NET and databases.*

```
using System;
using System.Diagnostics;
namespace Poker {
  public class MsgLog {
    public MsgLog(string errMsg) {
      DateTime now = DateTime.Now;
      errMsg = String.Format("{0} : {1}", now, errMsg);
      EventLog log = new EventLog("Application", ".", "Poker");
      log.WriteEntry(errMsg, EventLogEntryType.Error);
    }
  }
}
```

B.8 THE SIMPLEMACHINE CLASS

The SimpleMachine class is discussed in chapter 3, *Case study: a video poker machine.*

```
namespace Poker {
  public class SimpleMachine {
    public Hand Deal() {
      return new Hand();
    }
    public Hand Draw(Hand oldHand, string holdCards) {
      return new Hand(oldHand, holdCards);
    }
    public Hand Draw(string oldHand, string holdCards) {
      return new Hand(oldHand, holdCards);
    }
  }
}
```

The WinPok.cs listing

```
// file    : WinPok.cs
// compile : csc /r:poker.dll
//           /t:winexe
//           /win32icon:poker.ico
//           winpok.cs

namespace Poker {

  using System;
  using System.Runtime.InteropServices; // for API MessageBeep
  using System.Windows.Forms;
  using System.Threading;
  using System.Drawing;
  using System.ComponentModel;

  public class WinPokForm : Form {

    public static void Main() {
      // start the Windows message loop...
      Application.Run(new WinPokForm());
    }

    public WinPokForm() {
      initUI(); // create GUI controls
      newGame(); // init poker machine, user credits, etc.
    }

    private void initUI() {
      initForm();
      initMenu();
      initStartOverButton();
      initCredits();
```

```
    initMessage();
    initBet();
    initHoldCheckBoxes();
    initDealDrawButton();
    initPayoutTable();
    initMachineStats();
    initStatusBar();
    initCards();
}

private void initForm() {
    // initialize the form...

    // set title bar...
    Text = ".NET Video Poker  -  The Windows Forms Version";

    // set form height and width...
    Height = 510;
    Width= 445;

    // center form and disallow resizing...
    CenterToScreen();
    MaximizeBox = false;
    FormBorderStyle = FormBorderStyle.FixedDialog;

    // set the form icon...
    Icon = getIcon("poker");
}

private void initMenu() {
    // initialize the menu...

    // create the form's main menu...
    Menu = new MainMenu();

    // create the File menu...
    MenuItem fileMenuItem = Menu.MenuItems.Add("&File");

    startOverMenuItem = new MenuItem(
      "&Start Over",
      new EventHandler(startOverHandler),
      Shortcut.CtrlS);
    fileMenuItem.MenuItems.Add(startOverMenuItem);

    MenuItem quitMenuItem = new MenuItem(
      "&Quit",
      new EventHandler(quitHandler),
      Shortcut.CtrlQ);
    fileMenuItem.MenuItems.Add(quitMenuItem);

    // create the Help menu...
    MenuItem helpMenuItem = Menu.MenuItems.Add("&Help");

    MenuItem aboutMenuItem = new MenuItem(
      "&About",
      new EventHandler(aboutHandler),
      Shortcut.CtrlA);
```

```
      helpMenuItem.MenuItems.Add(aboutMenuItem);
   }

   private void initStartOverButton() {
      startOverButton = new Button();
      startOverButton.Location = new Point(8, 8);
      startOverButton.Size = new Size(424, 24);
      startOverButton.Text = "&Start Over";
      startOverButton.Font =
         new Font("Verdana", 10f, FontStyle.Bold);
      startOverButton.Click +=
         new EventHandler(startOverHandler);
      Controls.Add(startOverButton);
   }

   private void initCredits() {
      // display how many credits remaining...

      Label l = new Label();
      l.Location = new Point(8, 40);
      l.Text = "CREDITS";
      l.Size = new Size(88, 24);
      l.Font = new Font("Verdana", 10f, FontStyle.Bold);
      l.TextAlign = ContentAlignment.MiddleCenter;
      Controls.Add(l);

      creditsLabel = new Label();
      creditsLabel.Location = new Point(18, 64);
      creditsLabel.Size = new Size(60, 24);
      creditsLabel.Font = new Font("Verdana", 10f, FontStyle.Bold);
      creditsLabel.BorderStyle =
         System.Windows.Forms.BorderStyle.Fixed3D;
      creditsLabel.TextAlign = ContentAlignment.MiddleCenter;
      Controls.Add(creditsLabel);
   }

   private void initMessage() {

      Label l = new Label();
      l.Text = ".NET Video Poker";
      l.Font = new Font("Verdana", 10f, FontStyle.Bold);
      l.Location = new Point(104, 40);
      l.Size = new Size(232, 24);
      l.TextAlign = ContentAlignment.MiddleCenter;
      Controls.Add(l);

      // message to the player...
      messageLabel = new Label();
      messageLabel.Font = new Font("Verdana",10f, FontStyle.Bold);
      messageLabel.Location = new Point(104, 64);
      messageLabel.Size = new Size(232, 24);
      messageLabel.TextAlign = ContentAlignment.MiddleCenter;
      Controls.Add(messageLabel);
   }
```

```
private void initBet() {

  Label l = new Label();
  l.Text = "BET";
  l.Location = new Point(344, 40);
  l.Size = new Size(88, 24);
  l.Font = new Font("Verdana",10f, FontStyle.Bold);
  l.TextAlign = ContentAlignment.MiddleCenter;
  Controls.Add(l);

  betTextBox = new TextBox();
  betTextBox.Location = new Point(368, 64);
  betTextBox.MaxLength = 1;
  betTextBox.Font = new Font("Verdana",10f, FontStyle.Bold);
  betTextBox.Size = new Size(32, 22);
  betTextBox.TextAlign = HorizontalAlignment.Center;
  betTextBox.TabStop = false;
  betTextBox.TextChanged += new EventHandler(betChangedHandler);
  Controls.Add(betTextBox);
}

private void initCards() {

  card1 = new PictureBox();
  card1.Location = new Point(8, 104);
  card1.Size = new Size(72, 96);
  Controls.Add(card1);

  card2 = new PictureBox();
  card2.Location = new Point(96, 104);
  card2.Size = new Size(72, 96);
  Controls.Add(card2);

  card3 = new PictureBox();
  card3.Location = new Point(184, 104);
  card3.Size = new Size(72, 96);
  Controls.Add(card3);

  card4 = new PictureBox();
  card4.Location = new Point(272, 104);
  card4.Size = new Size(72, 96);
  Controls.Add(card4);

  card5 = new PictureBox();
  card5.Location = new Point(360, 104);
  card5.Size = new Size(72, 96);
  Controls.Add(card5);
}

private void initHoldCheckBoxes() {
  // init hold CheckBoxes...

  hold1 = new CheckBox();
  hold1.Location = new Point(12, 208);

  hold2 = new CheckBox();
```

```
  hold2.Location = new Point(100, 208);

  hold3 = new CheckBox();
  hold3.Location = new Point(188, 208);

  hold4 = new CheckBox();
  hold4.Location = new Point(276, 208);

  hold5 = new CheckBox();
  hold5.Location = new Point(364, 208);

  // set common HOLD checkbox attributes...
  hold1.Text = hold2.Text = hold3.Text =
    hold4.Text = hold5.Text = "HOLD";
  hold1.Font = hold2.Font = hold3.Font =
    hold4.Font = hold5.Font =
      new Font("Verdana", 11f, FontStyle.Bold);
  hold1.Size = hold2.Size = hold3.Size =
    hold4.Size = hold5.Size = new Size(80, 24);
  hold1.TextAlign = hold2.TextAlign = hold3.TextAlign =
    hold4.TextAlign = hold5.TextAlign =
      ContentAlignment.MiddleLeft;

  // add the HOLD checkboxes to the UI...
  Controls.Add(hold1);
  Controls.Add(hold2);
  Controls.Add(hold3);
  Controls.Add(hold4);
  Controls.Add(hold5);
}

private void initDealDrawButton() {
  dealDrawButton = new Button();
  dealDrawButton.Location = new Point(168, 240);
  dealDrawButton.Size = new Size(104, 24);
  dealDrawButton.Font =
    new Font("Verdana",10f, FontStyle.Bold);
  dealDrawButton.Click +=
    new EventHandler(dealDrawHandler);
  Controls.Add(dealDrawButton);
}

private void initPayoutTable() {

  // frame the payout table...
  GroupBox g = new GroupBox();
  g.Location = new Point(8, 272);
  g.Size = new Size(200, 168);
  Controls.Add(g);

  Label l = new Label();
  l.Location = new Point(5, 10);
  l.Text = Machine.PayoutTable; // payout text never changes
  l.Size = new Size(180, 150);
  l.Font =
```

```
       new Font(FontFamily.GenericMonospace, 8f, FontStyle.Bold);
    g.Controls.Add(l);
  }

  private void initMachineStats() {

    GroupBox g = new GroupBox();
    g.Location = new Point(216, 272);
    g.Size = new Size(216, 168);
    Controls.Add(g);

    machineStatsLabel = new Label();
    machineStatsLabel.Location = new Point(5, 10);
    machineStatsLabel.Size = new Size(190, 150);
    machineStatsLabel.Font =
      new Font(FontFamily.GenericMonospace, 8f, FontStyle.Bold);
    g.Controls.Add(machineStatsLabel);
  }

  private void initStatusBar() {

    statusBarPanel = new StatusBarPanel();
    statusBarPanel.BorderStyle =
      StatusBarPanelBorderStyle.Sunken;
    statusBarPanel.AutoSize = StatusBarPanelAutoSize.Spring;
    statusBarPanel.Alignment = HorizontalAlignment.Center;

    StatusBar s = new StatusBar();
    s.ShowPanels = true;
    s.Font = new Font("Verdana", 8f, FontStyle.Bold);
    s.Panels.AddRange(new StatusBarPanel[]{statusBarPanel});
    Controls.Add(s);
  }

  private void initPokerMachine() {
    // initialize the poker machine...
    machine = Machine.Instance;
    uiBet = machine.MinBet;
    uiCredits = machine.StartCredits;
  }

  protected override void OnClosing(CancelEventArgs e) {
    base.OnClosing(e);
    // make sure the player really wants to quit...
    DialogResult r = MessageBox.Show(
        "Quit?",
        "Closing",
        MessageBoxButtons.YesNo, MessageBoxIcon.Question);
    if (r != DialogResult.Yes) e.Cancel = true;
  }

  private void startOverHandler(object sender, EventArgs e) {
    // user selected "Start Over" from the File menu...
    newGame();
  }
```

```csharp
private void quitHandler(object sender, EventArgs e) {
  // user selected "Quit" from the File menu...
  Close(); // close this form
}

private void aboutHandler(object sender, EventArgs e) {
  // user selected "About" from the Help menu...
  string msg = ".NET Video Poker - Windows Forms Version\n";
  msg += "by Fergal Grimes\n";
  MessageBox.Show(
    msg,
    ".NET Video Poker",
    MessageBoxButtons.OK,
    MessageBoxIcon.Exclamation);
}

private void dealDrawHandler(object sender, EventArgs e) {
  if (dealDrawButton.Text == "&DEAL")
    deal();
  else
    draw();
}

private void betChangedHandler(object sender, EventArgs e) {

  int newBet;
  try {
    newBet = Int32.Parse(betTextBox.Text);
  }
  catch (Exception) {
    // use previous bet...
    beep(); // alert player
    showStatus("Error: Illegal bet!");
    newBet = uiBet;
  }
  betTextBox.Text = getBet(newBet).ToString();
}

private int getBet(int newBet) {
  Bet bet =
    new Bet(newBet,uiCredits, machine.MinBet, machine.MaxBet);
  if (bet.Amount != newBet) {
    beep(); // alert player
    string s =
      "Error: Minimum bet is " +
      machine.MinBet.ToString() +
      ".  Maximum bet is " +
      machine.MaxBet.ToString() + ".";
    showStatus(s);
  }
  return bet.Amount;
}

private void deal() {
```

```
        disableCommand("Dealing...");
        setBet();
        freezeBet();
        hideCards();


        // deal a hand...
        dealHand = machine.Deal();
        showCards(dealHand);

        // clear and enable the HOLD checkboxes...
        clearHoldCheckBoxes();
        enableHoldCheckBoxes();

        // tell player what to do...
        showMessage("Hold and Draw");
        showStatus("Hold cards and click the DRAW button.");
        enableCommand("&DRAW");
    }
    private void setBet() {
        int newBet = Int32.Parse(betTextBox.Text);
        Bet bet =
            new Bet(newBet,uiCredits, machine.MinBet, machine.MaxBet);
        uiBet = bet.Amount;
        uiCredits = bet.Credits;
        showMoney();
    }

    private void draw() {

        disableHoldCheckBoxes();
        disableCommand("Drawing...");

        // hold cards...
        string holdString = "";
        if (hold1.Checked) holdString += "1";
        if (hold2.Checked) holdString += "2";
        if (hold3.Checked) holdString += "3";
        if (hold4.Checked) holdString += "4";
        if (hold5.Checked) holdString += "5";

        drawHand = machine.Draw(dealHand, holdString, uiBet);

        // hide cards which have not been held...
        if (!hold1.Checked) hideCard(card1);
        if (!hold2.Checked) hideCard(card2);
        if (!hold3.Checked) hideCard(card3);
        if (!hold4.Checked) hideCard(card4);
        if (!hold5.Checked) hideCard(card5);
        pause(); // let the player see the backs of the cards

        showCards(drawHand);

        // update UI...
        int won = drawHand.Score * uiBet;
```

```
        uiCredits += won;
        showMoney();
        showMachineStatistics();
        showMessage(drawHand.Title);
        showStatus(drawHand.Title + "  -  Scores " + drawHand.Score);
        checkGameOver();
    }

    private void checkGameOver() {
        // check if player has enough money to go on...
        if (machine.MinBet > uiCredits) {
            disableCommand("Game Over");
            showStatus("Game over!");
            freezeBet();
            beep(); // alert player
        } else {
            enableCommand("&DEAL");
            focusCommand();
            unfreezeBet();
        }
    }

    private void newGame() {
        // start (again) with full credits...
        initPokerMachine();
        hideCards();
        clearHoldCheckBoxes();
        disableHoldCheckBoxes();
        unfreezeBet();
        showMachineStatistics();
        showMoney();
        enableCommand("&DEAL");
        focusCommand();
        showMessage("Click DEAL to Start");
        showStatus("Place Your Bet and Click DEAL to Start");
    }

    private void enableCommand(string s) {
        dealDrawButton.Text = s;
        dealDrawButton.Enabled = true;
        startOverButton.Enabled = true;
    }

    private void disableCommand(string s) {
        dealDrawButton.Enabled = false;
        dealDrawButton.Text = s;
        if (s.Equals("Game Over")) {
            startOverButton.Enabled = true;
            startOverMenuItem.Enabled = true;
        }
        else {
            startOverButton.Enabled = false;
            startOverMenuItem.Enabled = false;
```

```
      }
    }

    private void showMessage(string s) {
      messageLabel.Text = s;
    }

    private void showStatus(string s) {
      statusBarPanel.Text = s;
    }

    private void freezeBet() {
      betTextBox.ReadOnly = true;
    }

    private void unfreezeBet() {
      betTextBox.ReadOnly = false;
    }

    private void hideCards() {
      // display the backs of the cards...
      card1.Image = card2.Image = card3.Image =
        card4.Image = card5.Image = getImage("CB");
      Application.DoEvents();
    }

    private void hideCard(PictureBox card) {
      card.Image = getImage("CB");
    }

    private void showCards(Hand h) {
      card1.Image = getImage(h.CardName(1)); pause();
      card2.Image = getImage(h.CardName(2)); pause();
      card3.Image = getImage(h.CardName(3)); pause();
      card4.Image = getImage(h.CardName(4)); pause();
      card5.Image = getImage(h.CardName(5)); pause();
    }

    private void showMoney() {
      showCredits();
      showBet();
    }

    private void showCredits() {
      creditsLabel.Text = uiCredits.ToString();
    }

    private void showBet() {
      betTextBox.Text = uiBet.ToString();
    }

    private void showMachineStatistics() {
      machineStatsLabel.Text = machine.Stats;
    }

    private void clearHoldCheckBoxes() {
      hold1.Checked = hold2.Checked = hold3.Checked =
```

```
      hold4.Checked = hold5.Checked = false;
  }

  private void enableHoldCheckBoxes() {
    hold1.Enabled = hold2.Enabled = hold3.Enabled =
      hold4.Enabled = hold5.Enabled = true;
    hold1.Focus();
  }

  private void disableHoldCheckBoxes() {
    hold1.Enabled = hold2.Enabled = hold3.Enabled =
      hold4.Enabled = hold5.Enabled = false;
  }

  private void focusCommand() {
    dealDrawButton.Focus();
  }

  private Image getImage(string imgName) {
    string fileName = @"..\images\" + imgName + ".GIF";
    try {
      return Image.FromFile(fileName);
    } catch (Exception e) {
      MessageBox.Show(
        "Error loading card image file: " + e.Message,
        "Error!",
        MessageBoxButtons.OK, MessageBoxIcon.Error);
      return null;
    }
  }

  private Icon getIcon(string iconName) {
    string fileName = iconName + ".ICO";
    try {
      return new Icon(fileName);
    } catch (Exception e) {
      MessageBox.Show(
        "Error loading icon file: " + e.Message,
        "Error!",
        MessageBoxButtons.OK, MessageBoxIcon.Error);
      return null;
    }
  }

  private void pause() {
    pause(200);
  }

  private void pause(int n) {
    Application.DoEvents();
    Thread.Sleep(n);
  }

  private void beep() {
    MessageBeep(0);
```

```
        }

        // private form variables...
        private Machine machine;            // the poker machine
        private int uiCredits;              // amount of player credits
        private int uiBet;                  // amount of player's bet
        private Hand dealHand;              // hand dealt
        private Hand drawHand;              // hand drawn
        private Button dealDrawButton;      // click to deal/draw
        private Button startOverButton;     // click to start over
        private Label messageLabel;         // informational message
        private Label creditsLabel;         // display credits remaining
        private Label machineStatsLabel;    // display mechine stats
        private TextBox betTextBox;         // input player bet

        // start over menu item...
        private MenuItem startOverMenuItem;

        // display card images...
        private PictureBox card1, card2, card3, card4, card5;

        // display checkbox underneath each card...
        private CheckBox hold1, hold2, hold3, hold4, hold5;

        // status bar display...
        private StatusBarPanel statusBarPanel;

        [DllImportAttribute("user32.dll")]
        public static extern int MessageBeep(int type); // error beep
    }
}
```

index

checked operator 297
classes 17, 290, 302–303
Click event 220
client activation 130
client/server 11, 14, 56
client-activated objects 131
Close method 26
CLR 2, 6, 10–11, 34, 44
CLS 6, 11, 17
CLSCompliant attribute 6, 17
COBOL 2
<codeBase> configuration tag 37
CodeBehind attribute 165, 276, 278–279
COM 3–4, 56, 70–72
    COM-based poker game 70–77
COM+ 72, 119
Common Language Runtime. *See* CLR
Common Language Specification. *See* CLS
Common Type System. *See* CTS
CompareValidator, ASP.NET control 261
ComPok 70–77
Component class 209, 211
components, .NET 4
Conditional attribute 319
configuration file 33, 145
ConPok 77, 114–115
Console.WriteLine 23
const keyword 293
constants 291, 293
Container property 209, 211
ContainerControl class 214
ContainerControl.ActiveControl 214
Context property 166
continue statement 299
Control class 211
Controls property 222
controls, ASP.NET 248
controls, Windows Forms 205
controlToValidate property 263
CookieContainer class 185
cookieless 274
cookies 188
CORBA 4, 13, 164–165
CreateInstance method 43, 148

cross-language
    compatibility 11
    inheritance 6, 11
    interoperability 6
csc.exe 5, 318
CTS 2, 17
CurrentLeaseTime property 132
CurrentState property 132
CustomValidator, ASP.NET control 261

D

DAO 78
database management system (DBMS) 80
DataGrid, ASP.NET control 252, 254–255
DataList, ASP.NET control 252
DataReader class 79, 88
DataRelation class 87
DataRow class 82, 86
DataRowState enumeration 86
DataSet 79–80, 86–87
    and XML 83
    creating 81–82
    GetXml method 84
    Tables collection 80
    updating a database 85
DataSource property 255
DataTable class 82, 86–87
DB2 11
DCOM 13, 164–165
debugging 3
decimal type 17, 292
DefaultWsdlHelpGenerator 167
delegates 290, 314
Delete method 87
delta 94
deployment 4
DesignMode property 209
destructor 21
disassembling 28, 39
DISCO 190–192, 194
DiscoveryDocument class 194
display property 263
Dispose method 24–26, 209, 211
DLL 3, 16, 26, 69

System.Web.Services.Protocols namespace
　　SoapHttpClientProtocol class 175–176
System.Web.UI namespace 10
　　Control class 246
　　Page class 245, 274
System.Web.UI.HtmlControls namespace 252
System.Web.UI.MobileControls namespace 286
System.Web.UI.WebControls namespace 252
System.Windows.Forms namespace 10, 220
　　Form class 205
　　Message structure 240
　　Timer class 209
　　ToolTip class 209
System.Xml.Serialization namespace 102
System.Xml.XPath namespace
　　XPathDocument class 105

T

Table, ASP.NET control 252
TableCell, ASP.NET control 252
TableRow, ASP.NET control 252
TabStop property 223
TagName attribute 259
TagPrefix attribute 259
TCP 117, 121, 144, 146
　　and HTTP 127
　　channel 148
telnet 76
Text property 220, 222
TextAlign property 222–223
TextBox, ASP.NET control 252
TextBox, Windows Forms control 223
TextChanged event 223
TextMode property 252
TextWriter class 103, 105
this keyword 303
threading 319
ThreadStart delegate 320
throw statement 302
timeout attribute 274
Timer component 211
TimeSpan structure 133
ToolTip component 211
ToString method 22–23, 60
Trace.Warn 269

Trace.Write 269
traceMode attribute 272
tracing ASP.NET applications 269
Transform method 105
try statement 313
Type.GetType 43
TypeBuilder class 47
typeof operator 297
types 15–16

U

UDDI 164–165, 170, 191, 194, 198
　　API 198
　　registry 195–196
　　SDK 196–197
uint type 292
ulong type 292
unboxing 20, 38–39, 311
unchecked operator 297
Unicode 292
Uniform Resource Identifier. *See* URI
UNIX 12, 76
unmanaged applications 3
unsafe code 290
UNSPSC 196
Update method 85, 87
URI 119, 121, 124
URL 119, 148, 168, 173
URN 119
ushort type 292
using keyword 4, 245, 291

V

ValidationSummary, ASP.NET control 261, 264
value types 15, 18–19, 292, 310
variable-length parameter list 311
variables 291–292
VBScript 11, 242–243
　　and COM 71
　　poker game 71
verbatim string 293
version number 29
viewstate 141, 250
virtual methods 308

Visual Basic 11–12, 203, 228, 242, 295
Visual Basic .NET 5, 11–12, 16–17
Visual C++ 2, 11, 203
Visual Studio .NET 175, 211, 234, 248, 275–276
void return type 304

W

web controls 252
Web Forms 35, 56, 141, 248, 286
Web Service Description Language. *See* WSDL
Web service discovery. *See* DISCO
Web services. *See* XML Web services
Web.config file 265–267, 276
WebMailService example 179
WebMethod attribute 184, 318
WebPok 77, 279
WebService attribute 166, 200, 318
while statement 299
Win32 API 3
    MessageBeep function 233
Win32 applications 118
Windows event log 76
Windows Forms 10, 77, 203–204, 208
Windows SDK 238
Windows services 56, 117, 149
Windows Services Manager 100
WinPok 215–234

WndProc method 205, 238–239
WriteXml method 84
WriteXmlSchema method 84
WSDL 2, 165, 169–170, 173, 191, 194
    bindings 172
    contract 192
    messages 171
    portTypes 172
    services 173
    types 170
wsdl.exe utility 175, 185, 200
WSPok 77, 199–200

X

XCOPY command 29
XML 85, 101, 104
    and DataSets 83
    schema 84
    serialization 101–102, 106
XML Web services 56, 76, 164–165, 175
XmlElementAttribute 103
XmlRep program 106
XmlRootAttribute 103
XmlSerializer class 103
XPathDocument class 105
XSL 85
XSLT 102–106, 108